The New Geography of European Migrations

THE NEW GEOGRAPHY OF EUROPEAN MIGRATIONS

Edited by
Russell King

Belhaven Press
London and New York

Co-published in the Americas with
Halsted Press, an imprint of John Wiley & Sons, Inc., New York

Belhaven Press
(a division of Pinter Publishers Ltd)
25 Floral Street, Covent Garden, London WC2E 9DS, United Kingdom

First published in Great Britain 1993

Co-published in the Americas with Halsted Press, an imprint of
John Wiley & Sons, Inc., 605 Third Avenue, New York, NY 10158–0012

British Library Cataloguing in Publication Data

A CIP catalogue record for this book is available from the British Library

ISBN 185293 291 0

Library of Congress Cataloging-in-Publication Data

The New geography of European migrations/edited by Russell King.
   p. cm.
   Includes bibliographical references and index.
   ISBN 1–85293–291–0 (U.K.) – ISBN 0–470–22036–8 (Americas)
   1. Europe – Emigration and immigration. I. King, Russell.
JV7590.N49   1993
325.4–dc20   93–25980
                                                                                CIP

ISBN 0470–22036–8 (in the Americas only)

Typeset by Mayhew Typesetting, Rhayader, Powys
Printed and bound in Great Britain by Biddles Ltd of Guildford and King's Lynn

Contents

List of figures

List of tables

List of contributors

Corrado Bonifazi is Researcher at the National Institute for Population Research, Rome.

Grete Brochmann is Senior Researcher at the Institute for Social Research in Oslo and Guest Researcher at the Migration Studies Research Group, Catholic University of Louvain.

Malcolm Cross is Executive Director of the European Research Centre on Migration and Ethnic Relations at the University of Utrecht.

Antonio Golini is Professor of Demography at the University of Rome and Director of the National Institute for Population Research in Rome.

Vladimir Grečić is Deputy Director of the International Institute of Politics and Economics, Belgrade.

Bela Hovy is Associate Expert in the Population Division, Department of Economic and Social Development, United Nations, New York.

Russell King is Professor of Geography at the University of Sussex.

Wolfgang Lutz is Leader of the Population Project at the International Institute for Applied Systems Analysis, Laxenburg, Austria.

Philip Martin is Professor of Agricultural Economics at the University of California, Davis.

Christopher Prinz is Research Scholar on the Population Project at the International Institute for Applied Systems Analysis, Laxenburg, Austria.

Barbara Rhode is responsible for developing Social Sciences within DG XII (Science, Research and Development), Commission of the European Communities, Brussels.

Alessandra Righi is Researcher at the National Statistical Institute of Italy, Rome.

Richard Rowland is Professor of Geography, California State University, San Bernardino.

Krysia Rybaczuk is Lecturer in Geographical Information Systems at Trinity College Dublin.

John Salt is Senior Lecturer in Geography and Director of the Migration Research Unit at University College London.

Paul White is Senior Lecturer in Geography at the University of Sheffield.

Preface and acknowledgements

In March 1992 in Vienna one of the largest conferences ever held on European migration brought together some 300 migration scholars, journalists, politicians and policy-makers: the result was a unique dialogue between academics, migration administrators and the media on one of Europe's most burning social issues. The conference was titled 'Mass migration in Europe: implications in East and West' and its location in Austria was apt given the events of the past few years and the strategic position of Vienna as an intense contact point between Western Europe and the reforming countries of the East. Austria's front-line status in the new migratory movements emanating from Eastern Europe is revealed in its startling immigration figures: between 1989 and 1992 the number of immigrants living in the country doubled from 300,000 to an estimated 600,000; there has been a net addition to the labour force of 120,000, equivalent to 4 per cent extra workers; and about one-third of the 300,000 new arrivals are illegal immigrants.

The three main sponsors and co-promotors of the conference were the Institute for Advanced Studies, Vienna, the International Institute for Applied Systems Analysis (IIASA), Laxenburg, Austria, and the Institute for Futures Studies, Stockholm. Other sponsorship came from the Austrian Ministry for Science and Research, the Fritz-Thyssen-Foundation, Cologne, and the Centre for Economic Policy Research, London. The conference was structured into two plenary sessions and nine workshops. This book contains most of the papers from the Workshop entitled 'Why are people migrating? A socio-geographic approach'. This selection accounts for Chapters 1–5 and 11–13. Chapters 6–9 are drawn from other workshops held at the conference, and Chapter 10 was written especially for the book. As convener of the above workshop and editor of this volume, I should like to thank all the authors of the papers for making helpful revisions to their conference drafts and for allowing me considerable editorial freedom to fashion the contributions into what I hope is a coherent and useful book for students of European migration. Other materials from the conference will appear in books and journals around the world. For instance the plenary lectures and discussions have recently been published in *Framtider International*, vol. 2, 1992 (the English-language version of the journal of the Institute for Futures Studies).

Whilst focusing mainly on the East–West dimension of current European migratory movements, the book also tries to place this phenomenon within the larger global framework of international migrations. Thus the South–North dimension — which many believe to be the most vital axis in the long run — is by no means neglected, and there are (in Chapters 1 and 13) explicit attempts to compare European migratory trends with those in North America. Other chapters examine specific types of new migration, such as brain drain from Eastern Europe and asylum migration (Chapters 11 and 12). Whilst some chapters are essentially retrospective, looking back over the past few decades (Chapters 2 and 3), others look to the future – either the immediate future of the 1990s (Chapter 4) or by building scenarios for the first part of the next century (Chapter 5).

Of course, no one can predict with any degree of certainty the volume or nature of migration flows likely to take place over the next few years that span the transition to the twenty-first century. Demography remains an inexact science, especially when grappling with the migratory component of population change. Many migratory waves are simply unforeseeable, resulting from sudden political events or explosions of ethnic chauvinism; the dreadful series of conflicts surrounding the breakup of Yugoslavia are the most obvious testimony to the unpredictability of migration flows on Western Europe's doorstep. What is clear is that migration presents the contemporary world, including the new Europe, with one of its major challenges.

As geographers and social scientists, it is our job to describe and interpret the migratory events now taking place within and outside Europe. In doing this we can use the theories and models of the past, but not be overly reliant upon them. The best work from past geographies of migration can surely be used to inform our interpretation of current events, but we should always be alive to the space–time specificity of all migratory movements, and to the possibility that some at least of the new forms of migration now taking place in Europe may need new explanatory frameworks to understand them. Hopefully this book will be a step towards establishing such new frameworks, as well as describing the migrations in action.

In closing these introductory remarks, I should like to record my grateful thanks to several people who have been instrumental in the production of this book at various stages. First I thank my very good friend and colleague Sture Öberg, Professor of Social and Economic Geography at Uppsala University and Senior Researcher at IIASA, for inviting me to convene the workshop from which a large part of this book is drawn. Secondly, I really appreciated the fine organisational skills of Anne Babette Wils, also of IIASA, in setting up the workshop. Matthew Stout, Cartographer in the Department of Geography at Trinity College Dublin, produced or modified many of the maps published in this book. Finally I thank Eileen Russell and Margaret O'Flanagan for their invaluable assistance in the final stages of editorial work.

Russell King
Dublin and Brighton, June 1993

Chapter 1

The migration issue

Philip Martin

Introduction

Immigration has again risen towards the top of the international agenda. This is because unwanted newcomers are arriving in industrial societies which are experiencing economic insecurity and political uncertainty. These unwanted immigrants include foreigners arriving in Europe who request asylum, aliens who slip undetected across the US–Mexican border, and students and tourists in Japan who go to work.

For the first time, all of the major industrial countries in the OECD are immigration countries (Garson 1992). The volume, characteristics and degree of governmental control over this immigration varies greatly. For instance, Canada accepts about 250,000 immigrants annually, equivalent to almost 1 per cent of its population, and seems to believe that it can regulate with some precision the economic, family, and humanitarian mix of its newcomers. Germany may be at the other end of the spectrum. As a 'non-immigration country', it does not anticipate immigration, yet in 1990 over 1 million immigrants, asylees and illegal immigrants arrived, equivalent to over 1 per cent of its population.[1]

The OECD countries plan for immigration to add between 0 and 1 per cent to their populations annually. Yet a common feeling in these countries is that they are receiving 'too many' and the 'wrong kind' of immigrants. Furthermore, there is no natural end to today's immigration in sight.

Demography is ultimately destiny. If immigration continues, it will eventually change the population size and ethnic composition of the OECD countries. Political leaders are learning that compound interest also applies to population growth, and that their ageing populations are often uncomfortable with the demographic changes occurring around them. The probably apocryphal story is told of the American Indian chief who, in the 1850s, was asked by young braves about the single biggest mistake of the past generation's leaders. The reply was simple: we failed to preserve our way of life because we did not control immigration.

There are six dimensions of the migration issue in industrial countries that merit attention. First, immigration into industrial countries will increase in the 1990s. Second, there is a certain level of discomfort about high and rising levels of immigration everywhere, but the reactions of governments to this increased immigration are very different in Western Europe, North America and Asia. Third, migration flows are governed by demand–pull, supply–push and network factors, and regulating or reducing migration means intervening primarily in the industrial countries to affect migration flows in the 1990s. Fourth, Europe learned that there is nothing more permanent than temporary workers, or that immigration policy can not be made only on the basis of short-term labour market considerations. Fifth, the United States has 200 years of experience with immigration, but this experience has not enabled it to predict accurately the effects of changes in immigration policies. Sixth, large-scale immigration seems to reinforce other trends that are promoting economic inequality and reinforcing the isolation of the underclass in industrial nations.

How can the industrial democracies reassert control over immigration? Many thoughtful observers suggest some kind of 'Grand Bargain' in which effective controls over additional immigration are accompanied by renewed efforts to integrate the large number of recent newcomers.[2] However, they note that the industrial countries are instead drifting towards the worst of all worlds: continued large-scale immigration, which in turn fuels anti-immigrant political parties in Europe and contributes to compassion fatigue towards the poor in the United States. In both cases, immigration increases the need for social assistance, but there is in fact less help for newcomers. If this *status quo* continues, Europe (and the United States) may include an increasing number of poorly integrated immigrants, a sure recipe for escalating social tensions in the 1990s.

World population and labour force growth

The world's population is almost 5.5 billion, the world's workforce is 2.5 billion, and both numbers are increasing by almost 100 million annually. About 90 per cent of the world's population and labour force growth occurs in developing nations, which create 'real' jobs for perhaps half of their annual new crop of workers. In addition to creating more jobs for the youth who every year join the workforce, developing nations face three catch-up job creation tasks: they must find non-farm jobs for ex-farmers, as some of the world's 1 billion farmers seek non-farm jobs; they must create jobs for adults who are not now in the workforce, such as urban women; and they must reduce currently high levels of unemployment and underemployment.[3]

Despite widespread unemployment in developing nations, and wages and incomes that are 10–20 times higher in industrial than in developing countries, most poor people do *not* migrate. Most of the world's people will live and die within a few kilometres of where they were born. But even a small migrant percentage can translate into a large number of migrants — if 2 per cent of the annual increase in the world's labour force migrates, there are 2 million additional migrants each year.

There are about 80 million immigrants, refugees and asylees, and legal and unauthorised workers living outside their country of citizenship (Martin 1992). Only about half of the world's migrants are in industrial countries: 15 to 20 million are in Western Europe, 15 to 20 million are in North America, and 2 to 3 million are in the industrial nations of Asia, including Japan, Taiwan and Singapore. Some of these immigrants are living and working legally in their host societies, some are present illegally, and many have an intermediate legal status — such as applicants for asylum whose applications are rejected but who none the less are permitted to remain in the country.

Migration has become a major factor in the international economy. Remittances from migrants to their countries of origin are at least $70 billion annually, or 1.5 times the level of Official Development Assistance that OECD countries provide. Remittances from migrants in OECD countries are perhaps $50 billion annually, equivalent to $1,000 for each man, woman and child abroad, making remittances a major source of foreign exchange in southern European countries from Portugal to Turkey. Immigration and remittances are now major features of the international political economy, and their importance is likely to rise during the 1990s.

Industrial country reactions

The OECD countries have a population of about 775 million, or 15 per cent of the world total, and a GNP of $15 trillion, three-quarters of world GNP. As the major OECD countries become net immigration areas, some speculate that immigration may convert inequality between industrial and developing nations into inequality within industrial nations.

Many of the immigrants arriving in industrial countries today are unwanted, in the sense that illegal aliens, settled guestworkers, or rejected applicants for asylum were not expected to become residents, but the reactions of OECD countries to this unwanted immigration vary widely. In much of Western Europe, controlling immigration is a top domestic priority; if immigration is not perceived to be under control, political parties that have been in power since the Second World War fear that they may be dislodged or forced to share power with anti-immigrant parties.

The reaction in North America is different. In the United States and Canada, controlling immigration generally ranks well below controlling taxes and crime in public opinion polls. Indeed, in both countries restrictionist symbols, such as the introduction of employer sanctions in the

United States in 1986 and an annual cap on immigration in 1990 legislation, have permitted both countries to remain fairly open to newcomers. However, immigrants are concentrated in a few areas in each country and, in these areas, concern about out-of-control immigration is similar to levels of concern in Western Europe.

Asian countries such as Japan have been noted as exceptions to the tendency of industrial countries to rely on immigrants to fill undesirable jobs. These countries seem to have reached the limits of taking jobs to workers rather than importing workers to fill jobs, and they are initiating guestworker programmes to legalise growing influxes of illegal migrant workers (Martin 1991).

Immigration is a crisis in Western Europe, is treated with benign neglect in North America, and is seen as an economic asset if managed properly in Asia. These different perceptions of the immigration problem have led to rather different policy responses to the common problem of apparently rising immigration pressures. Such different responses to common challenges facing industrial nations tend not to persist. During the 1950s, for example, it was predicted that labour relations systems in industrial countries would converge despite very different labour histories because all industrial countries faced the common challenge of coping with assembly-line production systems. The different responses to immigration today in Western Europe, North America and Asia may reflect the fact that each area is at a different point on the experience-with-immigration spectrum, and not fundamental differences in how they will ultimately respond to this common challenge. What is not yet clear is whether the European 'crisis response' or the US 'benign neglect' policy will be typical early in the next century.

Why migration?

Migration occurs because of demand–pull factors that draw migrants into industrial countries, supply–push factors that push them out of their own countries, and networks of friends and relatives already in industrial societies who serve as anchor communities for newcomers. Although most of today's migration streams have their origins in colonial or recruitment policies of industrial countries, it appears that government-approved demand-pull factors are of waning importance in explaining current immigration levels, while supply–push and network factors are becoming more important. The fact that supply-push and network factors are not under the direct control of industrial country governments does much to explain the feeling in them of loss of control over immigration.

With most industrial countries closed to newcomers, or open to fewer immigrants than are arriving, there is a tendency to try to reduce current immigration levels by reducing supply-push factors such as joblessness and low wages that encourage emigration. Trade, aid and investment to accelerate economic growth in emigration nations should be encouraged to promote what has been termed 'stay-at-home' development, but there is no magic bullet development cure which is likely to reduce supply-push emigration in the 1990s. Indeed, it is more likely that the economic and social restructuring that is often necessary to accelerate economic growth may initially *increase* supply-push emigration. Development is the eventual remedy for supply-push emigration, but it is not the immediate solution for 1990s immigration pressures.

Tackling supply-push factors with development is an attempt by industrial nations to fix problems in other countries' backyards. However, 1990s remedies for 'out-of-control' immigration are more likely to be found if industrial countries deal with unofficial demand-pull factors in their own backyards (Straubhaar 1992). In today's deregulated economies and labour markets, there are job niches for immigrant workers to fill in industries that range from seasonal agriculture to construction to hotels and restaurants. Labour markets are flexible, and a supply of willing immigrant hands can soon create a demand for them tending children, lawns, or the elderly.

If immigration is going to be reduced in the 1990s, industrial countries would be wise to look more carefully at the demand-pull factors that attract migrant workers to jobs inside them. Hiring an unauthorised or semi-authorised worker is not considered a serious crime in most industrial countries. Without a social consensus that such employment is a serious offence, industrial countries ignore that part of the migration equation over which they have the most control.[4]

Demand-pull is not just hiring the unauthorised workers who are present; it is also at work when industrial countries protect industries that depend on immigrant workers from international trade (Weintraub 1990). As Mexico's President Salinas frequently reminds audiences, the United States seems to prefer Mexican tomato-pickers to Mexican tomatoes, since the United States does a much better job keeping out Mexican tomatoes than Mexican workers. One result is that Mexican tomato growers complain of labour shortages, while competing Florida growers report surpluses of workers. Similarly, European Community policies that exclude Polish farm products but accept Polish workers add to demand-pull factors that encourage immigration.

Some argue that industrial nations need immigrants to maintain their ageing and slow-growing populations. This argument can be misleading for four reasons. First, demographic projections are frequently wrong: few demographers predicted the baby boom or bust, and thus history would put little confidence in current projections of continued low fertility in the industrial countries. Second, importing even large numbers of youthful immigrants does not have nearly as much of an effect on 'youthening' the population as does more births. The reason is twofold: the number of births typically exceeds the number of immigrants, and babies begin at zero age, while immigrants are scattered across the age spectrum.

Third, admitting young immigrants to maintain pay-as-you-go pension plans is a never ending scheme, because ever more young immigrants must be admitted in the future to pay ever more pensions. Furthermore, if pension plans favour lower-wage earners, then admitting unskilled immigrants to maintain them can quickly turn a short-run benefit into a long-run cost. Fourth, immigration is usually more controversial when population growth is slow because the effects of the 'different' immigrants show up quicker in schools and other institutions. With fewer native children beginning school each year, immigrant children are more visible. If their presence is perceived negatively, native parents may feel compelled to shelter their children from too many immigrants in the schools.

Demand–pull and supply–push factors are like battery poles; both are necessary to start the car. Once started, networks affect who migrates where. Most migrants arrive in industrial countries with contacts in the established anchor community of previous immigrants; friends and relatives already there can provide information that the migrant can readily understand, and often jobs and housing for newcomers. Networks can be family or jobs-based. Individuals and families who have settled in an industrial country serve as anchors for family-based networks that bring relatives legally and illegally to settled families. Immigration countries can try to get families to wait in queues for their turn to enter legally, but many immediate relatives will enter immediately regardless of immigration policies.

Jobs-based networks often recruit young men for menial jobs in industrial countries. There are often enormous profits to be made in charging the migrant workers one-quarter of their first year's earnings to be smuggled into the country, perhaps charging the employer for access to the workers, and then providing at a profit the housing, transportation and other services that these unauthorised workers need. Rigorous immigration and labour law enforcement can break jobs-based networks but, as the experience with drug smuggling shows, it is very difficult to extirpate a profitable activity unless there is a strong social consensus to reinforce a massive enforcement effort.

Networks include more than helpful friends and relatives and employers eager to hire immigrants. Networks that bring immigrants into industrial countries have been likened to highways: what were once winding paths have become freeways because of the communications revolution which helped to raise expectations in emigration areas, the transportation revolution which increased access to and lowered the cost of migrating, and the rights revolution which makes it hard for industrial countries to prevent immigrants from staying and getting access to social services (Hollifield 1992).

Researchers know that demand–pull, supply–push and network factors

Table 1.1 Stocks of foreign population in selected EC and other European countries, 1980 and 1990: absolute numbers ('000) and as % of total national populations

	1980		1990	
	No.	%	No.	%
EC countries:				
Belgium	885.7	9.0	904.5	9.1
Denmark	101.6	2.0	160.6	3.1
France	3,714.2	6.8	3,607.6	6.4
Germany (West)	4,453.3	7.2	5,241.8	8.2
Italy	298.7	0.5	781.1	1.4
Luxembourg	94.3	25.8	104.0	27.5
Netherlands	520.9	3.7	692.4	4.6
United Kingdom	1,601.1	2.8	1,875.0	3.3
Other:				
Austria	287.7	3.7	413.4	5.3
Finland	12.8	0.3	26.3	0.5
Norway	82.6	2.0	143.3	3.4
Sweden	421.7	5.1	483.7	5.6
Switzerland	892.8	14.1	1,100.3	16.3

Note: Belgium 1981 instead of 1980, France 1982 instead of 1980, Luxembourg 1989 instead of 1990, UK 1984 instead of 1980. The data are collected on different criteria in different countries, hence they are not strictly comparable.

Source: SOPEMI 1992, p. 131.

explain much of today's migration, but they do not know how to assign weights to these factors, nor can they link a policy measure that affects one of these factors with a specific level of reduction in immigration pressure. However, if supply, demand and network factors each contribute one-third to overall migration pressure, it is clear that immigration into industrial countries in Europe and elsewhere will remain high during the 1990s. The reason is that industrial countries, even if they could reduce the demand–pull factors that affect immigration by 50 or 60 per cent, still leave unchecked most of the factors that stimulate immigration.

Immigrants in Europe

There are more than 13 million non-nationals in the 12 nations of the European Communities (EC), making foreigners 4 per cent of the EC population (see Table 1.1). About 40 per cent of these foreigners are from other EC countries, Italians in France, for example. But 60 per cent — some 8 million foreigners — are nationals of non-EC countries, e.g.

Turks in Germany. These foreigners from outside the EC are concentrated in the two countries that most actively recruited guestworkers in the 1950s, 1960s and early 1970s: France and (West) Germany. These two, with about one-third of the EC population, have two-thirds of the non-EC foreigners (Table 1.1). In addition to these legal foreigners, there are perhaps 1 million additional asylees and illegal immigrants from outside the EC in EC countries, such as Poles in Germany and Senegalese in France and Italy.

Only a third of the foreigners living in the EC are in the workforce. About 36 per cent of the intra-EC foreigners are in host-country workforces, but only 30 per cent of the non-EC foreigners. The low labour force participation rates of intra-EC migrants reflects in part the tendency of EC nationals to study or retire in another EC nation, and the low participation rates of non-EC foreigners reflects rules that restrict their employment together with the fact that they tend to have a relatively high proportion of children. EC nationals are on average 44 per cent of the foreigners in the EC workforce, but the proportion of EC nationals in the foreign labour force ranges from less than a third in Denmark, Germany and Portugal to three-quarters or more in Belgium and Luxembourg.

Immigration has been described as 'the biggest problem facing the whole European Community' (Horwitz and Forman 1990). During the 1950s, Western European nations sought temporarily to borrow workers from southern Europe and northern Africa, a labour transfer encouraged by international organisations. However, many migrants settled in Western Europe with their families, a process intensified by the decisions made in the mid-1970s to stop recruiting temporary workers abroad. High unemployment and immigration controls then kept immigration pressures down until the late 1980s, when more rapid economic growth created jobs, and when the maturing immigration networks increased immigration pressures throughout Europe. The fall of communism in 1989 and the lowering of national barriers symbolised by 1992 have made immigration control more difficult just as anti-immigrant sentiment is rising.

Since the mid-1950s, European migration has been largely labour migration. Economic recovery during the 1950s propelled migrants from lagging countries to boom areas. Italians went to Germany, and Spaniards to France. During the 1950s and early 1960s, there was little concern about the long-term consequences of these labour migrations because the migrants were expected to return to their countries of origin. Economic growth in migrant-receiving areas was expected to slow, and to accelerate in migrant-sending areas. Thus, it was assumed that labour migration would eventually stop because the economic incentive to migrate would disappear. The EC and other international organisations embraced the concept of moving labour across national borders until economic inequalities were reduced.

Some 20–30 million guestworkers were involved in the European labour migrations of the 1960s, making foreigners Europe's 'seventh man' (*sic*) because about 1 in 7 Europeans was a foreigner in his or her place of residence (Berger and Mohr 1975). Between 1960 and 1973, the number of migrant workers in Western Europe[5] jumped from 2 million to 7 million, and the total foreign population rose from 4 million to 12 million. Instead of coming from nearby Italy and Spain, more migrants in the early 1970s arrived from culturally and geographically more distant nations such as Turkey and Morocco. Concentrations of foreign workers in particular industries and cities in the early 1970s, and their steady movement from dormitories near factories into apartments with their families, made natives aware that the temporary guestworkers were becoming settled residents. But employers, governments and the migrants themselves claimed that the guests would eventually return home, and that both sending and receiving countries would enjoy economic benefits until then.

In 1973 and 1974, the countries that had been recruiting migrant workers from outside the EC halted further recruitment from non-EC nations such as Turkey, Yugoslavia and Spain. Rising unemployment in the wake of oil price hikes sent 2 to 3 million migrants home, and by 1988 the migrant workforce stabilised at 5 million. However, the total population of migrant workers and their families rose from 10 million in 1973 to 11 million by 1977, due to the onset of family reunion migration.

There are still about 5 million migrant workers in the European nations that recruited guestworkers, but the total migrant population reached 14 million in 1990. European labour migration, which began in the early 1960s on the basis of simple bilateral agreements a few pages long, is today governed by extensive regulations which cover topics ranging from the right of non-citizen migrants to vote in local elections to the pensions of migrants who retire to live in their countries of origin.

The European nations that recruited southern European workers in the 1960s started looking in the 1970s for effective means to control immigration. One of the first control mechanisms adopted was a system of penalties or fines on employers who hired illegal aliens. Germany enacted employer sanctions in 1971 to fine employers for hiring illegal aliens for working without the necessary permits. Today, all West European countries except the United Kingdom fine employers who knowingly hire illegal alien workers.

During the 1960s and early 1970s, European nations added up to 1 million foreign workers to their labour forces annually. The growing migrant labour force, plus a return flow of migrants, permitted the entry of 3,000–4,000 legal migrant workers daily, reducing pressures for illegal entry. Significant numbers of migrants did, however, continue to arrive in France, Germany and other recruitment countries illegally, sometimes because the official recruitment system was too cumbersome to suit employers and migrants. France routinely legalised the status of illegal workers who found jobs during the 1960s, and in Germany workers could be requested by name after they arrived illegally and found employers willing to hire them. Thus, illegal entrants could jump the queue of workers waiting at home to emigrate.

When recruitment stopped in 1973–4, migrants continued to arrive illegally, and policies towards these continued flows of illegal migrants diverged. France provided amnesty or legal status for many of the post-1974 arrivals who found regular jobs, under the theory that these newcomers had developed an equity stake in France and would be difficult to deport. Germany and Switzerland, on the other hand, refused to adopt legalisation programmes because they feared that legalisation would promote illegal immigration by encouraging more migrants to arrive and wait for another amnesty.

European nations are today embarked on a quest for control over unwanted immigration. Their sense of urgency arises from the fear that, if immigration is not brought under control, the political parties that have been in power for five decades may have to share power with single-issue, anti-immigrant parties. For this reason, many Europeans look to the United States for immigration solutions.

The US experience

The United States is a nation of immigrants unsure about taking more newcomers (Teitelbaum 1992). Despite this ambivalence, immigration is at an all-time high. About 9 million legal and unauthorised immigrants and refugees arrived during the 1980s, and projections suggest that 10–12 million may arrive in the 1990s.

American history celebrates *e pluribus unum* — from many, one. This motto explains the American confidence that people of diverse origins have forged and can continue to forge an American identity. Americans have always been ambivalent about additional immigrants, worrying that newcomers would reduce their own economic opportunities and be unable to become Americans. These competing themes of pride over the contributions of immigrants, and pressure to pull up the drawbridge so that even more immigrants do not undo the 'American experiment', are ever present in American immigration history.

Some Europeans believe that they can profit from the American experience to develop their own immigration policies. However, US experience in one area — predicting the effects of immigration policy changes — is not promising. Immigration reforms in 1965 that gave each eastern hemisphere country an equal annual immigration quota were not expected to alter the predominantly European origins of most US immigrants, yet this law unleashed the Hispanic and Asian immigration wave which continues today.

Other recent US immigration legislation has also had effects that were the opposite of what were intended. Efforts in 1986 to reduce illegal immigration with a legalisation programme for 3 million unauthorised aliens and employer sanctions to deter future illegal entries have in the early 1990s led once again to levels of illegal immigration that are similar to pre-reform levels. Reforms in 1990 to increase the number of professional immigrants admitted for economic reasons were accompanied by an overall enlargement of the annual immigration target so that over 80 per cent of immigrants continue to be mostly unskilled workers admitted for family reasons.

Recent US immigration reforms have relied on restrictionist symbols to cloak what are in fact expansionist measures. The restrictionist symbol of the 1986 reforms was employer sanctions, but these failed to prevent illegal migrants from finding jobs because of widely anticipated document fraud (Fix 1991). The restrictionist symbol of the 1990 legislation was a cap or annual quota on immigration, but this cap is flexible or permeable if many close relatives of US residents wish to enter, and it does not cover refugee admissions.

What might Europe learn from this American experience? First, immigration is cumulative and self-perpetuating. A country that thinks it can admit immigrants equivalent to, say, 0.5 per cent of its population may wish to announce a target or quota of 0.4 per cent, because immigrant channels tend to widen over time. Second, there is often a larger gap between policy goals and outcomes in immigration than in other areas, in part because managing flows of people is inherently difficult. Therefore governments should be modest in their promises to manage immigration with precision. Third, past waves of immigration to the United States have been followed by periods of little immigration. It is not clear how much time societies need to absorb a wave of newcomers, but the US experience suggests that, after 10–15 years of rising immigration, a decade or two was needed to absorb the newcomers.

It is this last point — the breathing-space that followed past waves of immigrants — that is troublesome today in areas such as California, whose population has been growing by 2.5 per cent annually, with two-thirds of this growth due to immigration.

California: wave of the future?

California is often a bell-wether for events that later appear throughout the United States and industrial nations. In California, the arrival of 3 million immigrants and refugees during the 1980s gave the state a population growth rate which was faster than that of Mexico and comparable to that of Morocco. If California continues to get one-third of all US immigrants, then the state's population of 30 million today is projected to be 38 million in 2000.

Most immigrants to California are unskilled Hispanics and Asians. The availability of such immigrant workers during the 1980s showed the economic growth that can be achieved with a First World infrastructure and a Third World labour force (Muller and Espenshade 1985). Los Angeles, for example, emerged as the nation's largest manufacturing centre despite rising housing costs and declining real manufacturing wages. One reason for this growth was defence, computer and other high-tech expansion, but rapid job growth also occurred in low-wage garment, footwear and furniture industries.

California and the United States have diamond-shaped labour forces. About one-quarter of their workforces are college-educated professionals and managers; one-half are semi-skilled and skilled operatives, craftsmen and clerks; and one-quarter are the less-than-high-school graduates who are often labourers, maids and janitors. Immigrants tend to have more or less education than American workers: 30 per cent are highly skilled, 20 per cent are in the middle, and 50 per cent are unskilled (Borjas 1990).

Large-scale immigration reinforces the other factors promoting economic inequality by adding workers to the top and bottom of the labour force. At the top, immigrant scientists and engineers fuel the growth of high-income education and high-tech industries. At the bottom, immigrant farm workers and labourers help to hold down wages and thus prices for fruits and vegetables and gardening services. The result is growing economic inequality which, in a state experiencing budget shortages, is not reduced with social service programmes. Indeed, the gap between the priorities of the older white population, which casts most of the votes in elections, and young minority immigrants who often do not vote, has been described as an important factor in making California a unique laboratory in which to determine whether the world's first 'universal' nation can function.

There are many reasons to believe that California can be prosperous with high levels of immigration. California is an export-oriented producer of products and services that immigrants can sell to their countries of origin. But California is also fraying around the edges. The older white population that supported a high-taxes, high-services model of government during the 1970s seems no longer willing to pay high taxes for services that are perceived to be ineffective efforts to assist poor citizen and immigrant residents. There was a great deal of discussion in the aftermath of the May 1992 riots in Los Angeles over the role that large-scale immigration plays in the lives of disadvantaged Americans. Although the evidence is likely never to be clear-cut, logic suggests that the availability of eager immigrants does make it harder for disadvantaged American workers to climb up the American job ladder (Briggs 1992).

The immigration which has helped to turn California from a diamond-shaped to a more hour-glass-shaped society — from a society with a broad middle class to one with relatively larger upper and lower classes

— has brought with it social tension. These tensions may worsen if economic and job growth remains slow during the 1990s. Benign neglect is likely only to aggravate such tensions. What is to be done? The solution most often suggested is a sort of Grand Bargain in which governments take steps to assure restrictionist-minded publics that immigration is under control, and this public reassurance then permits governments to spend more on assistance for the domestic poor and the newcomers who are already in their midst.

Immigrants no longer seem willing to wait the three generations that past arrivals required to be integrated, so efforts for adult immigrants to learn the host country language may have to be increased, since lack of host country language ability is perhaps the single most important obstacle to upward mobility. The institutions that successfully integrated immigrants in the past — schools, churches, the military, unions, political parties — are in many countries smaller and less sure of their ability to deal with newcomers.

The integration challenge is real, yet nothing is done, in part because admissionist-minded groups that want to get as many immigrants inside the country before the drawbridge goes up have blocked efforts by restrictionist groups to take probably unrealistic steps to stop all immigration or persuade some current immigrants to leave. This deadlock may lead, again, to the worst of all worlds. If the *status quo* continues, large numbers of unskilled immigrants will arrive in industrial countries, and right-wing movements in Europe and compassion-fatigued publics in the United States will support political parties that are not likely to make integrating newcomer immigrants or helping disadvantaged natives top priorities. Such a political gridlock would produce yet another deficit for later generations to grapple with: the deficit of uplifting those left behind.

Conclusions

Industrial nations are experiencing their highest ever levels of unwanted immigration, to which there is no end in sight. However, their responses to this immigration are very different, ranging from crisis management in Europe, benign neglect in North America, and confidence that migrant workers can be regulated in Asia. Although it is not clear whether these different reactions to the common challenge of unwanted immigration are temporary reflections of where these countries are on the immigration-experience spectrum, or are mirrors of each country's history and immigrant absorptive capacity, it is more likely that industrial countries' immigration policies will converge than diverge: hence the relevance of the US experience for Europe.

How might immigration policies converge? Political leaders are learning that the demand–pull, supply–push and network factors which govern migration can be reversed, but not easily or quickly. Reducing or reversing demand–pull factors are mostly within their control, but many seem to believe that it may be easier politically to spend more on aid abroad to reduce, with economic growth, supply–push emigration pressures than to spend more on immigration and labour law enforcement at home. However, aid is the least likely policy to reduce emigration pressure (Fielding 1993), and the trade and investment alternatives raise the same kinds of domestic issues that enforcement does.

Networks also offer few avenues for intervention to reduce emigration pressures. The communications revolution which exaggerates for poor peasants the riches of industrial countries is unlikely to be reversed; it has been observed that the popularity in developing countries of television shows such as 'Dallas' and 'Dynasty' may do much to raise expectations and stimulate emigration. Similarly, the expanding trade which industrial countries want to promote also makes industrial countries more accessible. Finally, industrial countries that extended rights to their own minorities may find it difficult to prevent immigrants from gaining access to social and educational services.

Experience is often a useful teacher, but it may not be in the case of today's immigration into industrial countries. Countries such as the United States with vast immigration experience have been unable to predict the results of changes in their immigration policies, and the lessons of the past, such as the three-generation transition to full integration, often seem inapplicable today.

Areas such as California that are experiencing high levels of unwanted immigration are groping towards a sort of Grand Bargain that involves better control over immigration, and more integration assistance for the newcomers who have been arriving. Achieving this compromise between control and integration is difficult because the debate between open-border admissionists and closed-border restrictionists is in some countries preserving the *status quo*. However, the *status quo* promises the worst of all worlds: immigration without integration.

Managing immigration and the tensions that surround it is a major challenge for the world community. The gaps in many research and policy discussions are the in-between policy responses — between changing a law or definition at one end of the response spectrum, and slowing world population growth at the other. During the 1990s, industrial countries are likely to explore much more carefully what they can really do about the forces that shape and control international migration.

Notes

1. In 1990, over 300,000 foreigners, most from former recruitment countries, moved into Germany. There were also almost 200,000 applicants for asylum, and almost 400,000 *Aussiedler* or ethnic Germans from the ex-USSR, Poland

and mostly East European nations. Additional illegal aliens arrived, but not all of them settled in Germany. See Kemper 1993.

2. Grand Bargains, which include new control measures and liberalizing policies, were common in Europe in 1973–4, when recruitment stops were accompanied by more liberal family unification policies, and in the US Immigration Reform and Control Act of 1986, which included both sanctions on employers who knowingly hired illegal alien workers and an amnesty for 3 million previously illegal aliens.

3. In most OECD industrial nations, half of the population is in the labour force. However, in high emigration nations such as Turkey and Mexico, only one-third of the population is employed or looking for work. These low labour force participation rates reflect both higher population growth rates, and thus a higher proportion of young people, and too few formal sector jobs, especially for women in urban areas.

4. Except when it comes to appointing women to high-level Cabinet posts, as President Clinton discovered when forming his new US administration in early 1993.

5. The major non-EC European nations which recruited guestworkers were Switzerland and Sweden; other non-EC nations with migrant workers include Austria and Norway.

References

Berger, J. and Mohr, J., 1975, *A seventh man: migrant workers in Europe*, Penguin Books, Harmondsworth.

Borjas, G.J., 1990, *Friends or strangers: the impact of immigrants on the US economy*, Basic Books, New York.

Briggs, V., 1992, *Mass immigration and the national interest*, Sharpe, Armonk, NY.

Fielding, A.J., 1993, 'Migrants, institutions and politics: the evolution of European migration policies', in King, R. (ed.), *Mass migrations in Europe: the legacy and the future*, Belhaven, London, 40–62.

Fix, M., 1991, *The paper curtain: employer sanctions' implementation, impact and reform*, Urban Institute Press, New York.

Garson, J.-P., 1992, 'International migration: facts, figures, policies', *OECD Observer*, 176: 18–24.

Hollifield, J., 1992, *Immigrants, markets and states: the political economy of immigration in postwar Europe and the US*, Harvard University Press, Cambridge, MA.

Horwitz, T. and Forman, G., 1990, 'Immigrants to Europe from the Third World face racial animosity', *Wall Street Journal*, 14 August 1990: 1.

Kemper, F.-J., 1993, 'New trends in mass migration in Germany', in King, R. (ed.), *Mass migrations in Europe: the legacy and the future*, Belhaven, London, 257–74.

Martin, P., 1991, 'Labor migration in Asia', *International Migration Review*, 25(1): 176–93.

Martin, P., 1992, 'International migration: a new challenge', *International Economic Insights*, 3(2): 3–7.

Muller, T. and Espenshade, T., 1985, *The fourth wave: California's newest immigrants*, Urban Institute Press, Washington, DC.

SOPEMI, 1992, *Trends in international migration*, OECD, Paris.

Straubhaar, T., 1992, 'Allocational and distributional aspects of future immigration to Western Europe', *International Migration Review*, 26(2): 462–83.

Teitelbaum, M.S., 1992, 'Advocacy, ambivalence, ambiguity: immigration policies and prospects in the United States', *Proceedings of the American Philosophical Society*, 136(2): 208–25.

Weintraub, S., 1990, *A marriage of convenience: relations between Mexico and the United States*, Oxford University Press, New York.

Chapter 2

Why do people migrate?
The geography of departure

Russell King

Introduction

Although this book is about recent, current and future patterns of European international migration, this chapter provides some historical context by throwing a backward glance. Its focus is the geography of outmigration, and the discussion is presented around a series of maps at scales which vary from the world to the village. Most of the maps are of peripheral parts of Europe — the main sending areas in the past — with special attention paid to Italian migration. The patterns shown by the maps are used to widen the discussion from a narrow description of spatial variations to interpretation by reference to historical, political, institutional and social processes. The characteristics of the migrants and the impact of emigration on the areas of departure are also dealt with. Although the chapter is retrospective in nature, the relevance of the mapping techniques and interpretative frameworks for new geographies of departure from countries and regions sending emigrants to Europe now and in the future should not be overlooked.

Curiously, attempts to generalise about spatial patterns in the intensity of outmigration have been relatively few, although there is an abundance of case studies and cartographic data sets scattered in the literature. White and Woods' (1980, pp. 21–41) analysis of the spatial patterns of migration flows devotes itself to measuring the shape, volume, length and direction of migratory movements; it does not consider the geography of out-migration — nor for that matter of in-migration or of return migration.

Four basic ways exist of enumerating migration flows — gross, net, emigration and immigration. Returning flows also should not be forgotten. Each of these can be indexed by relating it to the resident population of the area affected. For the purpose of this analysis we will mainly deal with net and emigration flows, with some brief reference to return migration. Where net migration is mapped (e.g. as a product of the census residual method of calculating migration), an important cautionary note must be sounded. Different groups of people migrate for different reasons; since net migration may be the balance of much larger inward and outward gross flows, the technique of ecological correlation in relating migration trends to independent variables such as income or employment is of questionable validity since it matches hypothesised causes to a non-existent 'net' migrant. This problem is partially overcome by studying the characteristics and spatial origins of the emigrants only. Thus emigration rates are measured by considering the number of emigrants leaving a specified area or group of areas over a period of time and expressing this number as a proportion of the average population of the area over the period in question, or of the population at the start of the period. Such rates — emigration indices — can then be mapped by areas to give a visual demonstration of the places where emigration has been most important. Maps of net migration and of some variety of return migration index (returning migrants as a proportion of resident population or as a proportion of outgoing migration, perhaps adjusted by an appropriate time-lag) can be added to complete the migration profile of a particular country or region. The fundamental problem of the ecological fallacy remains, however. To demonstrate that emigrants come mainly from areas of high unemployment does not necessarily mean that emigrants leave because they are unemployed. It could be that the unemployed stay and the emigrants are people leaving their jobs for better jobs abroad.

Some global and macro-regional patterns

Salt's (1989) series of world maps of migration flows for 1960, 1970 and 1980 provide a useful starting-point (Figure 2.1). The maps show a series of, to use his term, 'macroregional networks': regional core–periphery systems whereby labour migration flows constitute the 'human bond' (cf. King 1982) linking centres of capital accumulation and economic growth with peripheries of surplus labour. The location and scale of these systems changes from one period to the next but many are remarkably stable: central America to the United States, southern Europe and North Africa to north-west Europe, non-oil Arab and South Asian countries to the Gulf, and front-line and homeland states to South Africa. The common pattern here is clear: migrants move from areas of rural over-crowding, underemployment and limited peasant horizons to adjacent or not-too-distant countries where industrial, mining or service-sector growth provides higher incomes and the promise of a better life. The patterns of migration thus portray the global distribution of economic power and, at the international level, reflect simply the geography of economic opportunity between groups of countries. Where the gradients in standards of living are particularly sharp — as they are across the Mediterranean basin or the Rio Grande — migration pressures will be intense and the political debate may also be fierce (Salt 1989, p. 445).

Whilst the above explanation of international migration flows via

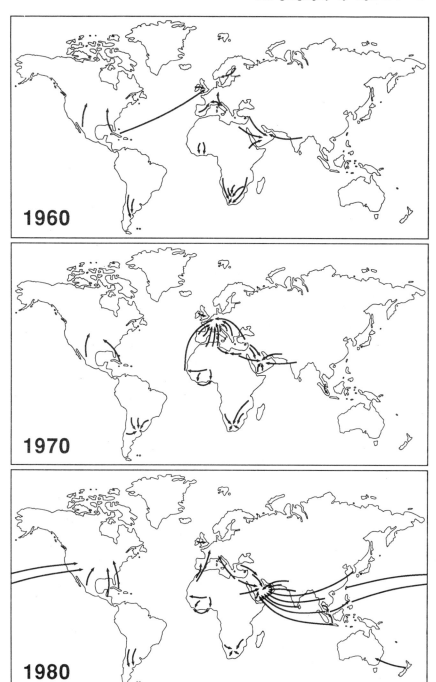

Figure 2.1 Main international labour migration flows at a world scale, 1960, 1970 and 1980

Source: Salt 1989.

economic push–pull concepts seems logical enough it has its flaws: for instance it does not explain why similar potential moves between pairs of poor and rich countries have *not* taken place, nor why spatial variations in the pattern of emigration from a given country exist. According to Portes and Borocz (1989, p. 608) the onset of international labour migration does not simply arise out of the theory of comparative economic advantage, but out of a history of prior contact between sending and receiving countries. The colonial stamp on the pattern of post-war labour flows into European countries like Great Britain (India, Pakistan, Jamaica), France (Algeria, Mali, Senegal) and The Netherlands (Indonesia, Surinam) would seem to bear this out. The history of prior contact tends to pass through a series of phases starting with coercion (slave migrations) and proceeding through colonial and post-colonial migrations based on specific recruitment policies to the more contemporary self-initiated labour flows.

The historical–political dimension to the explanation of the geography of international migration leads to a consideration of two other important issues: the institutional context of international movements, and migration as an essentially socially driven process. The institutional context is well expressed in Western Europe where so much of the labour migration channelled to France, West Germany and the Benelux countries between the mid-1950s and the mid-1970s resulted from a series of bilateral agreements. Figure 2.2 shows the pattern of the 33 bilateral recruiting agreements that existed in 1974, just before many of the agreements were repealed in the wake of the oil crisis. The map emphasises the wide geographical scale over which the European labour market has formally operated, including not only southern Europe but also North and West Africa. The bilateral links explain why, for instance, Yugoslavs are found in Germany but not in Belgium or The Netherlands, and why Tunisians are found in France and not in Germany. Of course, not all international labour migration in Europe is confined to these agreements. There has been much clandestine movement and settlement, both between countries governed by recruiting agreements (e.g. Portuguese to France) and between countries which are not (e.g. Turks and Moroccans in Belgium), and there has also been free movement of labour within the European Community (e.g. between Italy and the northern EC countries) guaranteed by the Treaty of Rome. Nevertheless the lines on Figure 2.2 constitute the main framework of the overall pattern of European post-war migration (Salt 1976, pp. 98–100).

The idea of emigration as a socially driven process emerges from numerous studies which show the relevance of personal networks in promoting international migration across space and time (Boyd 1989). The strength of kinship ties and of other personal relationships based on friendship and a shared community of origin expresses itself in the shape of many migration flows which are very particularistic in nature, linking specific origins and destinations through a self-sustaining process of

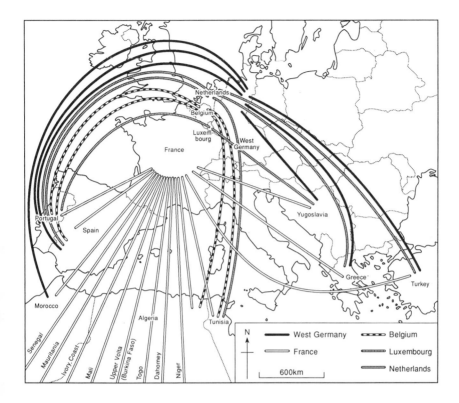

Figure 2.2   Bilateral labour migration agreements existing in Western Europe in 1974

Source: Salt 1976, p. 99.

chain migration which may eventually become more important than the contextual economic circumstances of income and employment disparities which gave rise to the original migration flow. Undoubtedly chain migration has been a key, yet under-appreciated, mechanism transforming a migration flow into an organised social system which then perpetuates the flow. Large-scale mapping of the spatial particularity of migration flows linking the myriad of individual migrant origins with the specific locations of settlement in destination countries is an almost impossible task, not least because of the lack of detailed data. But individual community studies give an idea of the unique character of the migration process at the locality level, as we shall see presently.

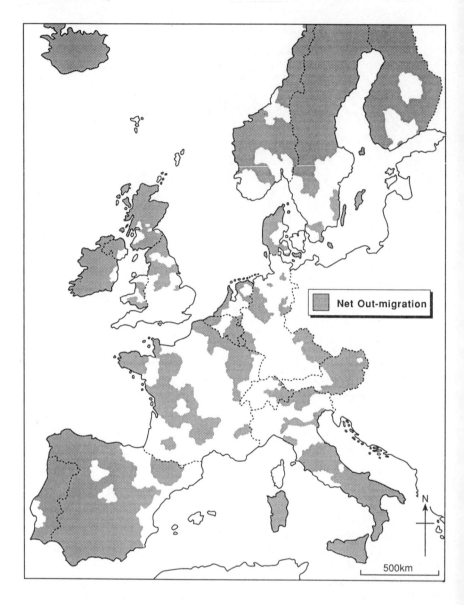

Figure 2.3 Areas of net out-migration in Western Europe, 1961–71
Source: Clout 1976, p. 37.

Some European examples of out-migration patterns

The first example (Figure 2.3), a simple map of net out-migration based
on the 1961–71 intercensal period, serves to pick out the spatial pattern
of migratory change in Western Europe at a time when there was great

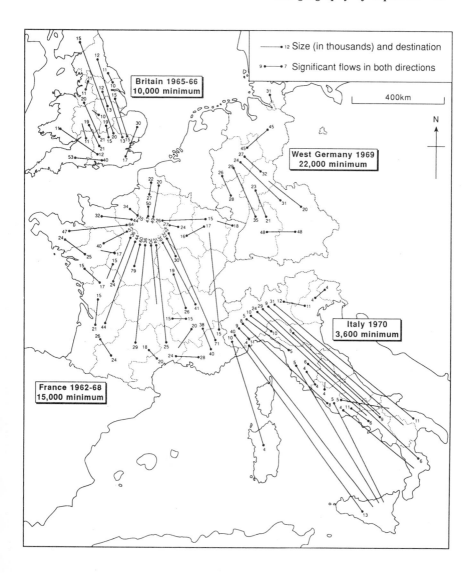

Figure 2.4 Gross inter-regional migration in selected European countries during the late 1960s

Source: Wood 1976, pp. 54–5.

mobility, both within countries and in terms of international periphery-to-core migration. The pattern is mainly one of out-migration from rural areas, with migratory loss also from more restricted areas of industrial decline, including mining regions (Clout 1976, pp. 36–8). Although revealing in its simplicity, the map also masks a lot — the degree of loss in individual regions, the variable importance of internal versus international migration, the specific direction of the outflows, and the pattern of migration 'fields' of various receiving towns and regions. And, as a net map, it gives no hint of gross flows.

For internal migration Wood (1976) provides some answers to these problems. His map of inter-regional migration, which in certain European countries reached the scale of a mass phenomenon during the period in question (the 1960s), shows the main flows of inter-regional migrants (Figure 2.4). The patterns are naturally conditioned by the large scale of the regions chosen and the slightly different time periods selected, but Wood has partially corrected for these problems by varying the threshold for mapping the flows in each country. The map shows the domination of London and Paris in the British and French flows respectively, and the importance of Piedmont-Lombardy and secondarily of Rome in the Italian pattern.

At this level of regional aggregation, however, a substantial number of the flows are two-way, especially those between urban regions. In attempting to explain the increasing importance of inter-urban migration and of exchange migration (with low net residuals) and the declining importance of periphery–centre patterns, Wood invokes the views of Richmond (1969) about the nature of migration in industrial and post-industrial societies. Richmond suggested that in post-industrial societies rural–urban migration would all but die out, to be replaced by dominant inter-urban flows between the main metropolitan areas. In this multi-directional, urban-dominated pattern the search for traditional push and pull factors to explain migration flows is no longer relevant since mobility is, at least for certain social and age groups, the norm. In such societies migration is less to do with geographical distance or the economically efficient spatial allocation of resources, and more to do with opportunity, choice and career development. These arguments are persuasive, although it can be noted in passing that the otherwise visionary views of Richmond failed to anticipate the switch to counter-urbanisation which started in many European countries about the time he was writing his seminal paper.

Turning now to a map of the spatial intensity of emigration abroad from the southern European countries in the 1960s (Figure 2.5), some further patterns may be identified and commented upon which are very different from Richmond's post-industrial world of north-west Europe. The map is constructed on the basis of regional deviations from national mean levels of emigration for the years 1963–8; the darker shading represent the heaviest emigration, although because of different national mean values the shading categories represent different emigration index levels for each country (see King 1976 for further details). The countries portrayed in Figure 2.5 fall into two groups as far as their emigration patterns are concerned. The first group — Portugal, Spain, Italy and Greece — consists of countries where the areas of highest emigration correlate with regions of high natural increase which are rural, poor,

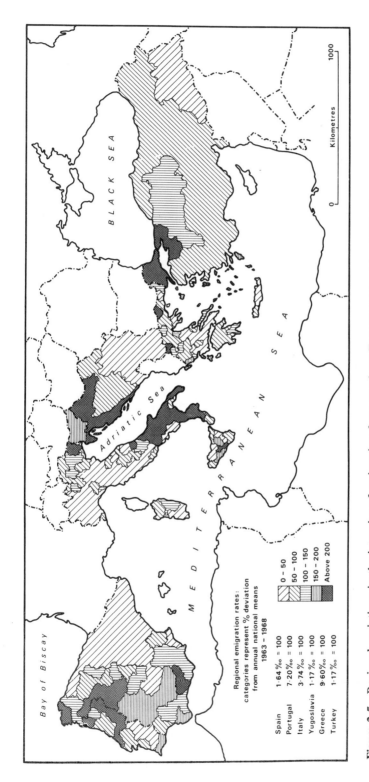

Figure 2.5 Regional variations in the intensity of emigration from southern European countries, 1963-68

Source: King 1976.

The following text labels appear within the figure:

Bay of Biscay

BLACK SEA

Adriatic Sea

MEDITERRANEAN SEA

Regional emigration rates:
categories represent % deviation
from annual national means
1963 - 1968

Spain	1·64 ‰ = 100
Portugal	7·20 ‰ = 100
Italy	3·74 ‰ = 100
Yugoslavia	1·17 ‰ = 100
Greece	9·60 ‰ = 100
Turkey	1·17 ‰ = 100

0 – 50
50 – 100
100 – 150
150 – 200
Above 200

0   Kilometres   1000

overpopulated and hilly or mountainous. Typical regions are Tras os Montes and Minho (Portugal), Galicia and Andalusia (Spain), and Friuli and the mainland Mezzogiorno (Italy). The second group consists of Yugoslavia and Turkey where more or less the opposite pattern can be observed: emigration was highest from those regions (Croatia, Slovenia, the Istanbul region) which are (or were) the most developed and urbanised in their respective countries. The answer to the apparently conflicting picture lies in the different historical development of emigration in the two sets of countries (King 1976). Portugal, Spain, Italy and Greece are all 'old' countries of emigration where migration abroad has a history extending back to the last century, if not earlier. When emigration first started from these countries, it was from the more developed, urbanised and accessible regions. Italian emigration in the mid- and late nineteenth century, for instance, developed initially from northern Italy, from where migrants moved either north across the Alps or overseas to South America. Only at a later state, after the turn of the century, did the centre of gravity of mass emigration shift south into the Mezzogiorno (King 1992). Yugoslavia and Turkey, on the other hand, are 'young' emigration countries where the main foci of movement abroad, at least in the mid-1960s, were still the more developed regions. In the case of Turkey, for example, the remote eastern regions were then too isolated and the people still too out of touch with the rest of Europe for emigration to be a large-scale phenomenon. However, in Turkey there remains the possibility that much emigration has been preceded by rural–urban step migration within the country. Thus for example internal migrants moving from eastern or southern Turkey to Istanbul and then, after a few years of urban 'acclimatisation', moving abroad would be recorded as departing from Istanbul and not from their rural provinces of origin. Such an explanation is less likely to hold for Yugoslavia where ethnic diversity has tended to keep people in their individual republics.

Generalising the historical process, we can see that the areas of origin of southern European emigrants have been extended from the main urban centres, which were the earliest migrant sources, to more remote rural districts in peripheral parts of the sending countries. As Salt and Clout (1976) point out, this has been accompanied by a gradual change in the types of migrant susceptible to foreign recruitment. The earliest migrants, from the more urbanised, developed regions, have had high levels of skill and education (relative to the average for their country). Later migrants, from rural areas, had fewer skills and less education. Salt and Clout (1976, pp. 154–60) provide a detailed account of how North Africa has experienced a spread of emigrant origins away from the more urbanised coastal regions into the more isolated areas of the interior; at the same time, an increasing proportion of the emigrants has been less well educated. However, since the 1970s another pattern has emerged. Rising standards of education in all parts of rural southern Europe and in some parts of North Africa have led to qualifications and job aspirations which cannot be satisfied locally. Provincial towns provide some job outlets for these newly educated rural labour market entrants, but many migrate longer distances, to national economic core areas, to other European countries, or overseas to the Gulf, Australia, etc.

Who migrates, and what are the effects of out-migration on the areas of departure?

I now widen the discussion from the essentially technical one of mapping spatial variations in rates of out-movement to a more human realm. A brief review of some of the literature on outmigration from Europe in recent decades will enable us to make some preliminary statements about the social character of emigration and of the impact on the 'sending' areas.

Migrants are rarely a random selection of the population of the place of origin. The following generalisations may be noted regarding rural out-migrants and emigrants from Europe in the last few decades (White and Woods 1980, pp. 12–17). A high proportion are young, unmarried adults. The gender balance varies from country to country. In many cases, for instance Turkey and the Maghreb states, males are overwhelmingly predominant, especially in the early stages of the migration process. In other cases the balance is much more even and in some countries (e.g. emigration from Ireland) females may be the majority. It seems frequently to be the case that females predominate in rural out-migration which is internal, while males are in the majority in emigration abroad. In both cases, migrants tend to be poor and have below-average levels of formal education — though this may be changing, as noted above. Finally, they tend to represent the more ambitious and innovative — but also dissatisfied and frustrated — sectors of the sending society. However these are very broad generalisations and many exceptions may be found. For instance, regarding the last point about innovation, migrants may be an innovative selection in the first stage but become a traditional aspect of society in the long run: such was the case of emigration from southern Italy to the Americas before the First World War. The Italian case will be considered in more detail shortly.

Where levels of out-migration from a set of areas or regions are of a significant magnitude and where the people leaving have certain definable characteristics which differentiate them from the societies from which they leave, the impact on the population left behind in the area of origin may be quite marked (White and Woods 1980, pp. 45–6, 53). Generalising once again on the picture for rural Europe over the past several decades, the rural areas of departure are deprived of young adults and of their labour and reproductive powers; hence activity rates and birth rates in the residual societies decline. However in countries like Turkey and Morocco where, at least initially, mainly males emigrated temporarily, the fertility decline due to emigration has been negligible. A second effect of sustained rural out-migration is the potentially dramatic loss of farm workers, which may distort the rural labour market. If too many people leave, agriculture becomes a largely female and part-time activity, with declining productivity. In any case out-migration is likely to remove the more innovative elements of the farm population so that agricultural improvement is hampered. The impact of emigration on agriculture and on rural society is a major field of research which has not yet been fully explored by geographers and rural sociologists, despite the fact that Lowenthal and Comitas (1962) pointed this out 30 years ago. Although unemployment may fall and incomes rise as a result of the removal by migration of surplus labour, a productive restructuring of the farm economy by the enlargement and consolidation of holdings tends not to take place since migrants hold on to land for sentimental reasons or as an insurance against failure abroad or in the city. To the extent that migrants are likely to be politically active or innovative, the communities left behind may become more conservative, deprived of both political and social leadership, or at least allowing traditional élites to consolidate their power. Feedback influences from emigration, such as return migration and remittances, should not be ignored, for they can act to sustain the rural economy, retexture rural social structure, and also promote further emigration (King 1986).

Evaluating the impacts of rural out-migration as harmful or beneficial to the sending area depends on the time, the place and also on value-judgements as to what is good or bad. For Spain, for instance, some authors (Douglass 1975; Iszaevich 1975) have argued that emigration has helped agricultural communities to preserve their stability by removing excess population at times of high natural growth or of agricultural difficulty (poor harvests or falling agricultural prices). Thus emigration nullifies demographic growth, stabilises rural social structures, and preserves economic integrity, or at least prevents economic difficulty. However, with the onset of fertility decline rural migration loss has become a problem rather than a cure (White 1980). Once fertility started to fall in rural communities — and that fall in natality was partly a function of the age- and sex-selective nature of past migration — the continuation of rural emigration loss has reduced total population. This process has been marked in Spain where the fertility drop in recent years has been cataclysmic and where counterurbanisation has made little impact on rural areas beyond the major metropolitan and touristic hinterlands.

Two brief case-studies in France illuminate the interaction between migration and other demographic variables, and enable us to return to the main cartographic theme of this chapter on the geography of departure. In his paper on rural migration loss in Normandy, 1962–75, White (1980) explores the geography of net out-migration and total population change in a sample of communes. Age-selectivity analyses show that the rate of out-migration at the peak cohort (20–24 years) is more than eight times the rate for the trough cohort (50–54 for men, 55–59 for women). Net migration loss characterised all communes over the period analysed, though in some cases there was a considerable immigration component as well (but always exceeded by out-migration). The net migration change was generally of much greater importance than natural change in its contribution to total population change. In most cases net migration loss more than nullified net natural growth, leading to a modest total loss; in a few cases, however, natural decrease compounded net migration loss to give 'true' depopulation (cf. Lowenthal and Comitas 1962).

The second case-study, Clout's (1974) map of population change in the Auvergne (Figure 2.6), shows a sixfold typology based on combinations of total, natural and migration change for the period 1954–68. Only a few areas, notably around Clermont Ferrand and other key employment centres, experienced both immigration and natural growth. Elsewhere, particularly to the south of the region in the Cantal upland area, there was migratory loss, leading often to total loss and sometimes accompanied by natural decrease.

The geography of departure: examples from Italy

The final major section of this chapter examines some of the rich material on the spatial dimension of migration intensities in Italy. The discussion will once again focus mainly around a series of maps. The order of the material is both chronological, starting with a brief discussion of the historical evolution of migration types in Italy, and geographical in that maps of a variety of scales from the nation to the village will be presented.

Until the early 1970s, when Italy started to become a country of immigration, this country had for at least a century been a classic place of emigration, sending emigrants to many parts of the globe in a series of waves of different types of migratory movement — permanent emigration, long-term emigration followed by eventual return, temporary emigration for short and medium terms, and cyclical and seasonal migration (Alberoni 1970). The first emigrants, setting out soon after Italian unification in 1861, came from northern regions like Piedmont and Veneto. They were seasonal migrants, mainly males, who crossed the Alps to France, Germany and Switzerland to work in farming or on construction projects building houses, roads, railways and tunnels. Since most of them were farmers in Italy, they returned regularly to their farms and families, thus minimising the deleterious impact of their departure on their home communities. After 1887 a new migratory flow came into force, directed towards South America, chiefly Argentina and Brazil. This, too, came mainly from northern Italy, especially the Veneto

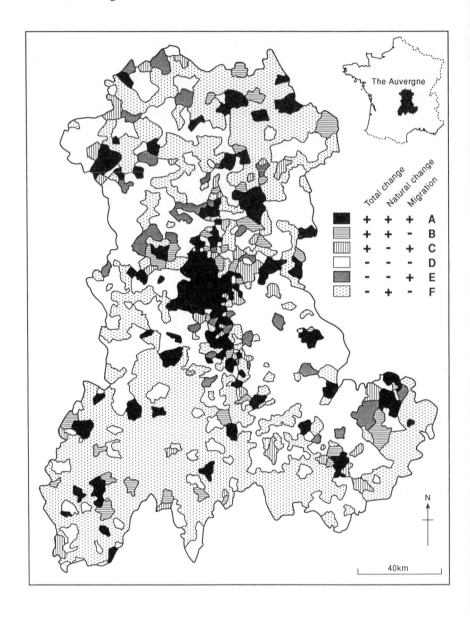

Figure 2.6   Types of population change in the Auvergne, 1954–68

Source: Clout 1974

region. It consisted above all of agricultural tenants who moved, with their families, to settle new land in a 'new' continent. It was perhaps the only phase of Italian emigration planned as permanent settlement. Thus it was very different from the exodus to Europe which was still going on. Gradually the South American flow became more south Italian in its origin and at the same time changed its character to a temporary or seasonal migration of agricultural workers. By the 1890s a major flow towards the United States developed. This also came initially from north Italy but very soon became dominated by huge numbers of southern Italians, especially those from Sicily, Calabria, Basilicata and the Abruzzi. Southern Italian emigration to the United States was different from both European and South American types. It involved mostly men, at least initially, and it was not seasonal or permanent but temporary or open-ended. The migrants left out of desperation at their conditions of poverty, landlessness and exploitation by landlords; they did not go to take up a specific job; they simply went to seek their fortune. Whether they succeeded in making their fortune or not, most stayed for good or for long periods of time. The heyday of this mass migration was the period 1900–14, with a brief resurgence during 1918–22. Another brief rise in emigration to both North and South America occurred after the Second World War, especially during the years 1948–55; this, too, mainly involved southern Italians. But the main destination of post-war emigrants, especially during the boom years of emigration during the 1950s and 1960s, was Europe with France, Switzerland and Germany again the predominant destinations. Southern Italians contributed 80 per cent of this movement. The regional geography of this post-war mass exodus has been documented in detail by the author (King 1992) and will be commented upon later. For the time being I return back in time to examine some interesting structural features of the geographical pattern of emigration at the height of the first mass exodus during the period between the turn of the century and the start of the First World War.

Regional variations in rates of emigration for this period have been examined in great detail in a series of papers by MacDonald (1956; 1958; 1963). Since each of MacDonald's papers uses somewhat different regional examples and data sets, the following account will pick out his main findings only. MacDonald starts by pointing out the crudeness of economic 'push–pull' theory for explaining regional and temporal variations in Italian emigration rates during the period 1902–13 — a period when national emigration rates were both extremely high and reasonably well documented. Although there is some superficial support for the expected inverse correlation at the regional level between emigration rates and wealth (i.e. poor regions generally had higher emigration rates), there are other questions to be asked, such as why some poor regions like Apulia and Sardinia had low emigration rates. MacDonald also points out that rural standards of living were fairly uniformly low over all parts of Italy at this time; therefore regional variations in wealth were largely explained by the contributions of major urban-industrial centres. Milan, Rome and Naples thus distorted the regional indices for Lombardy, Latium and Campania respectively. The key to explaining regional variations in emigration rates, according to MacDonald, is rural social structure — more specifically the distribution of landownership, agricultural

Table 2.1 Italy: selected emigration and other regional data for the period 1902–13

Administrative regions	Trans-oceanic emigration 1902–13 (per thousand, per year)	Net out-migration 1900–10 (per thousand, per year)	Mean prosperity index 1900–12 (Italy = 100)	Socialist vote, 1913 (%)	Members of agricultural labour unions, 1911 (as % males in agriculture)
Emilia	39	35	81	38	39
Tuscany	52	46	104	26	2
Umbria	52	73	46	15	3
Marche	164	77	52	11	2
Abruzzi	338	107	32	4	–
Basilicata	340	121	39	6	2
Calabria	368	91	37	2	1
Apulia	118	37	47	15	11
Sicily	263	56	53	3	5
Sardinia	37	40	41	6	–
Other areas:					
Alps	low	high	low	low	low
Campania (excluding Naples)	316	high	low	low	low

Source: After MacDonald 1958, pp. 68–9; 1963, p. 62.

tenancy arrangements, and the presence or absence of labour militancy as expressed in agricultural trade unions and other forms of class-based political activity.

Table 2.1 presents some of MacDonald's most relevant data; for further explanation of the measures chosen see especially MacDonald (1963). Ten administrative regions and two areas not conforming to precise administrative units are included in the table. The data for the areas tend to be qualitative estimates since geographical areas like the Alps comprise parts of several regions. Heavily urbanised regions such as Piedmont, Lombardy and Latium are left out of Table 2.1 for reasons indicated in the previous paragraph. The objective of the table is to show that emigration functioned as an alternative to class struggle and that emigration rates were lowest where there was greatest social solidarity amongst the rural labouring classes.

Moving down the table, we may first note the cases of the central Italian regions of Emilia-Romagna, Tuscany, Umbria and Marche, and the anomalous situation in the southern region of Apulia. All were regions of relatively low emigration, but they had very varying prosperity indices. Their key feature in common was the fact that their populations were engaged in militant working-class movements. Landownership was not widely distributed but polarised in the hands of a minority. Access to land was via the *mezzadria* system of stable share tenancy in central Italy; in Apulia such access was more difficult because of the survival of the *latifundia* system whereby large estates were worked by landless labourers. The key to the low emigration rates for these regions lies in the fact that their unequal land and income distributions led to a discrete class system within which a class struggle could take place: peasants and labourers had political channels to express their dissatisfaction and their aspirations for a better life, instead of being forced to emigrate. As Table 2.1 shows, agricultural labour unions and rural socialism were strongest in Emilia-Romagna, Tuscany and Apulia. It is true that emigration was quite high for Marche, but this emigration came mainly from the southern part of the region (provinces of Macerata and Ascoli Piceno) bordering on the Abruzzi. Southern Marche had a smaller-scale *mezzadria* system and less associative behaviour than other parts of the centre of Italy.

Abruzzi, Basilicata, Calabria and Campania (excluding Naples) constituted the 'Deep South', a region of mountains and rolling uplands overcrowded with people trying to extract a living from the difficult environment. Here land tenure was very complicated with large, medium and small holdings side by side and a variety of mostly insecure leasing and sharecropping arrangements. Rural society was thus complex and lacking the clear-cut strata of Apulia or the regions to the north. Instead property-based status was ranged on a continuous scale. In the absence of a class context appropriate to labour militancy, and with individual labourers, renters and small owners placed in a situation of fierce competition with each other for land, the peasants turned to emigration rather than to socialism as their best route to self-improvement.

The rural people of the Alps were also prone to emigrate, but in other respects they had little in common with their fellow *montagnards* at the other end of the peninsula. The Alpine economic system was based on a combination of small privately owned plots at lower elevations and communally owned summer pastures and forests on the higher levels. Private property was fragmented and often too small to support a farm family, even with the aid of communal rights. There were no large private holdings in this broadly egalitarian society. The Alps were politically tranquil and the communal traditions had no political colour. The equality of common poverty meant that there was no landed class to blame; hence the class struggle was ruled out, and emigration was the only option. The movement, however, was of a different type to that operating elsewhere in Italy, consisting of seasonal migrations of males to adjacent European countries. Because of its seasonality, much of this migration was unrecorded by the statistics, but the real rates were close to or even higher than those from the 'Deep South'.

Another regional situation is represented by Sardinia, an isolated island region sparsely populated by transhumant shepherds who lived outside the cash economy and accepted the *status quo*, neither emigrating nor entering into political activity. The low rate of emigration from Sardinia was basically due to its powerful clan-based cultural traditions and the insulation of its economy from national and international markets.

Finally in Table 2.1 there is the interesting case of Sicily which can be considered both in terms of emigration and of its socio-economic system as intermediate between Apulia and the regions of the Deep South listed earlier. Sicily's land tenure typically comprised large estates combined in most districts with a range of medium and small holdings. Some of the large estates were run along Apulian lines with large gangs of landless labourers hired on a day-to-day basis. Most, however, were subdivided into blocks for subletting in small allotments to peasant farmers on temporary and exploitative contracts. The intermediaries who administered these subleasing arrangements were the notorious *gabellotti*, a class of gangster-entrepreneurs who were closely connected to the early origins of the Mafia. The Sicilian case, however, was a changing one. During the 1880s membership of the island's rural labour unions, the *fasci*, was high, comprising perhaps a third of the males working in agriculture. Emigration rates were low, partly because the *fasci* were successful in controlling the worst excesses of the landlord and *gabellotto* systems. After the *fasci* were broken up by government military action in 1893, emigration from Sicily rose sharply. During 1902–13 it was intermediate in scale between Apulia and the 'Deep South' (Table 2.1) but by 1913 it was almost exactly on a par with the rest of the South (Sardinia excluded).

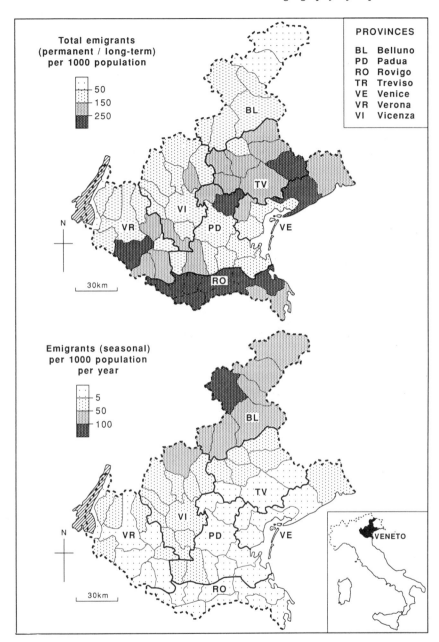

Figure 2.7 Temporary and long-term emigration from the Veneto, 1876–1903

Source: Brunetta 1983, pp. 154, 159.

Thus, to summarise, the Italian regional data at the beginning of the century indicate that emigration rates were a function of 'individualism' on the one hand, and 'solidarity' on the other. The economic aspirations of central Italy and Apulia were directed into cooperatives and trade unions, while those of the upland Deep South were more individualistic, leading to emigration as the principal means of mobility in the rural status hierarchy.

Although MacDonald produced no maps to illustrate his papers, his sophisticated socio-geographic analysis represents a classic of its kind. Two interesting maps produced by Brunetta (1983) for Veneto, an important emigration region not considered in detail by MacDonald, provide a useful cartographic complement to the latter's work. The maps (Figure 2.7) show permanent or long-term emigration (*emigrazione propria*) and seasonal emigration (*emigrazione temporanea*) for the period 1876–1903, when the Italian authorities distinguished between these two types of migratory movement. The mapping is by district (*distretto*), a now-obsolete (since 1912) administrative unit intermediate between the province and the commune.

Figure 2.7 shows that seasonal migration occurred mainly from the northern, mountainous districts of the region — from the province of Belluno and the northern part of Vicenza — whilst long-term emigration occurred from the hilly and, above all, the plain areas, especially the province of Rovigo which stretches along the banks of the lower course of the River Po. This important regional contrast can be interpreted as follows (Brunetta 1983, pp. 154–60).

Temporary emigration from the Alps of Veneto had quite deep historical roots in the pre-capitalist rural economy of the mountains which saw, every year, the seasonal migration of pastoralists with their animals to the lowland pastures of the Po Plain, of fruit and wood sellers to other districts of the region, and of artisans who sold their wares in lowland towns and cities. This type of fairly local-scale movement contributed to sustain the equilibrium of the mountain economy, together with mining, quarrying and small craft industries *in loco*. The decline and disappearance of these latter activities, and the fact that they were not replaced by new industries, together with a rapid population increase and worsening conditions in farming (leading to a progressive fragmentation of farm plots), were the causes which led to an intensification of temporary emigration. At the same time, the development of the economies of Central and Eastern Europe, easily reached by low passes through the Alps, enabled the seasonal migrants to be integrated into a wider geographical labour market. The movement was 90 per cent male and especially affected people who had construction skills. Official statistics, which almost certainly underestimated the phenomenon, enumerated 12,000 emigrants per year in 1882, rising to 60,000 by the end of the century. In Belluno province, where the average annual total was 25,000 over the period in question, 12 per cent of the total

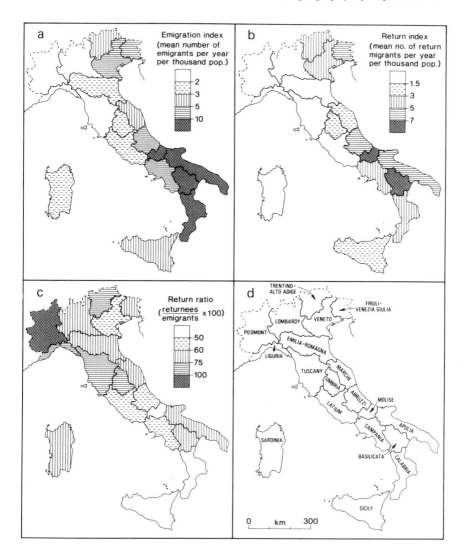

Figure 2.8 Regional patterns of Italian emigration and return migration, 1946–81

Source: King 1992.

population (16 per cent in some districts) were involved in this annual migration. The movement proved remarkably durable: as recently as 1961, 27,540 people, 13.8 per cent of the population of Belluno province, were temporary emigrants.

Overseas emigration, mainly to South America (Brazil, Argentina, Uruguay, Venezuela), developed only after Italian unification, and especially after 1887. This movement took away entire families; thus the emigration flow had high percentages of women and of children. The causes were familiar — demographic increase and crises in farming, especially in the wine and silk sectors. Declining conditions of rural life in the Veneto lowlands in the 1870s and 1880s led to widespread disease, especially pellagra — the 'disease of poverty'. The pull factors, as we saw earlier, were the opportunities for colonising land in South America, and the existence of regular shipping links from Genoa. This migration developed from the Veneto in two phases. The first phase involved fairly small numbers of smallholders and tenants from the foothill zones of Belluno, Treviso and Vicenza provinces who simply sold up and went to become colonising farmers. The second phase, which started in the mid-1890s, was more of a mass migration and took landless labourers from the lower plains of Verona, Rovigo and the north-east part of Venice province on assisted passages, paid for by the Brazilian government, to settle as owner–farmers.

Turning now to the post-war period, the second wave of Italian mass emigration, maps of various indices have been produced at the regional scale (King 1992). Figure 2.8 shows three such maps based on annual data for the period 1946–81. Emigration has been most intense in the mainland south and, secondarily, in the north-east Italian regions of Veneto and Friuli-Venezia Giulia. The return migration index (returnees per thousand population of the regions of return) is also strongest in these areas. The return ratio, however, which relates returnees to emigrants, shows the highest values in the north-western part of Italy, indicating that this part of the country has a higher propensity both to attract back its own migrants and to 'capture' returnees who originally left from other regions.

Migration data for the next levels of geo-statistical unit in Italy, the 95 provinces and the 8,000 or so communes, can only be reliably created by the intercensal migration residual method. Such a technique fails to quantify gross movement and to distinguish internal migration from emigration and return from abroad. Some annual data on foreign emigration and return are available at these levels, but they are widely regarded as flawed (King 1992, pp. 2–4). Figure 2.9 shows the provincial mosaic for the 1971–81 intercensal period. The picture is one of net out-migration from the southern half of the peninsula, including Sicily and Sardinia, from Alpine provinces such as Sondrio and Belluno, and from certain provinces of the lower Po Plain such as Mantua, Rovigo and Ferrara. Most of the north gains by net in-migration, the greatest gains being registered by provinces with medium-sized cities which are fast-growing and adjacent to the main metropolitan centres (e.g. Varese to Milan, Latina to Rome).

Examples of the micro-geography of Italian migration are based on commune-level data. There are several such examples in the literature, usually for individual provinces or regions, and usually for southern regions and provinces, these being the ones most affected by migratory

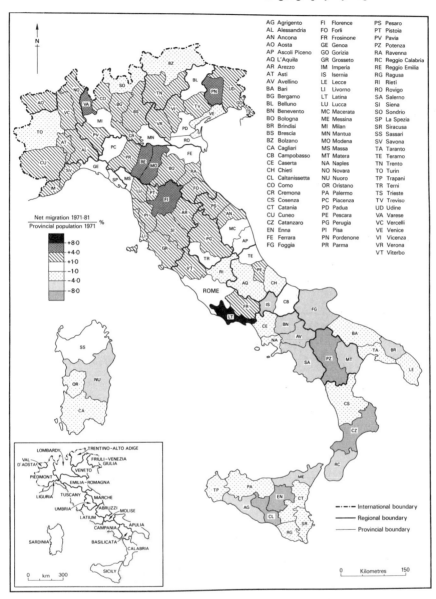

Figure 2.9 The provincial pattern of net migration in Italy, 1971–81
Source: King 1985.

loss in recent decades. Figure 2.10 shows the intercensal net migration pattern for Sardinia during 1961–71 — the decade of maximum mobility of the Sardinian population (King and Strachan 1980). Areas of net in-migration are very few (only 19 out of the island's 350 communes) and are limited to developing coastal towns and tourist areas (Porto Torres,

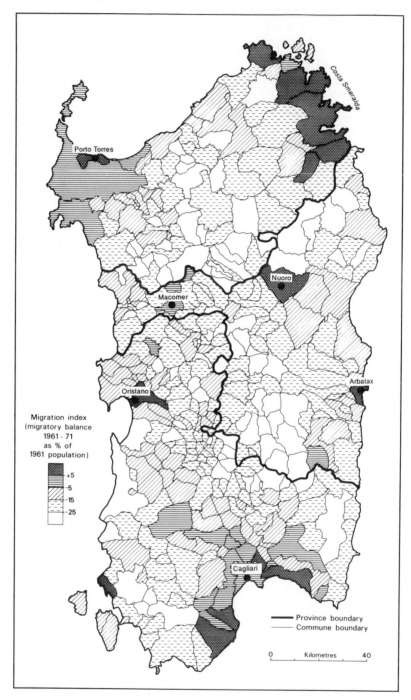

Figure 2.10   Sardinia: net migration index by commune, 1961–71
Source: King and Strachan 1980.

Costa Smeralda, Oristano, Arbatax, Gulf of Cagliari) and the two main towns of the interior (Nuoro and Macomer). Large numbers of communes in the interior, especially in the east-central highlands, lost over 15 per cent (some more than 40 per cent) of their populations owing to out-migration during the decade as the agro-pastoral economy of the island collapsed and people left for the mainland, abroad (mainly European destinations) or the main towns of the island. King and Strachan (1980) found that the trend in service sector employment 'explained' the greatest percentage of the spatial variation in migration. In other words, communes with net in-migration or low out-migration were those where growth in tertiary sector employment was the greatest.

The problems of mapping and interpreting net migration without reference to the gross flows which produce the net figures have been mentioned more than once. In most of southern Italy during the 1960s and 1970s there was a very considerable 'turnover' of migrants, giving relatively small net balances. The in-migration component of the net figure consisted overwhelmingly of returning migrants.[1] Strachan and King (1982) tried to relate the various patterns of gross flows to each other and to a range of hypothesised independent variables for the southern regions of Apulia, Basilicata and Calabria for the 1970s; this was done via cluster analysis of commune data on emigrants, returnees and socio-economic variables. The results of this analysis show that most of Apulia has moderate rates of emigration but, relative to these emigration levels, high incidences of return, whereas Basilicata and Calabria have higher levels of gross emigration and lower rates of return. A long series of cluster and component maps in Strachan and King (1982) shows that the high rates of return in Apulia and in other favoured zones (northern Basilicata, pockets on the west coast of Calabria, etc.) are correlated with a buoyant tertiary and commercial sector, above-average housing quality, and richer farming.

Communes are not, in fact, the lowest common denominator for recording population in Italy. The decennial censuses also record population (but not migration) figures for each *frazione* (small village or hamlet) and for dispersed dwellings (*case sparse*) in each commune. In a study of the Cilento region of southern Campania, White (1985) analysed population change, 1961–71, and other data for the 77 *frazioni* of the district. Multiple regression analysis of these data showed that the presence or absence of tourism was the main factor explaining population change; the greatest positive population change was thus found along the coast where embryonic resort development was under way during the period analysed.

For really local-scale study of the geography of departure field mapping is necessary. This enables the recording of the migration history and status of each family and its dwelling. The mapping of such on-the-spot enquiries inevitably involves restricted areas such as villages and small rural districts. This has been done in a number of settings including the

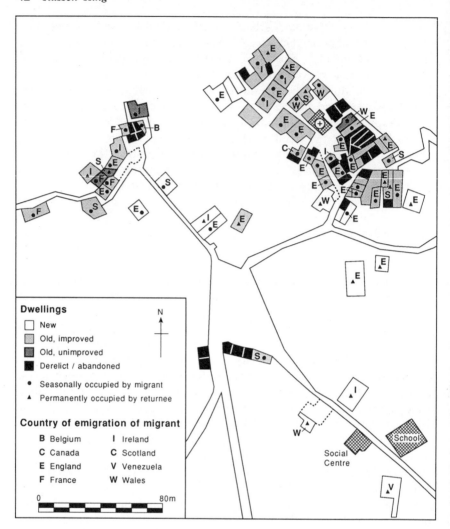

Figure 2.11   Housing and migration in the village of Monforte, Latium, Italy
Source: Reynolds 1993.

Aeolian Islands (King and Young 1979), the village of Casalattico in the southern Apennines (Reynolds 1993), and two villages in the Giulian Prealps (Meneghel and Battigelli 1977). Although there is a danger that such micro-geographical studies get bogged down in detail, they are effective in portraying the migration personality of an area, and the impact of the out-migration process (and perhaps also the return) on the rural landscape and built environment.

When such studies are compared and analysed, certain spatial regularities are observed. One is the tendency for small settlements to be affected to a greater extent by out-migration than larger settlements; thus, within a given rural *comune*, it is generally the higher, more remote and inaccessible *frazioni* which are abandoned first. Within individual village settlements, there is a tendency for old, cramped (but often historically valuable) dwellings to be abandoned and not reoccupied and for returning migrants to build new, spacious housing on the fringes of the village. Usually the abandoned dwellings are in the older, higher parts of hilltop and hillside settlements, perhaps clustered round the church or a ruined castle: in this way emigration progressively destroys the *centro storico* of the towns and villages of origin. The new dwellings built by returnees with savings garnered from their years of hard work abroad are often found in a valley location, near a main road or railway station, or along a coastal strip. Such dwellings need more space for their gardens and patios; their expansiveness and 'showiness' are a symbolic statement of the returnees' economic achievement and aspirations for social status within the village. For returnees the ancestral dwellings in the village core are merely a reminder of a time when life was much harder; a return to the decaying alleys of the *centro storico* would thus confer little prestige as well as being impracticable for modern vehicular access. Figure 2.11 shows these processes of abandonment and resettlement for part of the commune of Casalattico in southern Latium. The map shows both the physical state of each dwelling (derelict, unimproved, improved, new) and, where owned or occupied by a migrant or migrant family, the destination of the migration. As can be seen from the map, this village has a particular migration history to the British Isles (see Reynolds 1993), but many other countries are represented as well. The main contrast in the map is between the decay and abandonment evident in the *centro storico* of Monforte (especially the oldest section of the village south-east of the church), and the growth of new returnee-financed building scattered along the lanes away from the main village nucleus.

Conclusion

This chapter has presented a large number of maps which document the geography of emigration at a range of scales from the global to the village. Such maps are only a selection of those theoretically available, either as existing maps in the literature, or as potential maps that could be drawn from migration data sets. The maps demonstrate that not only is migration a socially and demographically selective process, it is spatially highly selective as well. Although generalisations always have their exceptions, most of the departure areas are poor, rural, over-populated relative to their resources, and have high rates of population growth and unemployment. When individual countries and regions are examined, the real situations are seen to be much more complicated.

Attention also needs to be paid to the history of emigration in particular areas, to the key role of chain migration mechanisms, and to the political and institutional contexts of migration.

For each geography of departure, there is a geography of destination. Whilst mapping the spatial patterns of settlement at the destination is not the concern of this chapter, it is important to devote some attention to the way in which certain origin areas develop links to specific destinations. Such links are revealing when mapped and fascinating to unravel, although such unravelling can only be done on a region-by-region and community-by-community basis — an endless task. Where this has been done, migration is revealed to be an intriguing social process in which the functioning of kinship networks is often as important as the macroeconomic structures of international and inter-regional inequality which provide the wider context to human mobility and displacement.

So many studies have been carried out of immigrant settlement and integration (or non-integration) in destination areas that the impact of out-migration on the rural areas left behind is often neglected. This chapter has attempted to redress this imbalance somewhat by describing both in general terms and with reference to Italian case-study material the social geography of areas abandoned by emigrants. The impacts are usually clear: emigration leads to reduced total populations, both directly and by reduced fertility, and undermines the economic and social viability of rural communities. Such a process may become cumulative and irreversible, posing formidable problems for rural planning.

Although this chapter has been essentially retrospective, taking its examples mainly from recent decades but also from the end of the last century, its relevance for future studies of emigration should not be overlooked. The techniques of mapping and of interpretation presented here can be applied to areas of out-migration for the new European migrations currently under way and likely to increase in the future. These studies will need to be carried out in different areas — in Poland rather than Portugal, in Senegal rather than Sardinia, in Cape Verde rather than Calabria.

Note

1.   Foreign immigrants into Italy have, it is true, grown spectacularly during the late 1970s and throughout the 1980s, even into the south, but many of these were not recorded by the annual migration figures.

References

Alberoni, F., 1970, 'Aspects of internal migration related to other types of Italian migration', in Jansen, C.J. (ed.), *Readings in the sociology of migration*, Pergamon, Oxford, 285–316.

Boyd, M., 1989, 'Family and personal networks in international migration: recent developments and new agendas', *International Migration Review*, 23(3): 638–70.

Brunetta, G., 1983, 'Veneto', in Gentileschi, M.L. and Simoncelli, R. (eds), *Rientro degli emigrati e territorio*, Istituto Geografico Italiano, Naples, 149–209.

Clout, H.D., 1974, 'Population changes in the Auvergne region of central France 1954–68', *Erdkunde*, 28(4): 246–59.

Clout, H.D., 1976, 'Rural–urban migration in Western Europe', in Salt, J. and Clout, H.D. (eds), *Migration in post-war Europe: geographical essays*, Oxford University Press, London, 30–51.

Douglass, W.A., 1975, *Echalar and Murelaga: opportunity and exodus in two Spanish Basque villages*, Hurst, London.

Iszaevich, A., 1975, 'Emigrants, spinsters and priests: the dynamics of demography of Spanish peasant societies', *Journal of Peasant Studies*, 2(3): 292–312.

King, R.L., 1976, 'The evolution of international labour migration movements concerning the EEC', *Tijdschrift voor Economische en Sociale Geografie*, 67(2): 66–82.

King, R.L., 1982, 'Southern Europe: dependency or development?' *Geography*, 67(3): 221–34.

King, R.L., 1985, 'Italian migration: the clotting of the haemorrhage', *Geography*, 70(2): 171–5.

King, R.L., 1986, 'Return migration and regional economic development: an overview', in King, R.L. (ed.), *Return migration and regional economic problems*, Croom Helm, London, 1–37.

King, R.L., 1992, *Italian migration: the historical and geographical background*, University of Bristol, Centre for Mediterranean Studies, Occasional Paper 5.

King, R.L. and Strachan, A.J., 1980, 'Patterns of Sardinian migration', *Tijdschrift voor Economische en Sociale Geografie*, 71(4): 209–22.

King, R.L. and Young, S.E., 1979, 'The Aeolian Islands: birth and death of a human landscape', *Erdkunde*, 33(3): 193–204.

Lowenthal, D. and Comitas, L., 1962, 'Emigration and depopulation: some neglected aspects of population geography', *Geographical Review*, 52(2): 195–210.

MacDonald, J.S., 1956, 'Italy's rural social structure and emigration', *Occidente*, 12(5): 437–56.

MacDonald, J.S., 1958, 'Some socio-economic emigration differentials in rural Italy, 1902–1913', *Economic Development and Cultural Change*, 7(1): 55–72.

MacDonald, J.S., 1963, 'Agricultural organisation, migration and labour militancy in rural Italy', *Economic History Review*, 16(1): 61–75.

Meneghel, G. and Battigelli, F., 1977, *Contributi geografici allo studio dei fenomeni migratori in Italia*, Pacini, Pisa.

Portes, A. and Borocz, J., 1989, 'Contemporary immigration: theoretical perspectives on its determinants and modes of incorporation', *International Migration Review*, 23(3): 606–30.

Reynolds, B., 1993, *Casalattico and the Italians in Ireland*, Belfield Italian Library, Foundation for Italian Studies, Dublin.

Richmond, A.H., 1969, 'Sociology of migration in industrial and post-industrial societies', in Jackson, J.A. (ed.), *Migration*, Cambridge University Press, Cambridge, 238–81.

Salt, J., 1976, 'International labour migration: the geographical pattern of demand', in Salt, J. and Clout, H.D. (eds), *Migration in post-war Europe: geographical essays*, Oxford University Press, London, 80–125.

Salt, J., 1989, 'A comparative overview of international trends and types, 1950–80', *International Migration Review*, 23(3): 431–56.

Salt, J. and Clout, H.D., 1976, 'International labour migration: the sources of supply', in Salt, J. and Clout, H.D. (eds), *Migration in post-war Europe: geographical essays*, Oxford University Press, London, 126–67.

Strachan, A.J. and King, R.L., 1982, *Emigration and return migration in Southern Italy: a multivariate, cluster and map analysis*, University of Leicester, Department of Geography, Occasional Paper 9.

White, P.E., 1980, 'Migration loss and the residual community: a study in rural France 1962–75', in White, P.E. and Woods, R.I. (eds), *The geographical impact of migration*, Longman, London, 198–222.

White, P.E., 1985, 'Modelling rural population change in the Cilento region of southern Italy', *Environment and Planning A*, 17(12): 1401–13.

White, P.E. and Woods, R.I., (eds), 1980, *The geographical impact of migration*, Longman, London.

Wood, P., 1976, 'Inter-regional migration in Western Europe: a reappraisal', in Salt, J. and Clout, H.D. (eds), *Migration in post-war Europe: geographical essays*, Oxford University Press, London, 52–79.

Chapter 3

The social geography of immigrants in European cities: the geography of arrival

Paul White

Introduction

It is important to recognise at the outset that the motivations for the massive volumes of post-war international migration both within and into Europe have been extremely diverse, reflecting a very full range of human aspirations, objectives and fears. Whilst it has been customary to regard the most important reasons for mass migration as economic, we should also remember the existence of considerable flows of political refugees at various stages over the last 45 years, coupled with other movements where familial factors have proved the catalysts with economic considerations playing only a permissive role.

Since the end of the last war migrants have arrived at European frontiers from every corner of the world; the diversity of origins is far greater than occurred during previous important migratory periods in human history. Diversity affects not only geographical origin but also ethnicity, religion, language, family structures, clothing habits, food customs, skill levels, educational backgrounds, literacy and many other variables.

It is clear that the three important migration parameters of motivation, origin and destination have undergone constant evolution, albeit with certain particular periods (such as the mid-1970s or the late 1980s) witnessing more substantial changes. Trends have differed between countries, and individual phases of particular migration processes have operated at different times for specific origins and destinations.

For these reasons most successful models of international migration affecting post-war Europe have dealt only with limited time-periods and migratory subsystems. This is the case with Böhning's (1972) influential model of labour migration to north-west Europe and with the analysis by Castles *et al.* (1984) of the later evolution of these streams into ethnic minority communities. Any model which seeks to encompass a wider range of migration experience must operate at a greater level of abstraction. This chapter attempts to produce such a model, highlighting three waves of migration during the post-war period. The focus is placed on changes in the context of migrant reception as influencing the spatial sorting of migrant arrivals and the spatial characteristics of later ethnic minority community evolution. The model suggested here is based on experiences in north-west Europe, since until recently the eastern part of the continent has played only a very limited role in the European migration system, whilst southern Europe has been a source rather than a destination of migrants. These features have been changing in recent years, and the final section of the chapter briefly reviews the factors likely to influence the future development of ethnic minority communities of migrant origin throughout Europe.

Three waves of movement

In discussions of international migration in post-war Europe the greatest attention has been focused on labour migration. Explanations of the need for such movement have highlighted demographic and especially economic considerations (Böhning 1972; Castles and Kosack 1973), whilst other studies have emphasised changes in the character of supply involving the countries of origin (Castles *et al.* 1984). However, today's ethnic minority communities of migrant origin have not solely been created by labour migration but also by a variety of other types of movement. It is useful to explore these in terms of three migratory waves — labour migration, family reunification, and a third wave that might be loosely described as 'post-industrial'.

Although Figure 3.1 suggests that these three waves peak at different points in time, it must be made clear that they are not purely consecutive but, in fact, overlap at the level of Western Europe as a whole, although in certain individual countries the three are more or less discretely identifiable. It must also be added that certain post-war mass movements associated with the migration of Germans from Eastern Europe and with European decolonisation elsewhere are not fully encompassed within this classification.

Labour migration

The labour migration wave, generally commencing in the 1950s and extending through to the 1970s, has been extensively covered in the literature. The responsiveness of migration to economic conditions at the place of destination was nearly always clear, whether driven by free market forces or by specific recruitment by employers and governmental agencies.

Patterns of migrant origin were extremely diverse, partly reflecting the old colonial connections of certain of the destination countries, but in the classic 'guestworker' countries (West Germany, Switzerland and Austria) new national labour supply relationships were negotiated by governments. The geographical patterns of supply therefore involved far-

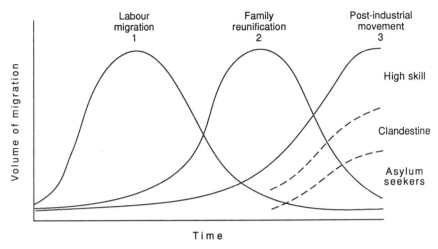

Figure 3.1 Three waves of international migration

flung colonies, ex-colonies and overseas possessions (in the West Indies, South Asia and sub-Saharan Africa) as well as more regional supply sources, predominantly in countries around the Mediterranean Basin (King 1976). As certain of these 'local' suppliers reached more advanced stages of economic development (Italy and Spain being the most important), greater diversity of migrant origins came into being, a factor of considerable significance in the subsequent history of ethnic minority formation (Castles *et al.* 1984).

Family reunification

It has become conventional to date the halting of large-scale labour migration to north-west Europe to the events accompanying the 'oil shock' and related economic recession of 1973–5, although it has been argued (White 1986) that bans on further labour recruitment were in fact motivated by a much more complex series of political and social arguments than such a straightforward economic explanation implies.

As stated earlier, however, the attempt to assign a single date to the end of one migration wave and the start of another is implausible since there is a degree of overlap. Much labour migration into France had historically involved family movement taking place within a few years of the arrival of the worker (Ogden 1989), and in the United Kingdom, where the first moves to halt labour migration date back to the early 1960s, a considerable amount of family movement had already occurred well before 1970.

In many countries, however, the latter half of the 1970s was a crucial period for family movement. Taking the European experience as a whole, for each migration stream the bulk of family reunification generally occurred over a relatively short space of time — little more than a decade in most cases — leaving a small and slowly diminishing number of single workers whose families had not joined them.

Post-industrial movement

Whilst the first two major post-war migration waves were relatively homogeneous in their broad outlines, the third — which can loosely be termed post-industrial — has been much more diffuse in character. This in part reflects the changing nature of European economies and societies away from an industrial base towards a more varied economic structure in which the significance of industrial and manufacturing employment is generally diminishing, coupled with other changes tending towards a greater polarisation in social structures. The role of international migration has been very important within certain of these developments.

As Figure 3.1 shows, it is possible to identify three major aspects of the European post-industrial international migration system. Each of the three types of migration has existed to some extent before, but each has come to much greater prominence over the past decade. A further observation is that in many cases family movement is common from the outset in this new evolutionary system.

When the first discussions were held in the European Community about the freedom of movement of labour, the expectation was that such movement would be mainly of the semi-skilled; today, at the inception of the Single European Market and of the European Economic Area the prospects are rather different. During the 1980s it became clear that increased intra-Western European mobility would not simply be 'more of the same' from the past. Changes in demand within labour markets, together with changes in the organisational structure of many employing enterprises, meant that labour shortages became most marked in highly skilled occupations. Growing transnational and multinational corporations increasingly created their own international internal labour markets, or recruited internationally (Salt 1988). By the later 1980s flows of international migrants in the working age group in and out of various north-west European countries consisted predominantly of the high-skilled in technical, managerial and professional occupational sectors, rather than the manual workers of the past.

High-skilled movement has therefore become a major feature of international migration over the past decade, involving both intra-European movements and migratory connections with other parts of the world, particularly North America and Japan. Most of this migration is much more temporary than the earlier labour migration, with short-term contracts and a circulatory system being common features. There are also increasing trends for repeated movements between two or more base areas for certain self-employed people, as well as increasing international movement among the affluent retired and semi-retired.

The second major and rapidly increasing form of migration involves rather different source areas and economic connections. The extent of *clandestine migration* is inevitably unknown, but all estimates show its rapid increase in significance in recent years, especially as part of the growing migratory influx into southern Europe. Clandestine migration is permitted by relatively weak frontier and internal controls, but it is also closely related to the growth of the informal economy and the significance of that economy in supplying certain important services. This latter fact means that in many cases the authorities have been reluctant to move against the complex informal and formal organisational systems that link clandestine migrants and employment, often in highly exploitative situations.

The third recently growing migration stream affecting Western Europe has involved *asylum-seekers*. Numbers of refugee arrivals at Western European frontiers rose dramatically during the 1980s (White and Kesteloot 1990), and further pressures are occurring in the 1990s. Part of the reason may relate to the effect of more restrictive immigration policies in various Western European countries forcing would-be immigrants to attempt to claim refugee status (Norro 1990), but other causes reflect increased political instability and ethnic tension in various parts of the world, coupled with greater economic hardship and the realisation of stronger feelings of relative deprivation. As with clandestine movement, the vast bulk of asylum-seeking migration has in the past originated in Third World countries, although conflicts in former Yugoslavia are also now generating massive refugee flows.

Whilst these three aspects of post-industrial migration have all grown in significance in recent years none of them is new: skilled migration has a long history, albeit at a lower level of intensity; clandestine migration has been present from the start of labour movement; and refugee flows have played a varying role in Europe over the last few decades, with early post-war movement generally involving European populations themselves, supplemented with particular flows in 1956 (Hungary), 1968 (Czechoslovakia), the late 1960s (East African Asians) and the late 1970s (refugees from South-East Asia).

The position of southern Europe in these three waves is of particular interest. Countries such as Portugal, Spain, Italy and Greece were all source countries for migrants of the first two waves. Since the late 1970s these countries have themselves become destinations, and to some extent their receipt of migrants has bypassed the first two waves, being concentrated instead on the third. The case of southern Europe in the migration system of post-industrial Europe is considered in detail in Chapter 10.

Changing contexts of reception

Migrants arriving in a particular country do not then spread out randomly throughout all possible destinations. The migrants use specific paths and routes, and these are influenced and in some cases manipulated by a variety of agencies to produce particular spatial outcomes. Such paths can be conceptualised as existing in a variety of dimensions — economic, social, political and geographical. In considering the geography of arrival of the migrants it is therefore necessary to evaluate the forces influencing the emergent distribution patterns.

It must be accepted, however, that these forces have not remained static throughout the post-war period, but have themselves evolved in response to changing economic and political structures, changing attitudes, and to the very presence of the migrants themselves. While the processes outlined here are arguably of general significance, their actual operation often involves mediation through particular local circumstances.

Explanations of the spatial distribution of ethnic minorities generally only focus on a limited set of causes. At the regional scale, explanations are usually couched in terms of economic and employment factors (Peach 1968), with chain migration processes playing a secondary role. By contrast, at the local scale the causes of ethnic distributions are usually felt to depend on a combination of three factors — the economic status of the migrants; levels of prejudice expressed towards them by the 'host' society and translated into controls on their freedom of choice; and the extent of 'in-group orientation' within the ethnic minority group, leading to voluntary segregation.

In relating the changing conditions of migrant reception to our earlier discussion of the three migratory waves, the material that follows is ordered around four sets of contextual factors that partly overlap with these more traditional explanations — employer involvement in migrant reception; governmental involvement (including both national and local government policies); evolving free market structures, particularly relating to economic activities, social attitudes and changing housing markets; and finally in-group orientation amongst migrants and ethnic minorities.

Employer involvement

Employers played a major role in much of the first wave of migration, a much reduced role in the second, but in the third wave employer involvement for certain aspects of international migration is once again at a high level.

Much labour migration, especially in the *Gastarbeiter* countries but also to some extent elsewhere (such as the United Kingdom or France), took place under direct employer recruitment of labour (Böhning 1972; Castles and Kosack 1973). Such recruitment resulted in a very high degree of selectivity amongst the migrants, but it also usually involved considerable employer involvement in the housing and therefore the residential location of the migrants. All aspects of the geography of arrival, from region of employment to the locality of residence, were decided either directly by the employer or with employer involvement in consortium situations, as for example in the financing of migrant worker hostel construction.

Labour migrants progressively moved out of their employer-provided accommodation into the free market (White 1984), a move accelerated by the desires for family reunification which meant that employer-provided hostels were no longer appropriate. It was only arguably in France that employers retained a role in deciding the housing of employees with families, through their decision-making roles in certain types of social housing (Pinçon 1981). Generally, however, the second wave of mass migration saw the virtual elimination of employer involvement in either recruitment or the regional or local placing of migrants.

The reception circumstances surrounding two groups within the third wave are, however, strongly influenced by employers. Movements of skilled workers are, as suggested earlier, very largely the result of direct recruitment within internal labour markets or through international advertising. Employer involvement in the residential location of such movers is often very great, creating discernible residential geographies of such migrants in the biggest European cities (Glebe 1986; White 1988).

Although statistical evidence is lacking, it is also certain that employer involvement is high in aspects of clandestine migration, where the arrangement of international travel, of an exploitative employment situation and of a place to live may form part of a single employer-driven system.

Government involvement

National governments are involved in the contexts of reception of migrants both through their formulation of policies on immigration and through their policies towards immigrants once arrived: many of the policy effects in the latter set may, in fact, be indirect ones resulting from policies designed for other purposes. A significant policy role is also played by local government in terms of policies towards immigrants after their arrival, except in Switzerland (and there only in conjunction with the federal ministries) where local authorities do not have general policy-making roles on immigration.

For the first wave of labour migrants national government immigration policies had both permissive and regulatory aspects, but had little effect on the geography of arrival of the migrants, since policies towards 'immigrants' were virtually non-existent. Changes in government policies during the 1970s and the introduction of bans on new labour recruitment form part of the process leading from the first to the second wave of migration. Here the regulatory element in immigration policies grew at the expense of permissiveness, and it was during this period of the late 1970s and early 1980s that policy conflicts became apparent between desires to improve the circumstances of existing ethnic minority communities ('immigrant' policies) and desires to persuade as many as possible to return 'home' (Gans 1990). Such repatriation schemes have since been identified as being important in creating a social climate whereby ethnic minorities were increasingly seen as a 'problem' (Freeman 1989).

National policies aimed at improving integration often brought in their wake specific local policies to influence the processes identified as leading to ethnic residential segregation and clustering. Throughout the decade from 1975 to 1985 a number of Western European countries and cities saw the introduction of measures to prevent or restrict foreigners moving into particular city districts or being allocated certain social housing properties under the control of municipalities (Arin 1991; Flett 1982). The conclusions from evaluative studies of these policies are that they in fact did little to promote the residential dispersal that they were aimed at.

During the 1980s the direct involvement of local and national government policy in the circumstances of immigrant arrival and reception weakened, in part through the steady dilution of the state's role in social housing in a number of European countries. It could be argued that certain of the difficulties and elements of deprivation faced by ethnic minorities today are the result of them being left to the free market.

However, governmental interest in the third wave of migrants has been considerable. It has been argued above that governments have actually connived at those types of clandestine migration that most closely serve particular interests of capital and host societies, but in general Western European governments have been keen to reduce clandestine movement and to deport illegal immigrants. The level of concern over asylum-seekers has also grown rapidly and, apart from measures to try to reduce flows, several governments have adopted, with varying degrees of success, policies for the spatial dispersion of refugees in the hope of avoiding the creation of further zones of ethnic minority concentration (Norro 1990).

Government involvement in the reception conditions for international migration in Western Europe has consistently been driven by a belief that ethnic minority segregation is a bad thing and that measures of social engineering should be used towards an objective of integration and assimilation. Such an aim does not tally with the working of the free market, nor with many of the aspirations of the migrant groups themselves.

Evolving free market structures

In macro-scale terms, the European economy has undergone a number of processes over the last forty years, moving from rapid growth to prolonged stagnation, from industrial strength to deindustrialisation, and from individual national economies to international economic structures. These economic changes have brought very different labour requirements, some of which have been indicated earlier in this chapter in the change from shortages of low-skill to shortages of high-skill personnel. The rise of the informal economy and its opportunities for clandestine migrants is a further important dimension of the contemporary scene: this issue is discussed further in Chapters 7 and 10. It should also be noted that economic restructuring today presents a threat to many of those ethnic minority communities that are still dependent on a role taken on during the first great period of labour migration (Gordon 1991).

It is not only European economies that have changed: societal attitudes have also shifted. Public opinion towards mass immigration was at first equivocal but over the years opinions have generally hardened. Hierarchies of the 'acceptability' of different ethnicities to the indigenous population have been uncovered, generally indicating a 'preference' for those of European origin, with Islamic groups (such as Algerians, Moroccans and Pakistanis) at the opposite pole (Girard 1977). According to Marxist theories on labour processes, the ethnic origins of the migrants should have lost significance through time as they are drawn into a particular class position. In fact, ethnicity has emerged as a crucial variable in Western European societies, with blocked assimilation and acceptance in some cases leading to the reassertion of a separate identity.

A further general socio-economic feature of significance to ethnic minority community evolution in Western Europe concerns changes in the housing market. Much attention has been paid by geographers to housing market explanations of residential segregation, but it is notable that European housing markets have changed considerably over recent decades, with the significance of the social housing sector generally peaking in the early 1970s followed by the privatisation of part of the stock, a lack of new construction, and the increasing association in political and public opinion of social housing with marginalised groups in society (Krätke 1989). It is arguably only in Dutch cities, because of the very high degree of social ownership still present in the housing stock, that large numbers of low-status ethnic minority groups are now to be found in good-quality accommodation (van Amersfoort 1990); elsewhere the operation of the free housing market has acted to squeeze housing opportunities for migrants. That is, of course, particularly true for clandestine and refugee migrants of the third migration wave who are effectively debarred from certain housing sectors.

One distinctive development in the housing market has been the emergence of subsectors catering specifically for certain ethnic groups, with in-group sources of finance, group-specific information channels and search patterns, and complex organisational networks holding the whole structure together. Such subsectors have evolved for migrants drawn from each of the three great migratory waves, but they increased in importance particularly during the change-over period from the wave of labour migration to that of family reunification in circumstances where securing satisfactory family accommodation was not possible through existing channels. The significance of such subsectors has grown further for certain groups of the third wave.

The total picture, therefore, is of a set of socio-economic structures that have evolved considerably during the past 40 years and that have resulted in new circumstances for ethnic minority reception and community evolution. One important observation, putting these trends together, is that as a result of economic restructuring, societal hostility and changes in housing markets, many ethnic minority groups have been thrown back on to their own resources to a considerable extent.

In-group orientations

It was Dahya (1974) who coined the phrase 'voluntary non-participation' to describe the tendency of certain groups to stay apart from the surrounding host society. This was hypothesised to relate to a 'myth of return' whereby the migrant group kept itself in a condition that would facilitate reintegration to its place of origin at some future date. Such a conceptualisation may now appear over-simplified since, as suggested above, in-group orientation may also result from problems encountered in dealing with the rest of society.

At the time of the first wave of labour migrants the general expectation in many European countries was that assimilation was not going to be an issue since the migrants were on short-term contracts and would retain their orientation to their places of origin where they had left their families, and to which they sent remittances. However, in certain countries, France being the most notable case, there was a genuine hope for long-term settlement with expectations of assimilation favouring a policy for the in-movement of those who might rapidly become 'French' — notably Italians and Spaniards (Ogden 1989).

With the inception of the second wave, of family reunification, assimilation became a significant issue everywhere. It quickly became apparent that the 'myth of return' was no longer sufficient to sustain 'apartness', but that the reasons for observable in-group orientation lay as much with reactions from outside the ethnic minority communities as from pressures from within. Nevertheless it has remained useful to many involved to retain the myth — for politicians to argue that ethnic minority groups constitute a 'fifth column', and for the leaders of minority communities to reassert group cultural identity (Heisler 1986). Such questions of identity have grown in significance with the growth to maturity of a 'second generation' of ethnic minority origin who have no direct experience themselves of migration.

Whilst official views, as indicated above, became mistrustful of cultural retention and its associated features during the family reunification stage, it is clear that an introversion of minority communities has served many beneficial purposes to the individuals involved in terms of mutual support and defence, collective cultural consumption, and a degree of bargaining power.

However, as Lichtenberger (1984) pointed out in her study of Yugoslavs in Vienna, the standpoints of many migrants are highly ambivalent. Whilst for those least susceptible to racial labelling and discrimination assimilation processes may indeed occur, although the example of the Irish in the United Kingdom suggests that the time-scale is a long one (King *et al.* 1989), for other groups a reassertion of apartness seems to be becoming the norm, sometimes involving the emergence of a new identity, as amongst the *beurs* (young people of North African ethnic origin) in France.

Amongst migrants of the third wave the remarks above may apply to all groups. In the case of highly skilled migrants the forces of in-group orientation (perhaps most especially for the Japanese) are as high as for many lower-status migrant groups of the past and present.

Spatial sorting

Regional patterns

Whilst descriptions of the spatial distributions of ethnic minority groups abound at a variety of scales, the problems generally lie in making the causal connections between these descriptions of the observable patterns and the sets of determining factors suggested earlier.

It is clear that in many Western European countries not only are there different levels of ethnic minority concentrations in different regions, but that the minority groups are differently composed. Inter-regional variations have been present in each of the three great waves of migration, with the draw for labour migration being the big cities and industrial regions in all countries, and with family reunification thus inevitably developing a similar pattern.

Amongst the third wave, skilled international migrants have concentrated in the great cities that provide the tertiary and quaternary economic sector jobs in which they are employed but have shunned the old industrial zones. Refugee flows have also concentrated in the big cities, partly relating to points of entry through airports, and partly for the infrastructural facilities and help that may be available through existing communities. National and local authorities may try to counter-balance these trends through policies of regional dispersal, but these have not, in general, been successful over anything other than the shortest time-periods. A special case is that of the Eastern European *Aussiedler* in Germany where different regional patterns have emerged amongst those originating from Poland, the former Soviet Union and Romania, with some elements of dispersion present (Sprink and Hellman 1989).

Contemporary Third World and clandestine migration also shows regional concentration, generally in the big cities such as Madrid or Rome which offer employment in the informal sector. But the case of Italy is an unusual one where, after the regions containing Rome and Milan, the next biggest foreigner presence in 1990 was estimated to occur in Sicily (Montanari and Cortese 1993). Here Third World immigrants have formed a labour force substituting for departed Sicilian migrants, although their distribution shows a close relationship to the points of entry through Sicilian ports.

With few exceptions post-war mass migration in Europe has been an important element in retaining population growth in metropolitan regions, even to the extent of counterbalancing recent trends of popula-tion loss amongst the indigenous populations of such city regions. The consequences of these 'replacement effects' are highly significant for aggregate processes of urban change. However, it has been the more micro-scale levels of intra-urban distributions that have been accorded greater attention.

The intra-urban scale

The post-war years have seen the addition of an ethnic dimension to the residential patterns of almost all European cities. Certainly ethnic elements were observable earlier on in cities (such as Paris or Vienna) where international or ethnically diffuse migration had been present in earlier decades. However, the post-war period, through the rising scale of migration, the increasing diversity of the migrants, and the spreading of flows to many more destinations, has seen a rise both in the significance of intra-urban spatial sorting on the basis of ethnicity, and of public perceptions of that significance.

International migrants have not been spread evenly within their destination cities. Instead they have become concentrated in particular districts as a result of the interaction of the processes outlined earlier. Although there are dangers of a loss of specificity, it is nevertheless worth drawing out the most general features of intra-urban ethnic minority distributions through time.

The wave of post-war labour migration, with its high degree of employer and government involvement and its highly selective character, brought two types of residential situation to the fore. The first consisted of residences in industrial areas, often suburban in location, where housing was provided by employers, as in Germany, or where unused land proximate to factories could be used for self-build accommodation, as with the *bidonvilles* in France. Although micro-scale segregation in these districts was often complete, at the neighbourhood level this was mitigated by the nearby presence of large numbers of the indigenous working class living in normal housing.

The second type of residential area for the first wave was that of the inner-city district of privately rented property at low rents, often in slum housing. Foreign migrants were excluded from both social housing and the owner-occupier sectors at the outset, and with low wage levels and a desire to keep costs low for reasons of saving or remittance transfer, concentrations in districts offering cheap but low-grade property became seen as a 'natural' process by all those involved. It was in an attempt to break such further 'natural' concentration that governments brought in interventionist 'immigrant' policies, as outlined earlier. However, such intervention did not come until the second wave of migration started to transform the population structures of the ethnic groups, making them more 'visible' through the presence of women and children.

Thus the first migratory wave was associated both with some suburban dispersal, and with the emergence of clear concentrations in inner-city slum districts in which the provision of community facilities quickly led to a feedback process encouraging further in-movement and the growth of in-group orientations.

The second wave of migration, that of family reunification, brought new circumstances to bear, both in terms of changing migrant composition and in terms of policy responses. The establishment of family structures amongst migrant groups also brought a change in their place within the housing market, with two particular features being of importance.

The first was the accession of ethnic minority families to social housing in many (but not all) destination countries. Where this occurred, as in The Netherlands, Sweden, the United Kingdom and France, it had the potential to create a marked suburbanisation of the ethnic group. Thus in Amsterdam the 1970s saw a rapid deconcentration of Moroccans and Surinamers from the inner city and their relocation in suburban social housing (van Amersfoort 1990). In Paris the present-day distribution of 'foreigners' is inexplicable without reference to the great movement into suburban social housing that occurred during the 1970s, although there are clear indications of selective allocation policies both between and within estates (Sporton and White (1989). In Britain suburbanisation through accession to social housing was not as common because in many cities urban renewal was creating high-rise council estates in inner-city areas to which ethnic minority families were allocated, for a variety of reasons including their own preferences, instead of to lower-density estates on urban peripheries.

The second housing market change that came about during family reunification was the movement of selected migrant groups in certain countries into owner-occupation, albeit at the cheapest end of the market in poor-quality properties not unlike those of the privately rented tenancies previously occupied. This particularly occurred amongst South Asians in the United Kingdom, but it also affected certain older migrant groups in France. Spatial change resulting from this process was generally slight, but it did create a high degree of segregation *between* ethnic groups since the propensity to purchase property was seen to be group-specific, being particularly high amongst the Spanish and Portuguese in France, and amongst Indians, Pakistanis, Bangladeshis and the Chinese in the United Kingdom.

It must be noted, however, that in Germany, Switzerland and Austria the housing sector changes associated elsewhere with family reunification did not occur to the same extent. Thus the dominance of private renting remained throughout, albeit with certain adjustments within that sector in relation to changed accommodation needs. Such adjustments often involved the movement out of suburban employer-provided accommodation into the 'open' market to rent an inner-city family apartment (O'Loughlin 1987). However, a certain continuation of employer involvement in accommodation provision also occurred amongst the largest firms where factory housing previously occupied by the indigenous workforce passed to the foreigner tenants who had replaced the upwardly mobile German workers in the least-skilled jobs.

Over the last decade the strengthening of in-group orientations has tended to reduce the rapidity of residential change for many groups, reinforced by the general decline in social housing opportunities in Europe referred to earlier. Major urban renewal programmes are also much less in evidence now than in the past, so that the locations of ethnic minority populations that evolved during the family reunification phase and especially during the 1970s are now stable and an established part of the urban social map.

However, the arrival of the third wave of post-industrial migrants has added certain new features. In particular the expansion of high-skilled migration has brought new areas of ethnic population growth to many cities. The housing market circumstances of these skilled movers are superficially similar to those of the first guestworker families of the past (with a lack of access to social housing, and the inappropriateness of owner-occupation, although caused by short time-horizons for the skilled migrants rather than by poor economic circumstances). However, their involvement in the private market is at a much higher level of quality, often with the assistance of their employers, and the residential areas that have emerged are therefore very distinct from those inhabited by other migrant groups (White 1988). In-group orientation may, however, be as strong or even stronger, such that in certain cities it is these skilled migrants who form the most highly segregated groups of all (Grimmeau and David-Valcke 1978).

Evidence on the residential distributions of clandestine migrants is obviously extremely difficult to obtain, but the indications are of very marked encapsulation within 'legitimate' communities. Recent research amongst the developing Moroccan community in Madrid (of both 'legal' and 'clandestine' movers) suggests patterns of residential location that are familiar from the past with both run-down inner-city rented properties and more suburban locations proximate to industrial and other employment being of great significance (Pumares 1991).

Consideration of the outcomes of the various processes operating amongst the different migration waves quickly shows that European cities now generally display significant levels of ethnic minority segregation, but that various explanations are needed. As Cross points out in Chapter 7 of this volume, true comparative studies measuring segregation have been few, but there are general indications that segregation levels are lower than in the cities of the United States, and that ethnic minority neighbourhoods are rarer than across the Atlantic. Instead most ethnic minority groups in Europe live amongst indigenous peoples, albeit in a series of asymmetric distributions.

In fact, if account is taken of stages in the life cycle and other standardising variables, it is sometimes found that some subgroups of the ethnic minority population actually display relatively low degrees of spatial separation from similar subgroups of the indigenous population. In Dutch cities, for example, there is little segregation between single-person households composed of Dutch or of foreign individuals (van Amersfoort and de Klerk 1987), and there are also indications in Sweden of life-stage residential sorting becoming more important than ethnic sorting (Lindberg and Lindén 1986). However, these observations concern only the older groups who arrived earliest during the first and second waves of labour migration and family reunification, and who anyway displayed the least cultural distinctiveness from local populations. In very many cases the more recently arrived populations are more segregated and the normative expectation of a reduction in such segregation through time is unlikely to occur given the present set of circumstances faced by such migrants from more 'different' origins.

Just as important as indigenous/minority segregation, therefore, is the high degree of segregation between ethnic groups of different origins, reflecting a series of influences such as different dates of arrival, different occupational status, reactions to different levels of prejudice, and the minutiae of identity formation and retention processes within groups.

It has been argued here that patterns of residential location and segregation were more fluid in the past than they are today, and that relative stability is now the norm. Earlier commentators identified 'classic' invasion and succession processes at work (Nebe 1988), or couched their explanations of change more in terms of the attractions of suburbanisation for the indigenous population than the push of recently arrived immigrants (O'Loughlin 1987). Processes of locational change require relatively high rates of intra-urban mobility: evidence today suggests that such mobility has fallen in a number of cities as a result of tight housing market conditions (Glebe 1990).

In total, therefore, apart from the establishment of new ethnic minority communities in southern European cities and the growth of high-status minority neighbourhoods in the largest financial centres, the general picture of ethnic minority residential distributions in Europe today is one of relative stability, affected in specific cities by processes of urban gentrification or renewal, but overall with few signs of major relocation at work, unlike the picture of two decades ago.

Towards the future

The classical labour migration and family reunification waves have now been all but completed, certainly in north-west Europe. The future of international migration into and within Europe in the next decade or so will depend on the continuation of the third wave of movement or on the generation of completely new flows.

The possibilities for enhanced skilled labour transfer appear equivocal. On the one hand there is likely to be a further strengthening of the internationalising trends within the European and global economy, which might be expected to create more skilled labour movement. But at the same time improved telecommunications links might reduce the need for actual face-to-face dialogue and decrease the need for movement. Simon (1991) has also pointed out that the development of a more 'European' attitude amongst the post-1992 generation might encourage the real establishment of a single European labour market, at least in some employment sectors. If this were to happen it might counteract the existing trend towards lower mobility rates within the European Community.

It is likely, in fact, that future migration pressures on Western Europe will be driven more by external forces than by internal labour demand within the region. Amongst these external forces the potential for East–West movement within the new Europe and for South–North migration from the Third World will be the two most significant features.

The scope for East–West migration is obviously immense, but the reality (except in the case of mass refugee movement, for example occasioned by a collapse of Eastern economic structures or further large-scale ethnic strife as has occurred in the former Yugoslavia) will almost certainly be highly controlled by Western governmental policies including, conceivably, the restriction by Germany on the entry of further *Aussiedler*, particularly from the former Soviet Union. Thus, although the logic of the integration of Eastern Europe into the European economy as a whole should, according to neo-classical economic theory, be a flow of capital to the East and of labour to the West, at least part of this equation will almost certainly be prevented by Western policies. The reverse flow of capital, where it does occur, will bring the new creation of high-status migrant neighbourhoods composed of entrepreneurs and managers in Eastern European cities.

Immigration policies throughout Europe will predictably attempt to control South–North flow (Grečić 1991), but here the probability of successful control is less, given the greater extent of the possible pressures from the source countries and of the propensity of the potential migrants to accept clandestine movement and informal labour conditions in the face of a far worse alternative at home.

If the argument that future migration streams are likely to be determined more by conditions at the sources of supply is correct, then those movements that do occur in the future will be *confronted* by conditions in the host economies and societies rather than *responding* to them. Clearly much will depend on the future course of European economic growth, and on the way such aggregate growth is translated into local circumstances. However, one of the most likely future trends appears to be the continued deindustrialisation of the core economies of Western Europe, with consequent economic restructuring altering the balances of employment away from further manual work and towards the tertiary and quaternary sectors. Within this trend the role of future South–North or East–West migration may be crucial in giving a further impetus towards the growth of the informal economy. A feature already apparent in various parts of Eastern Europe is the attraction of clandestine migrants to perceived informal sector opportunities in nearby countries, as with the rapidly growing circulatory systems of Russians crossing into Poland: with any perception of entry possibilities into Western Europe such informal sector moves could develop significantly.

There are strong signs that one important dimension of the future context of migrant arrival both in Western and in Eastern Europe will be a resurgent racism, currently seen in the *Vlaamse Blok* in Belgium, in the rise of neo-Nazism and right-wing pressure groups in Germany and Austria, in Le Pen's *Front National* in France, in the extreme-right MSI party in Italy, and in talk of 'ethnic cleansing' in various parts of Eastern Europe. Whilst such racism will be aimed at halting immigration it will also have profound repercussions on the tone of the agenda surrounding the existing presence of ethnic minority communities, with the likely effect of producing further restrictions to assimilation and the encouragement of greater identity and consciousness-raising among such groups. In recent years in certain European countries there have been tentative moves away from a normative expectation of ethnic minority assimilation, and towards the recognition of a 'multicultural' model of society. With a growth of racism such developments will be halted or reversed.

It is unlikely that the housing markets of the rest of the 1990s will again become as favourable as they were during the 1960s and 1970s to the creation of new areas of ethnic minority concentration. Where new migration does occur it will most likely lead to further pressure on those sectors of the housing stock already used by existing communities.

Finally, it must be remembered that the composition and aspirations of existing ethnic minority communities will themselves alter over the next decade or two. Pressures leading to inter-generational change are already strong, as a population with no direct experience of migration comes to maturity. Their search for identity both as individuals and as groups involves complex processes of negotiation which appear to vary markedly in response to a large number of both in-group and out-group circumstances (Bolzman *et al.* 1987).

The effects of post-war international migration in Western Europe have arguably been as profound as those created in the past during the great periods of urban-industrial growth fuelled by internal movements of population. The presence of ethnic minority communities of migrant origin is now felt in almost every Western European urban area. The diversity of experiences for all concerned has been very great indeed, but underpinning these experiences there has been a relatively limited set of macro-scale economic, political, societal and geographical processes which have evolved differentially in time and space throughout the post-war period. The significance of migration has been such as to bring about profound changes even within those structural processes. Mass international migration has not therefore been simply a series of 'events' but has also become part of the underlying structure of European life. The extension of the European migration field to the eastern part of the continent will be one of the great transformations of the 1990s.

References

Arin, C., 1991, 'The housing market and housing policies for the migrant labor population in West Berlin', in Huttmann, E. *et al.* (eds), *Urban housing segregation of minorities in Western Europe and the United States*, Duke University Press, London, 199–214.

Böhning, R., 1972, *The migration of workers in the United Kingdom and the European Community*, Oxford University Press, London.

Bolzman, C., Fibbi, R. and Garcia, C., 1987, 'La deuxième génération d'immigrés en Suisse: catégorie ou acteur social?' *Revue Européenne des Migrations Internationales*, 3(1): 55–72.

Castles, S. and Kosack, G., 1973, *Immigrant workers and class structures in Western Europe*, Oxford University Press, London.

Castles, S., Booth, H. and Wallace, T., 1984, *Here for good: Western Europe's new ethnic minorities*, Pluto, London.

Dahya, B., 1974, 'The nature of Pakistani ethnicity in industrial cities in Britain', in Cohen, A. (ed.), *Urban ethnicity*, Tavistock, London, 77–118.

Flett, H., 1982, 'Dimensions of inequality: Birmingham council housing allocations', *New Community*, 10(1): 46–56.

Freeman, G.P., 1989, 'Immigrant labour and racial conflict: the rôle of the state', in Ogden, P.E. and White P.E. (eds), *Migrants in modern France*, Unwin Hyman, London, 160–76.

Gans, P., 1990, 'Changes in the structure of the foreign population of West Germany since 1980', *Migration*, 7: 25–49.

Girard, A., 1977, 'Opinion publique, immigration et immigrés', *Ethnologie Française*, 7: 219–28.

Glebe, G., 1986, 'Segregation and intra-urban mobility of a high-status ethnic group: the case of the Japanese in Düsseldorf', *Ethnic and Racial Studies*, 9(4): 461–83.

Glebe, G., 1990, 'Segregation and migration of the second generation of guestworker minorities in Düsseldorf', *Espace, Populations, Sociétés*, 1990–2: 257–78.

Gordon, I., 1991, *The impact of economic change on minorities and migrants in Western Europe*, University of Reading, Department of Geography, Discussion Paper 2.

Grečić, V., 1991, 'East–West migration and its possible influence on south–north migration', *International Migration*, 29(2): 241–52.

Grimmeau, J.P. and David-Valcke, A., 1978, 'Les cadres étrangers à Bruxelles', *Revue Belge de Géographie*, 102: 33–41.

Heisler, B.S., 1986, 'Immigrant settlement and the structure of emergent immigrant communities in Western Europe', *Annals American Academy of Political and Social Science*, 485: 76–86.

King, R., 1976, 'The evolution of international labour migration concerning the EEC', *Tijdschrift voor Economische en Sociale Geografie*, 67(2): 66–82.

King, R., Shuttleworth, I. and Strachan, A., 1989, 'The Irish in Coventry: the social geography of a relict community', *Irish Geography*, 22(2): 64–78.

Krätke, S., 1989, 'The future of social housing: problems and prospects of "social ownership": the case of West Germany', *International Journal of Urban and Regional Research*, 13(3): 282–303.

Lichtenberger, E., 1984, *Gastarbeiter: Leben in Zwei Gesellschaften*, Hermann Böhlau, Vienna.

Lindberg, G. and Lindén, A.-L., 1986, 'Housing market segmentation in Swedish local authorities; immigrants and Swedes, young and old', *Scandinavian Housing and Planning Research*, 3: 233–48.

Montanari, A. and Cortese, A., 1993, 'Third World immigrants in Italy', in King, R. (ed.), *Mass migrations in Europe: the legacy and the future*, Belhaven, London, 275–92.

Nebe, J.M., 1988, 'Residential segregation of ethnic groups in West German cities', *Cities*, 5(3): 235–44.

Norro, P., 1990, 'Accueil et répartition des candidats-réfugiés politiques en Belgique', *Espace, Populations, Sociétés*, 1990–2: 191–205.

Ogden, P.E., 1989, 'International migration in the nineteenth and twentieth centuries', in Ogden, P.E. and White, P.E. (eds), *Migrants in modern France*, Unwin Hyman, London, 34–59.

O'Loughlin, J., 1987, 'Chicago an der Ruhr or what? Explaining the location of immigrants in European cities', in Glebe, G. and O'Loughlin, J. (eds), *Foreign minorities in continental European cities*, Steiner, Wiesbaden, 52–69.

Peach, G.C.K., 1968, *West Indian migration to Britain*, Oxford University Press, London.

Pinçon, M., 1981, *Les Immigrés et les HLM*, Centre de Sociologie Urbaine, Paris.

Pumares, P., 1991, *Inmigración Marroqui en Madrid: el caso del Poblado de Ricote*, Instituto de Economía y Geografía Aplicadas, Madrid.

Salt, J., 1988, 'Highly-skilled international migrants, careers and internal labour markets', *Geoforum*, 19(4): 387–99.

Simon, G., 1991, 'Une Europe communautaire de moins en moins mobile?' *Revue Européenne des Migrations Internationales*, 7(2): 41–61.

Sporton, D. and White P.E., 1989, 'Immigrants in social housing: integration or segregation in France?' *The Planner*, 75(4): 28–31.

Sprink, J. and Hellmann, W., 1989, 'Finanzielle Belastung oder ökonomisches Potential? Regionale unterschiedliche Konsequenzen des Aussiedlerzustroms', *Informationen zur Raumentwicklung*, 5: 323–9.

van Amersfoort, H., 1990, 'La répartition spatiale des minorités ethniques dans un état-providence: les leçons des Pays-Bas 1970–1990', *Espace, Populations, Sociétés*, 1990-2: 241–55.

van Amersfoort, H. and de Klerk, L., 1987, 'Dynamics of immigrant settlement: Surinamese, Turks and Moroccans in Amsterdam, 1973–1983', in Glebe, G. and O'Loughlin, J. (eds), *Foreign minorities in continental European cities*, Steiner, Wiesbaden, 199–222.

White, P.E., 1984, *The West European city: a social geography*, Longman, London.

White, P.E., 1986, 'International migration in the 1970s: revolution or evolution?' in Findlay, A.M. and White, P.E. (eds), *West European population change*, Croom Helm, Beckenham, 50–80.

White, P.E., 1988, 'Skilled international migrants and urban structure in Western Europe', *Geoforum*, 19(4): 411–22.

White, P.E. and Kesteloot, C., 1990, 'Les migrations internationales en Europe Occidentale durant les années quatre-vingt', *Espace, Populations, Sociétés*, 1990-2: 316–23.

Chapter 4

A general framework for the European migration system in the 1990s

Antonio Golini, Corrado Bonifazi and Alessandra Righi

Introduction

Even though only a small proportion of the world's population is involved, international migration has an importance that goes beyond the actual figures. In fact, at the beginning of the 1980s there were about 50 million people or 1 per cent of the world population who were living in a country other than the one in which they were born (United Nations 1989). To this we should add the overall stock of temporary immigrants which, according to Appleyard (1989), stood at about 20 million individuals worldwide during the same period. The figures relating to the flows were also low, relatively speaking. The World Bank (1991) estimates the average annual net migration for the period 1985–90 at 1 million persons made up of those who move to take a permanent residence, legally admitted refugees and illegal immigrants. Of this 1 million, 58 per cent of the net migration is into the United States.

Despite the relatively small size of these migration figures when set against global population, there is a growing interest in international migration in academic and political circles. This attention is fired by the growing imbalances between different parts of the world and by the political uncertainty which now reigns not only in the South of the globe but also in most of the ex-communist countries. From the perspective of Western affluent societies, international migration is one of the most dramatic problems that the world is facing. Their fear is that if the migratory flows acquire an intensity proportionate to the size of the push forces, the social and economic equilibrium of the world would be upset. This would not only affect the well-being of the developed countries but would also deprive the developing countries of their human resources.

For the last 20 years the European migratory system has been shaped by a dual polarisation on North–South and West–East lines, to which demographic and economic factors have contributed. A good example is the increasing gap between the two shores of the Mediterranean (Montanari and Cortese 1993). Political changes in the East in the last few years have further complicated the situation; the ex-Comecon countries which were formerly excluded from the international migration system have already become involved and will become even more so in the future.

The size of migratory flows from the East will depend on the economic and social reforms that the Eastern countries manage to introduce. We can assume that in the short and medium term economic restructuring will cause high unemployment and create even more severe economic imbalances between a rich Western population and a poor Eastern population — at least for the more deprived social groups. Over the next few years these factors will encourage people to move towards the richer countries. The fact that in the East the age structure of the population is younger than in the West will also encourage migration, as will the cultural and geographical closeness of the two parts of Europe. Moreover, Western European countries will probably be more favourably inclined to accept immigrants from Eastern Europe — because this is an area of strategic importance — than from the South.

Although in this chapter we are mainly interested in the situation in Europe, many of the characteristics of international migration in general lead us to consider a larger area than that of the European continent alone. Certainly the south-east Mediterranean and Eastern Europe plus the ex-Soviet Union are natural reservoirs for future European migration, but the possibility of migration flows from other world areas — Black Africa, Latin America, South East Asia — cannot be ruled out.

European international migration flows in recent decades

In the 1980s there was a clear trend of expansion in international migration, as demonstrated by the progressive entry into the system of countries (for instance in Central Africa and Eastern Europe) which were not previously involved in the migratory flows. In the past, colonial links and geographical proximity fashioned international migration in a very precise way but this is no longer the case (Gesano 1991). The current situation is characterised by a growing contrast between supranational areas which are at different levels of development. This is expressed in geographical terms along the 'fault lines' which divide 'North' from 'South' and 'West' from 'East'.

Salt (1989) has identified the following characteristics in the new map of international migration: a large decline in permanent settlement and a consequent increase in temporary migration (at least as regards intention); the increasing importance of family reunion; an increase in the scope of international migration; the fact that institutions are playing a more important role; an increase in the number of refugees; and growing pressures towards illegal immigration. Migration flows work within a highly interdependent global system but are further characterised by greater cultural differences than in the past (Chiarello 1990). The flows work in a context in which the push forces — of a demographic, economic, social and political nature — have gained importance in the countries of origin, whereas the official demand for immigrants on the part of countries of traditional or possible destination has declined (Bonifazi 1988; Golini 1988).

A common element in the changes that have taken place in international migration in the 1980s is the prevalence of the political factor over the other factors competing to determine the migratory system. If, generally speaking, 'it is precisely the control which states exercise over borders that defines international migration as a distinctive social process' (Zolberg 1989, p. 405), never before has such a connection been so obvious. In almost all of the developed countries, immigration policies — the result of balancing the needs and moods of the various social groups — now play a role which probably exceeds the scale necessary to deal with the specific problem. However, this policy intervention determines the size and character of legal immigration and thus makes the first basic distinction between legal and illegal or clandestine immigrants. Let us not forget that hundreds of thousands of people all over the world are encouraged to emigrate precisely for political reasons.

In the post-war history of international migration in Europe a phase of strong immigration flows and markedly positive net migration can be identified. For most of the main immigration countries, this stage lasted up to the mid-1970s. The turning point occurred when the 'stop migration' policies were introduced in the two-year period 1973–4. In the following years the in-flows declined and, for the first time since the war, in some countries (Germany and Switzerland, for example) net migration was temporarily negative. Between 1975 and 1980, the in-flows picked up again and there was a growth in net migration, but it was nothing like the level reached during the boom period of European labour migration.

In 1990, the overall foreign population in the various countries was as follows: Germany had reached 5,241,800, Switzerland 1,100,300, it was 904,500 in Belgium, 692,400 in The Netherlands, and 3,607,600 in France. Once a community has created ties with the departure areas, extensive and deep-rooted links are established and new legal and illegal migratory flows begin to emerge even in the face of restrictive regulations and strict controls. It is not easy to understand completely the changes that have taken place in the traditional immigration countries because the new factors and the effects of past migration history tend to overlay each other. For this reason there is growing interest in what is happening in the new immigration countries of southern Europe and, in particular, in Italy.

We can look at the difference between today's and yesterday's trends by considering the different sending areas and the different way in which immigrants enter the labour market in Italy today and in Germany at the beginning of the 1970s. In Italy, more than 44 per cent of foreigners with valid sojourn permits (at 31 December 1990) came from outside Europe and the Mediterranean area, i.e. they came from sub-Saharan Africa,

America and Asia (excluding the Middle East). In contrast, in Germany at the time of the 1970 census this proportion was little more than 5 per cent. These figures demonstrate the different geographical context in which international migration now operates. In the space of 20 years the links and the interdependences between geographical areas are so extensive and highly ramified that migration can develop even without geographical or colonial ties between the sending and the receiving countries and without there being any particularly strong quantitative imbalances in the labour markets of the receiving countries.

In Italy, foreign workers mainly enter the labour market in the following sectors: fishing, agriculture (especially in some zones of southern and central Italy), and services (street vendors, domestic helpers, portering, catering, etc.); whereas relatively few find a job in industry (Gesano 1991; Pugliese 1991). On the basis of one of the most recent and comprehensive surveys carried out (see Censis 1991), of the 1,525 foreigners interviewed, 67.2 per cent had a job (45.7 per cent a steady job and 21.5 per cent occasional work) and 20.9 per cent were unemployed. Taking the group in work, 10.7 per cent were working in the primary sector (10.4 per cent in agriculture and 0.3 per cent in fishing); 13.5 per cent were working in industry (8.6 per cent as unskilled workers and 4.9 per cent in the building trade); 5.1 per cent worked as craftsmen; and, lastly, 70.7 per cent were working in the service sector (25.4 per cent in domestic help, 15.9 per cent as street vendors, 14 per cent in hotels and the catering trade, 9.4 per cent were working in other services, 2.8 per cent as white-collar workers and 3.2 per cent did other kinds of work). The comparison with the German immigrant employment situation is extremely interesting and cannot, evidently, be explained only by structural differences in the two economies. In 1970, foreign workers in Germany were distributed over the various sectors of economic activity as follows: 0.9 per cent in agriculture; 3.3 per cent in the mining sector; 16.7 per cent in the building trade; 62.7 per cent in industry; and 16.4 per cent in services (Böhning and Maillat 1974).

In the past, then, immigrants tended to be absorbed mainly by industry but today their working area is largely the unqualified section of the tertiary sector. In fact, in the advanced capitalist countries, the pull forces increasingly tend to be concentrated at the lower levels or — but to a much lesser extent — at the highest levels of the occupational hierarchy. As a result, this new immigration is only a part substitute for the national labour force within the official labour market; cases of 'parallel supply' are to be found in sectors and jobs where the border between 'legal' and 'illegal' work is less clear (domestic help, fishing, the building trade, light industry, etc.).

In the 1950s and 1960s foreign workers were considered the cheapest possible way to face the increasing labour demand. Now foreign labour makes it possible to fill the supply gaps in specific labour market areas which exist even in a situation of relatively high unemployment. In this somewhat more complex situation, the weight of non-economic factors — demographic, social and political — in determining the migration flows has increased. Links of various kinds also play their part, in particular the information links which are beginning to be established even between very distant areas in our 'global village'. It is precisely the existence of these links — which may vary in nature — that leads to the birth and consolidation of many immigration flows, guaranteeing a flow of information that is needed by immigrants in order to 'colonise' a space of their own in the receiving country.

Demographic imbalances

For a better understanding of the present migration situation it is necessary briefly to examine the demographic trends in various regions of the world. Table 4.1 summarises some key demographic contrasts at world level and for those regions which most directly affect the European migratory area. The South of the world is presently going through the third stage in its demographic transition: fertility is declining, the population growth rate is beginning to fall, and the proportion of the young population is still high, even if beginning to fall. On the other hand, the North has gone beyond the fourth stage into what has been defined as the 'post-transitional' stage, with growth rates of around zero and a sharp decline in fertility (total fertility rate or TFR) which has now fallen to 1.9, below the replacement level of 2.1 births per woman. In this situation the population is ageing, tending to remain stationary in the medium term and to decline in the long term.

The differences are more marked if we compare the various continental areas. In this case the range is from 1.7 children per woman in Europe to 6.2 in Africa. The gap between the two continents over the last 30 years has in fact increased since the TFR in Africa in this period has only fallen by 8 per cent whereas in Europe it has fallen by 35 per cent. There has, however, been a sizeable decline in Latin America and Asia even if fertility remains at about 3.5 children per woman, still well above the figures recorded in the developed areas.

In the European migratory area, the lowest fertility is to be found in the countries with market economies. At the end of 1980s the highest rate was to be found in Northern Europe (1.8 children per woman) and the lowest in Western and Southern Europe (just below 1.6). The countries of Eastern Europe and the ex-Soviet Union remain around the replacement level (2.1 children per woman). North Africa is well above this limit (5.1) as is Western Asia (just below 5.1). We should, however, bear in mind that although Western Asia includes high emigration countries such as Turkey, it also includes the oil-producing Gulf states which have high immigration levels and high fertility.

In 1960 the population of the poor countries exceeded that of the rich

Table 4.1 Indicators of fertility and mortality in major world areas, 1960–90

Areas	Total fertility rate		Life expectancy at birth				Infant mortality rate (%)	
			Male		Female			
	1960–65	1985–90	1960–65	1985–90	1960–65	1985–90	1960–65	1985–90
World Total	4.98	3.45	51.7	61.8	54.7	65.9	118	70
More Developed Regions	2.69	1.89	66.7	70.3	72.7	77.4	32	15
Less Developed Regions	6.09	3.94	47.7	60.1	49.3	62.8	136	78
Europe	2.63	1.72	67.2	71.1	72.4	77.7	37	13
Northern America	3.34	1.81	66.9	72.1	73.6	79.2	25	10
Oceania	3.94	2.51	61.9	68.4	67.0	74.5	55	26
USSR	2.54	2.38	65.5	65.0	73.0	74.2	32	24
Africa	6.79	6.24	40.3	50.3	43.4	53.6	165	103
Latin America	5.96	3.55	55.4	64.0	59.2	69.5	100	54
Asia	5.71	3.48	48.1	61.7	49.1	63.9	133	72
Northern Europe	2.78	1.81	68.6	72.6	74.0	78.5	21	8
Southern Europe	2.72	1.59	66.1	71.9	70.7	78.1	52	16
Western Europe	2.69	1.58	67.7	71.9	73.8	79.0	26	9
Eastern Europe	2.33	2.02	66.6	68.0	71.3	74.8	44	17
Northern Africa	7.08	5.11	45.3	57.8	47.6	60.4	165	79
Western Asia	6.54	5.07	50.7	63.1	53.1	65.9	157	71

Source: United Nations 1991.

countries by 1.1 billion, rising to 2.9 billion in 1990. By 2010 this figure may reach 4.6 billion (see Table 4.2). Between 1960 and 1990, 11.6 per cent of the increase was in the rich countries and 88.4 per cent in the poor countries. In the first decade of the next century the proportions will probably be 4.8 per cent and 95.2 per cent. In 1960, 3 people in 10 lived in the rich countries, whereas by 2010 the figure will be approximately 2 in 10. In only 50 years there will have been an all-out demographic revolution both within nations and between nations.

The South will continue to grow much more rapidly than the North; even though this growth will slow down, the gap in the velocity of growth will not be bridged. The enormous demographic potential of the South is coupled with persistently high mortality levels, and particularly high infant mortality despite the considerable improvements of the past 30 years. The gap between the two geographic areas has narrowed, but the differences between the rich and the poor countries are still enormous. Life expectancy at birth in the South has increased during the period 1960–90 from about 48–49 years to 60–63 years. In the North it has risen from 67 to 70 years for men and from 73 to 77 years for women over the same period. In the North, the battle against premature death has been almost completely won, but not in the South. A child born in the South still has a life expectancy that is 10 years less than a child born in the North, and 15 years less in the case of a girl.

It is in the area of infant mortality that the differences and disparities are even greater — we need only compare the eight deaths in the first year of life for every 1000 live births in Northern Europe with the 103 in Africa. The high level of infant mortality in many countries is one of the most powerful indicators of the degree of socio-economic inequality that exists in the world, and it is also the first significant constraint on the full expression of the potential population vitality which exists in the South.

The differences are also marked as regards the working-age population (Table 4.3). For this parameter — whose projections for shorter time intervals are much more reliable than those for the total population — there will be a very slow growth in the more developed countries (MDCs) over the next two decades (0.3–0.4 per cent annual average), and in the less developed countries (LDCs) there will be very steady growth (2.1 per cent annual average). There are big differences within the European and Mediterranean area ranging from a slight fall in the sizes of the aggregate in Southern and in Western Europe to an increase of 3 per cent in North Africa and 3.2 per cent in Western Asia in the present decade (1990–2000) and respectively 2.7 per cent and 3.4 per cent from 2000 to 2010.

Even though it is not necessarily the case that the demographic factor must automatically lead to an increase in migratory pressure, it is unlikely that international development and cooperation policies can ignore a factor of such importance. In other words, demographic dynamics will make a decisive contribution to the nature and dimensions

Table 4.2 Population trends by major world region, 1960–2010

Areas	Absolute values (million)				Absolute increase (annual average)			Annual change (%)		
	1960	1990	2000	2010	1960–90	1990–00	2000–10	1960–90	1990–00	2000–10
World Total	3,019.7	5,292.2	6,260.8	7,204.3	75.8	96.9	94.4	1.9	1.7	1.4
More Developed Regions	944.9	1,206.6	1,264.1	1,309.6	8.7	5.8	4.5	0.8	0.5	0.4
Less Developed Regions	2,074.8	4,085.6	4,996.7	5,894.8	67.0	91.1	89.8	2.3	2.0	1.7
Europe	425.1	498.4	510.0	515.7	2.4	1.2	0.6	0.5	0.2	0.1
Northern America	198.7	275.9	294.7	311.2	2.6	1.9	1.6	1.1	0.7	0.5
Oceania	15.8	26.5	30.1	33.6	0.4	0.4	0.3	1.7	1.3	1.1
USSR	214.3	288.6	308.4	327.1	2.5	2.0	1.9	1.0	0.7	0.6
Africa	279.3	642.1	866.6	1,148.5	12.1	22.5	28.2	2.8	3.0	2.9
Latin America	218.1	448.1	538.4	628.7	7.7	9.0	9.0	2.4	1.9	1.6
Asia	1,668.3	3,112.7	3,712.5	4,239.5	48.1	60.0	52.7	2.1	1.8	1.3
Northern Europe	75.6	84.2	86.1	87.2	0.3	0.2	0.1	0.4	0.2	0.1
Southern Europe	98.2	117.1	119.1	119.4	0.6	0.2	0.0	0.6	0.2	0.0
Western Europe	151.7	173.1	175.6	175.4	0.7	0.3	-0.0	0.4	0.1	-0.0
Eastern Europe	99.5	124.0	129.2	133.7	0.8	0.5	0.5	0.7	0.4	0.3
Northern Africa	65.1	140.6	178.9	219.6	2.5	3.8	4.1	2.6	2.4	2.1
Western Asia	55.9	131.8	172.0	216.5	2.5	4.0	4.5	2.9	2.7	2.3

Source: United Nations 1991.

Table 4.3 Evolution of working-age population (15–64) by major world region, 1960–2010

Areas	Absolute values (million)				Absolute increase (annual average)			Annual change (%)		
	1960	1990	2000	2010	1960–90	1990–00	2000–10	1960–90	1990–00	2000–10
World Total	1,743.0	3,254.2	3,869.3	4,616.7	50.4	61.5	74.7	2.1	1.7	1.8
More Developed Regions	594.8	803.6	838.7	868.2	7.0	3.5	3.0	1.0	0.4	0.3
Less Developed Regions	1,148.2	2,450.6	3,030.6	3,748.5	43.4	58.0	71.8	2.6	2.1	2.1
Europe	274.2	334.0	339.7	342.4	2.0	0.6	0.3	0.7	0.2	0.1
Northern America	118.5	182.4	197.9	211.3	2.1	1.5	1.3	1.4	0.8	0.7
Oceania	9.4	17.1	19.7	22.3	0.3	0.3	0.3	2.0	1.4	1.2
USSR	134.1	187.4	199.6	215.2	1.8	1.2	1.6	1.1	0.6	0.8
Africa	148.6	333.5	455.5	627.2	6.2	12.2	17.2	2.7	3.2	3.3
Latin America	117.7	266.0	333.6	405.6	4.9	6.8	7.2	2.8	2.3	2.0
Asia	940.4	1,933.8	2,323.4	2,792.8	33.1	39.0	46.9	2.4	1.9	1.9
Northern Europe	48.8	55.2	56.5	57.8	0.2	0.1	0.1	0.4	0.2	0.2
Southern Europe	63.9	79.3	79.8	78.9	0.5	0.1	-0.1	0.7	0.1	-0.1
Western Europe	98.5	117.6	117.1	116.0	0.6	-0.1	-0.1	0.6	-0.0	-0.1
Eastern Europe	63.0	81.9	86.3	89.7	0.6	0.4	0.3	0.9	0.5	0.4
Northern Africa	34.7	77.2	104.1	136.2	1.4	2.7	3.2	2.7	3.0	2.7
Western Asia	30.3	73.8	97.9	129.6	1.5	2.4	3.2	3.0	2.9	2.8

Source: United Nations 1991.

of the problems that European (and non-European) countries will have to face in the next few years.

Economic imbalances

In the 1980s the economic imbalances between the OECD countries and the South were generally accentuated; only in a few cases were they partially reduced. Taking an economic indicator like the per capita gross domestic product, the present inequalities are very evident, and in all cases greater than those found in preceding historical periods.

The differences in per capita GDP in relative terms are all growing to the disadvantage of the South, except for Asia. Nevertheless, the absolute North–South differences are growing strongly to the disadvantage of the whole South, from US$2,459 in 1950 to US$7,308 in 1989 (in real terms, based on 1980 values) — a significant increase considering the burden on a sharply growing number of people (World Bank 1991). In 1950, the inhabitants of those countries today classified as MDCs numbered 832 million and those in LDCs were 1.65 billion, while in 1989 they were 1.2 billion and 4.0 billion respectively.

The International Labour Office provides another set of useful figures to compare — albeit approximately — the situation of the European labour market with those of the migration source areas (Table 4.4). The data refer to the situation prior to the political upheavals in Eastern Europe and must therefore be interpreted in the light of these profound changes. To the existing differences shown in Table 4.4 we must obviously add the tensions deriving from the processes of economic transformation which will, at least initially, determine a big increase in unemployment in the Eastern European labour markets (see Chapter 8 in this book).

The problems in comparing labour market indicators between different types of economies at different levels of development are well known. Activity rates differ by gender and for the different age groups in a developed society and in a developing society. The activity rates are also different in a market economy compared to a planned economy.

The low rates of female activity in North Africa (8.2 per cent) and Western Asia (18.7 per cent) may be also explained by the difficulty of giving definitions to certain activities in traditional sectors by using concepts (e.g. employment, unemployment) typical of a capitalist economy. The high figures for female activity recorded in the planned economies (46–7 per cent) were a result of the greater participation (partly ideologically motivated) on the part of women in productive activities. On the other hand, demographic factors such as the greater weight of the younger age groups explain the low male activity rates in North Africa (47.7 per cent) and Western Asia (50.5 per cent).

Differing levels of economic development are suggested also by the

Table 4.4 Some indicators of economically active population in European
migration areas

Areas	Total activity rates (1985) Male	Female	% in agriculture (1980)
Northern Europe	60.2	38.4	4.7
Southern Europe	55.9	24.5	20.3
Western Europe	58.9	33.7	6.8
Eastern Europe	57.6	46.1	22.1
USSR	56.3	47.1	20.0
Northern Africa	47.7	8.2	47.5
Western Asia	50.5	18.7	46.8

Source: International Labour Office 1986.

very different percentages of agricultural workers. The figures are very
high for the two non-European areas where almost half the total active
population work in agriculture. One worker in five is in agriculture in
Southern and Eastern Europe and Russia whilst only one in 20 workers
is in agriculture in Northern and Western Europe, the areas with the
most advanced economic structure.

It is very likely that the economic changes that are taking place in the
ex-communist countries will have the effect of reducing female and
agricultural employment. These are two components of the labour
market where for various reasons low productivity jobs tend to concentrate.

As a consequence of these economic changes, it is very likely that there
will be many candidates ready to leave their own countries. Whether all
kinds of workers or only certain types decide to leave will depend on
migration possibilities. Those most tempted to emigrate will almost
certainly be young qualified workers looking for better living conditions.
This threatens to create a brain drain from some of the Eastern countries, especially the ex-Soviet Union. Such a brain drain could cause an
impoverishment of the ruling and intellectual classes, although in the
long term the knowledge acquired abroad could be regarded as a heritage
which the emigrants would bring back when (and if) they return and
which could be used to improve the human capital of the home country.
These issues are discussed in more detail in Chapter 12.

Social and cultural imbalances

Inequalities tend to decrease slowly and with difficulty — or to persist
— not only in the economic and demographic fields, but also in the
social, scientific and cultural realms. Indicators of such imbalances are
increasingly being dealt with in the reports of international organisations.

In 1983 (the most recent year for which data are available) 73 per cent of the expenditure on research and development was concentrated in the industrial countries, 24 per cent in the ex-socialist European countries and the ex-USSR, and only 3 per cent in the developing countries. This is perhaps one of the greatest (and most important) developmental contrasts that can be observed. For every million inhabitants, 533 books were published in the North as compared to 67 in the South, giving a ratio of 8:1; the ratio between Europe (plus the USSR) and Africa was 23:1.

In the field of television productions and programmes, the hegemony of the Western countries is creating a new and important boundary. There is an 'army of images and words' in the North which is moving southwards and eastwards. This international 'image management' is also linked to a certain extent to migratory movements from the South and the East. On the one hand, the diffusion of Western television helps to sensitise people of other countries to their own conditions, and, furthermore, encourages them to emigrate. On the other hand, the fact that the images are only one-way means that Northern countries do not really know much about the South, which does not help them to overcome the idea of 'otherness'.

The world is becoming increasingly interdependent. The boundaries that separate national markets for goods, capital and labour have continued to be eroded. Worldwide trade has expanded by more than 6 per cent a year since 1950, which is more than 50 per cent faster than the growth of output. Global integration processes in trade, investment, factor flows, technology and communication have been tying economies together (World Bank 1991, p. 2). This interdependence is not only economic but it encompasses the movement and exchange of people, knowledge, ideas and news. It strengthens the reality of the 'global village' and, at the same time, on a political level, often tends to reduce the degree of national autonomy of many countries.

Weighing up the pros and cons of this increasing integration at the macro-level, we might conclude that to date it seems to have harmed the South and the East, whose role and importance in the international arena have been reduced. Above all, the South is now less free to specify its own needs, including cultural ones, and dialogue with the North is less productive. At the time of the great leaders of the LDCs such as Tito, Nehru and Nasser, dialogue was much more intense and beneficial and it respected reciprocal interests. The role of the non-aligned movement (instituted in the far-off 1950s) has suffered greatly as has Southern solidarity in general in the face of a substantial growth in Northern solidarity.

Therefore, only a new awareness on the part of the Western countries can nourish the hope of rebalancing relations between different areas of the world. Along with the moral imperative of reducing poverty in the South, the North must realise that, in a climate of growing economic integration, a recession in the South could severely damage the North. It is sufficient to consider the fact that the contraction of the Southern markets due to the unfavourable economic situation of the 1980s cost North America half a million jobs in the manufacturing industries (Ravenhill 1990). Likewise an increasing debt can cause a crisis not only for the Southern debtor countries, but also for the banking system of the North.

The problems of South–North relations are by now common knowledge even if the solution appears to be a long way off, but total uncertainty reigns as to the nature of East–West relations. One of the risks of the present situation is that of fierce competition between the East and the South to secure commercial and political agreements with the West and to reap the benefits of cooperation. Given the greater geographical and cultural proximity of the East and its more attractive markets, it is not unreasonable to predict that the loser in this war will be the South.

Conclusions

Generally speaking, social scientists conclude that, in the future, the 'excess' of economic development in the developed world resulting from reduced or negative demographic growth, together with the lack of development associated with the 'excess' of demographic growth in the less developed world, will bring about a strong increase in migratory flows from the world's most backward areas towards the more developed ones. Taking this general comment as a starting point, the following reflections may be made.

Firstly, there is the dualism that characterises current migratory flows in Europe. A clear distinction exists between, on the one hand, people who emigrate to take up well-paid jobs at the middle and high levels of the occupational scale, who move without difficulty, and who experience few or no problems integrating and, on the other hand, those who find only menial work with low rates of pay, who suffer entry and residence problems, and who have serious problems in integration. This differentiation correlates to particular geographical areas. It is the citizens of the industrialised Western countries who generally move easily and who integrate well. Those coming from the South of the world have greater difficulty. Those who want to emigrate from the East have seen their situation worsen radically in the last few years. The easier it becomes to leave an ex-communist country, the more difficult it is to enter a Western country.

A second consideration is that under current conditions there is the risk that development may remain a dream for many of the LDCs. In this regard, we often quote encouragingly the case of the relatively rapid development of the four Asian 'dragons' (South Korea, Hong Kong,

Taiwan and Singapore). In reality, their experience seems to be specific and cannot be simply extended and generalised, not only for cultural reasons, but also for structural ones.

The Official Development Assistance (ODA) as a percentage share of the GNP of the OECD members dropped from 0.48 in 1965 to 0.33 in 1989. The ODA of the OPEC members dropped extremely sharply from 2.32 per cent of the GNP in 1976 to 0.45 per cent in 1988 (World Bank 1991). Now that computers and robots are more widely used, the importance of the large supply of low-cost labour offered by the LDCs tends to be reduced to the extent that in many cases this factor has become a less attractive investment option for transnational corporations. Moreover the alternatives available for the Southern countries are limited in that the economies of Eastern Europe and the ex-Soviet Union (countries whose social stability and military peace are more important — to Western Europe and the United States than those of the LDCs — with a few exceptions) have required large-scale and growing international capital flows.

On this last point, the most important (perhaps the only) hope is that the enormous current military expenditure be reduced and that the money be directed towards productive investments. In the late 1980s military expenditure totalled more than $1,000 billion a year, £860 billion in high-income countries and $170 billion in developing ones. In 36 countries, most of which are developing, military expenditure amounts to more than 5 per cent of the GNP, and at the same time takes up a very high quota of the available resources (World Bank 1991).

Even if the collective effort to reduce the developmental disparities is only partially successful, the general modernisation process will encourage the impetus towards individual mobility as a means of professional and social advancement. While we are waiting to see if and when this new awareness will be adopted, South–North migration will continue to play an essential role in the relations between the two sides. Migrations are needed to satisfy the demand of the labour markets of the North, to lighten the demographic pressure of the South, to favour the economy of the South by means of the remittances of the emigrants, to favour the more rapid process of development of human resources in the South, and to promote the fastest possible transfer of knowledge and technology.

The West, and in particular Europe, cannot ignore this situation and it must adjust its behaviour accordingly. In fact it is very likely that what will happen in the domain of international migration depends more on Western policies and popular attitudes than on any other factor. Therefore, it is much more positive for Europe to attempt to manage the form and intensity of the migratory flows rather than give in to the temptation to put up barriers around itself which would in any case be overcome. Indeed, American experience shows us that, to make the borders of the Rio Grande invincible, severe laws, heavy fines for employers taking on illegal workers and borders guarded night and day with sophisticated surveillance systems were just not enough. We may well ask what instruments are necessary to manage immigration flows. A commonly used instrument is the quota system, but in Europe this does not seem to be sufficient in itself. According to Böhning (1991), a second instrument could be 'project-tied migration'[1] and a third 'migration for training'.

Besides the necessity of keeping the doors open to new moderate immigration, there is the need to encourage and foster an environment of full acceptance and integration for immigrants. If this is not done, the democratic structure of the Western countries is in danger. It seems that there is no other choice: it is a question of integration or conflict. If a society wants to remain democratic, it must treat foreigners in the same way as it treats its own citizens, giving them full rights. The ultimate objective is to guarantee equal rights to immigrants while fully protecting their cultural identity and making sure that they are not pushed out on to the fringes of society. If the immigrants are left as misunderstood strangers on the margins of society, regression towards a weakened democracy would be inevitable. Growing political–social tensions would be provoked by native citizens trying to preserve their 'right' at all costs and the foreigners trying to avoid having to live a life of social, economic and political deprivation.

Note

1. The term 'project-tied migration' refers to a migrant who is admitted to a new country to undertake a specific assignment of employment.

References

Appleyard, T.R. (ed.), 1989, *The impact of international migration on developing countries*, OECD, Paris.
Böhning, W.R., 1991, 'Integration and immigration pressures in Western Europe', *International Labour Review*, 130(4): 445–58.
Böhning, W.R. and Maillat D., 1974, *The effects of the employment of foreign workers*, OECD, Paris.
Bonifazi, C., 1988, 'Migrazioni internazionali ed immigrazione straniera in Italia: alcune considerazioni', *Studi Emigrazione*, 25(91–2): 566–9.
Censis, 1991, *Immigrati e società italiana*, CNEL, Rome.
Chiarello, F., 1990, 'Teorie dell'immigrazione e flussi migratori: applicazioni e implicazioni', in Ancona, G. (ed.), *Migrazioni mediterranee e mercato del lavoro*, Cacucci, Bari, 69–90.
Gesano, G., 1991, 'Mercato del lavoro e tipologie occupazionali', in Sergi, N. and Carchedi, F. (eds), *L'immigrazione straniera in Italia: il tempo dell'integrazione*, Edizioni Lavoro, Rome, 107–25.
Golini, A., 1988, 'L'Italia nel sistema delle migrazioni internazionali', *Studi Emigrazione*, 25(91–92): 544–65.

International Labour Office, 1986, *Economically active population, 1950–2025*, ILO, Geneva.

Montanari, A. and Cortese, A., 1993, 'South to North migration in a Mediterranean perspective', in King, R. (ed.), *Mass migrations in Europe: the legacy and the future*, Belhaven, London, 212–33.

Pugliese, E., 1991, 'La portata del fenomeno e il mercato del lavoro', in Macioti, M.I. and Pugliese, E., *Gli immigrati in Italia*, Laterza, Bari, 3–89.

Ravenhill, J., 1990, 'The North–South balance of power, *International Affairs*, 66(4): 731–48.

Salt, J., 1989, 'A comparative overview of international trends and types', *International Migration Review*, 23(3): 431–56.

United Nations, 1989, *World populations at the turn of the century*, UN, New York.

United Nations, 1991, *World population prospects 1990*, UN, New York.

World Bank, 1991, *World development report*, Oxford University Press, New York.

Zolberg, A.R., 1989, 'The next waves: migration theory for a changing world', *International Migration Review*, 23(3): 403–30.

Chapter 5
Modelling future immigration and integration in Western Europe

Wolfgang Lutz and Christopher Prinz

Introduction

When analysing the volume, structure and consequences of international migration the demographic scientist finds very few certainties on which to base calculations. Much more than the other demographic components of population change, mortality and fertility, migration depends on short-term changes in the field of policy and other hard-to-predict areas. While in modern societies mortality tends to change very slowly from year to year and even fertility, which is largely the result of individual behaviour, only shows annual increases or decreases by a few percentage points, migration intensities can double or quadruple from one year to another. And the European experience of the past few decades provides vivid examples of such unpredictable irregularities.

What can forecasters, who are asked to prepare population projections, do in the face of such tremendous uncertainties, that sometimes seem to come close to chaotic behaviour, when the death of a politician or the passing of a new law out of a very specific political situation can trigger the migration of millions? One possible reaction for scientists is to abstract from short-term fluctuations and look at the longer-term trends. Under a long-term perspective, patterns are certainly more stable than on an annual basis. But still when looking at immigration levels since 1950 in industrialised countries one finds that only in the classic immigration countries (the United States, Canada and Australia) have there been fairly stable levels of immigration. All European countries show significant long-term changes. Even France and Germany, the biggest immigration countries in Europe, experienced great ups and downs with a peak in the 1960s and a low in the early 1980s. A number of smaller countries (Austria, Denmark, The Netherlands, Norway) switched from migration losses to migration gains at around 1960. Another group (Finland, Greece, Italy, Portugal, Spain) experienced this reversal of pattern around 1975. In a number of Eastern European countries net migration has been continuously negative at varying levels (see Wils 1991) with a new spur to emigration in recent years.

Another possible approach for the scientist interested in future migration is to look at the economic push and pull factors that underlie the decisions to migrate, or to study the socio-cultural aspects and identify established channels of migration, since one of the basic findings of the analysis of international migration over the centuries seems to be that migrants follow existing paths. Such analyses can certainly help us to understand the potential for migration better. But talking about potentials is different from talking about actual migration. The latter is very much dependent on specific short-term policies. The introduction of a new and rigorously enforced visa regulation can effectively interrupt a migratory stream no matter how great the migration potential. In this sense migration policies have two aspects: first the content of the policy itself and second the degree to which the policy can be enforced. The proportion of illegal immigrants seems to vary greatly from one country to another. A final interesting question in this context is whether legal immigration restrictions can in the long run resist strong push factors from outside and especially pull factors from inside that will find their lobbies within the domestic political establishment.

In this chapter a third general approach was chosen that neither relies on the extrapolation of past trends nor exclusively refers to migration potentials as a proxy for actual migration. The chosen approach accepts the inherent uncertainty about future migration levels and studies the implications of alternative hypothetical immigration patterns without passing judgement on their likelihood. A systematic comparison of such alternative scenarios, which are nothing but a number of alternative 'if-then' calculations, can provide us with a better understanding of those aspects of the population structure which are rather sensitive to alternative immigration patterns and which ones would be hardly affected.[1]

A multi-state population projection model considering integration as well as immigration

Figure 5.1 depicts the basic structure of the model considered in this chapter. First, a distinction is made between the 'native' population in Western Europe and the 'non-natives'. Immigrants into Western Europe are grouped into two broad categories according to their region of origin: Eastern Europe and the rest of the world. Since all countries of Western Europe — defined as EC plus EFTA — are considered as forming one population in this context, migration streams within Western Europe are treated as internal migration and remain unaccounted. The distinction between migrants from Eastern Europe and the rest of the world (which mostly refers to less developed countries) was introduced because of the belief that these two migratory streams are of a very different nature. This difference is reflected in the magnitude and timing of the migration stream: we assume a shorter-term peak in East–West migration which should weaken over the next two decades due to economic progress in

Western Europe

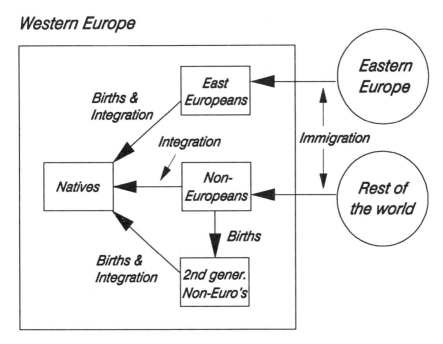

Figure 5.1   Structure of the multi-state population projection model

the East, possibly even leading to some return migration because Eastern Europeans tend to retain some links to their country and culture of origin (Öberg and Boubnova 1993). For the less developed countries we assume a virtually infinite potential for migration that will not weaken in the future. These two groups also show different rates of integration into the 'native' population. In the group of non-European immigrants we further distinguish between the first-generation and second-generation immigrants because we believe that integration rates are different for foreigners already born in Western Europe than for their parents.

When we speak about integration in this context we do not attempt to apply or evaluate complex sociological criteria, but give it a purely technical definition: integration is the transition at a specific assumed rate from a 'non-native' group within Western Europe to the 'native' group. Above all, in this study, integration implies changing demographic behaviour, especially fertility. The transition rates applied are open and can be chosen freely by the user of the model. In the following scenario calculations we chose annual integration rates of between 0 per cent (no integration) and 10 per cent (very rapid integration). These rates are choices made to illustrate the consequences of alternative assumptions and do not necessarily reflect the most realistic cases. Judgements concerning the likelihood of alternative integration and immigration assumptions in this model go beyond the scope of this chapter and should be made by the individual reader. This analysis merely attempts to demonstrate what will happen if certain alternative conditions of immigration and integration come true. As expressed by the title of the chapter, our aim is to study the impact of alternative immigration and integration levels on future population size, on the relative sizes of the four subgroups of the population, and on age structure.

Definition of scenarios

Western Europe for the present purposes includes the following 16 countries: Austria, Belgium, Denmark, Finland, France, Germany, Greece, Ireland, Italy, The Netherlands, Norway, Portugal, Spain, Sweden, Switzerland and the United Kingdom. Eastern Europe as a region of origin for migrants includes Albania, Bosnia Herzegovina, Bulgaria, Croatia, the Czech and Slovak Republics, Hungary, Poland, Romania, Slovenia, the remaining former Yugoslavian republics, and the republics of the former Soviet Union. The non-European region includes the rest of the world, with Africa being quantitatively most significant.

For our alternative projections the population for the initial year 1985 has been divided into four subgroups: West European natives (97.5 per cent in 1985), East Europeans living in Western Europe (0.4 per cent), non-Europeans living in Western Europe (2.1 per cent), and second-generation non-Europeans (defined as zero in 1985). The composition of the foreign population by region of origin and sex was estimated using data from France (census of 1982) and Germany (1987), the two countries which together hosted more than half of the total foreign population of Western Europe in 1989. The age structure of the foreign population was estimated using the most recent census information for Belgium (1981), France (1982), Italy (1981) and Sweden (1985).

Since this particular study is mainly interested in the effects different migration patterns have on population size and structure, fertility and mortality rates are assumed to follow only one path. The total fertility rate (TFR) for natives and Eastern Europeans is assumed to remain constant (1.63 children per woman in 1989). Constant fertility was assumed because it seems to be entirely open and unclear in which direction European fertility will move over the next few decades. Some countries currently exhibit an increase in fertility (Scandinavia), while others still experience a strong decline (southern Europe) or a stabilisation at low fertility rates. For the non-European immigrant population, TFRs of 3.0 and 2.0 for first- and second-generation immigrants, respectively, were assumed because many studies show that the fertility of immigrants is somewhere between the fertility level of the country of origin and that of the host country.

Life expectancy at birth is assumed to increase linearly from 71.9 years for men and 78.6 years for women in 1985 up to 83.5 and 89 years,

Table 5.1 Definition of the demographic assumptions for six scenarios of population change

Scenario	Total fertility rate	Life expectancy M/F	Annual net migration	Annual integration rate (%) Newborn	Others
Observed around 1985	1.63	71.9/78.6	500,000		
Scenario 1					
(low migration, low integration)					
Natives	1.63	83.5/89	–	–	–
East Europeans	1.63	83.5/89	500,000/0[1]	100	10
Non-Europeans	3.0	83.5/89	500,000/0[1]	–	0
Second-generation non-Europeans	2.0	83.5/89	–	100	5
Scenario 2					
(medium migration, low integration)					
Natives	1.63	83.5/89	–	–	–
East Europeans	1.63	83.5/89	500,000/0[1]	100	10
Non-Europeans	3.0	83.5/89	500,000[2]	–	0
Second-generation non-Europeans	2.0	83.5/89	–	100	5
Scenario 3					
(medium migration, high integration)					
Natives	1.63	83.5/89	–	–	–
East Europeans	1.63	83.5/89	500,000/0[1]	100	10
Non-Europeans	3.0	83.5/89	500,000[2]	–	5
Second-generation non-Europeans	2.0	83.5/89	–	100	10
Scenario 4					
(high migration, low integration)					
Natives	1.63	83.5/89	–	–	–
East Europeans	1.63	83.5/89	500,000/0[3]	100	10
Non-Europeans	3.0	83.5/89	1,500,000[4]	–	0
Second-generation non-Europeans	2.0	83.5/89	–	100	5
Scenario 5					
(high migration, high integration)					
Natives	1.63	83.5/89	–	–	–
East Europeans	1.63	83.5/89	500,000/0[3]	100	10
Non-Europeans	3.0	83.5/89	1,500,000[4]	–	5
Second-generation non-Europeans	2.0	83.5/89	–	100	10
Scenario 6					
(high migration, low integration of offspring)					
Natives	1.63	83.5/89	–	–	–
East Europeans	1.63	83.5/89	500,000/0[3]	10	10
Non-Europeans	3.0	83.5/89	1,500,000[4]	–	0
Second-generation non-Europeans	2.0	83.5/89	–	10	5

Notes:
[1] 500,000 from 1985 to 2000, no immigration after 2000.
[2] constant from 1985 to 2050.
[3] 500,000 from 1985 to 2010, no immigration after 2010.
[4] increase from 500,000 to 1,500,000 by 2010, then constant.

respectively, in 2050 (see Table 5.1). The assumed increase in life expectancy is somewhat lower than a continuation of the trend during the last two decades would suggest.[2] Mortality is assumed to be identical in all three population groups. This mortality assumption corresponds to the average between the high and low mortality scenarios in a recent book prepared for the Council of Europe (Cliquet 1993) and it differs from the assumption used in Lutz and Prinz (1992).

Concerning immigration flows, we assumed three alternative levels: (1) 'low immigration': no immigration after the turn of the century with constant immigration during the period 1985 to 2000, i.e. 500,000 immigrants annually from Eastern Europe and another 500,000 annually from outside Europe; (2) 'medium immigration': continuation of present flows with 500,000 immigrants annually from Eastern Europe (only until the year 2000) and 500,000 annually from non-European countries (until 2050); and (3) 'high immigration': 500,000 immigrants annually from Eastern Europe (only until 2010) and another 1.5 million annually from non-European countries (linear increase from 500,000 in 1985 to 1.5 million in 2010, then constant).

The assumptions on immigration levels are complemented by alternative assumptions concerning the integration of foreigners. We chose to define integration by annual integration rates, i.e. the proportions of members of the East European and non-European subpopulations that annually move to become like the native population. Unlike some similar calculations (e.g. Steinmann 1991), this does not assume automatic, complete integration of foreigners after a specific time-period but it assumes heterogeneity of the immigrant population with respect to integration probabilities. Because a constant rate implies a decrease over time in absolute numbers integrated out of the initial stock of foreigners, an integration rate of 10 per cent annually would result in the integration of approximately 90 per cent after 25 years, or, as another example, a 5 per cent integration rate annually would result in approximately 70 per cent integration after 30 years.

The integration rate of Eastern European immigrants was assumed to be constant at 10 per cent per year under all scenarios. Children of Eastern European immigrants, the second generation, are assumed to be integrated immediately, i.e. they are assumed to be born as natives (with one exception). For non-European immigrants we distinguish three groups that are assumed to be integrated at different rates: the first, the second and the third generation. Three levels of integration are compared: (1) 'low integration': assuming no integration for the first generation, a 5 per cent integration rate annually for the second generation, and immediate, full integration for the third generation, i.e. the child of a second-generation immigrant is born as a native, as is the child of a first-generation Eastern European immigrant; (2) 'high integration': assuming a 5 per cent integration rate annually for the first generation, a 10 per cent integration rate annually for the second generation, a rate that is equal to the integration rate of Eastern Europeans, and again immediate, full integration for the third generation; and (3) 'low integration with low integration of offspring': assuming the lower 0 per cent and 5 per cent rates of integration for the first and second generation, together with 10 per cent integration rates annually for the third generation of non-European and the second generation of Eastern European immigrants.

Basing our calculations on a cross-classification of the different immigration and integration assumptions, we defined the following six scenarios that are also listed in Table 5.1. Scenario 1 considers low immigration and low integration, i.e. no integration of first-generation and 5 per cent annual integration rates of second-generation non-Europeans, 10 per cent annual integration rates of East Europeans, together with full integration of third-generation non-Europeans and second-generation East Europeans. Scenarios 2 and 3 both assume medium immigration levels, the former in combination with low integration, the latter with high integration. They are labelled 'medium immigration, low integration' and 'medium immigration, high integration', respectively. Both scenarios assume full integration of third-generation non-Europeans and second-generation East Europeans. Scenarios 4–6 consider the high immigration alternative. They only differ with respect to integration of foreigners, comparing the low integration alternative (both with full and low integration of third-generation non-Europeans and second-generation East Europeans) to the high integration alternative. Scenarios 4, 5 and 6 are labelled 'high immigration, low integration', 'high immigration, high integration' and 'high immigration, low integration of offspring', respectively.

Results

Total population size

Table 5.2 gives the total population size of the 16 Western European countries calculated up to the year 2050 under the alternative scenarios considered. These figures include all four subgroups of the population. Since mortality and fertility rates are kept constant, one can expect that the differences in future population size rates should have an independent impact on population size because we have assumed higher fertility rates for the non-European population, and if their size increases less quickly due to greater integration they will have a smaller weight and hence reduce the average fertility of the total population.

As expected, only the low immigration scenario 1 will result in a decline in the total size of the Western European population. This is the consequence of subreplacement fertility. Mostly as a result of the young

Table 5.2 Total population size by scenario (million)

Year	Scenario 1 Low migration, low integration	Scenario 2 Medium migration, low integration	Scenario 3 Medium migration, high integration	Scenario 4 High migration, low integration	Scenario 5 High migration, high integration	Scenario 6 High migration, low integration of offspring
1990	379	379	379	379	379	379
2000	398	398	398	402	401	402
2010	407	410	409	426	424	426
2020	406	416	414	450	447	450
2030	401	419	416	472	467	472
2040	389	417	413	490	483	490
2050	373	411	405	506	496	506

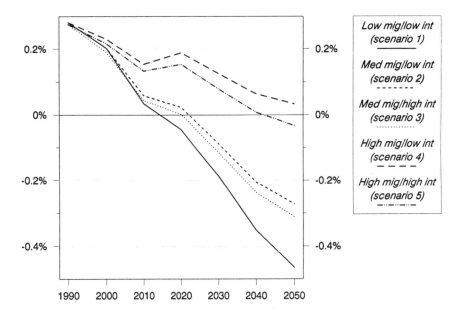

Figure 5.2 Average annual rates of natural population increase, 1990–2050, by scenario

age structure, the total population would continue to increase from 379 million at present to around 407 million in 2010 and decline thereafter. As we will see later, the low immigration case will also result in an extreme ageing of the population.

Scenarios 4, 5 and 6 all assume high immigration into Western Europe and will result in a significant increase of the total population to between 496 and 506 million by the year 2050 depending on the different average fertility levels which are the result of alternative integration assumptions. Scenarios 2 and 3, which assume immigration to continue around the present level, have an intermediate position resulting in a more moderate increase of the Western European population to between 405 and 411 million by 2050.

Figure 5.2 plots the annual growth rates that underlie the changes in population size given in Table 5.2. Due to the assumption that immigration would only gradually increase to its maximum level by 2010 and remain constant thereafter, we see a slight discontinuity for all growth rates around that year. Under all scenarios growth rates show a long-term decreasing trend that at some point will result in decreasing population sizes. As mentioned above, under the low immigration scenario 1 this will already be the case around 2015; in the medium immigration scenarios 2 and 3 it will happen around 2025; and even under the high immigration scenarios the Western European population will start to shrink by the middle of the next century. This clearly demonstrates that in the very long run the effect of low fertility can outweigh even very strong immigration if immigrants at some point adopt European subreplacement fertility levels.

Population ageing

Considerations of age structure are of great importance in a country's economic and social life. The proportion of economically active people as compared to the pensioners has been changing in an adverse direction for some time mostly due to population ageing plus a decline in the mean age at retirement in some cases. For the next 30–50 years a dramatic worsening of this relationship is foreseen for purely demographic reasons. The large birth cohorts of the baby boom of the early 1960s will reach retirement age while the number of people in the economically active ages is significantly shrinking due to the generally very low fertility since the 1970s. Alternative population projections for Europe and North America (Lutz *et al*. 1991) have shown that the mean age of the population in Western Europe could even increase by 20 years from 37 years at present to 57 years by 2050 in a scenario of fertility and mortality decline.

It is evident that immigration may have a direct impact on demographic dependency ratios if it is age-selective, i.e. if the age distribution of immigrants is different from that of the resident population. And since immigrants tend to come in their young adulthood, they increase, at least in the short run, the proportion of the population in the active age group 15–64. In the long-run the positive effects of immigration on demographic dependence is less clear-cut because, unless they return to their home country, migrants will also age and eventually draw retirement benefit. What will happen to demographic dependency in the long term will depend on the specific conditions assumed, in particular whether migrants have higher fertility than the rest of the population, and whether the stream of new immigrants increases, decreases or remains constant. Generally, under homogeneous fertility and mortality conditions, the stream of immigrants would have to be continuously increasing to have a long-term positive effect on demographic old-age dependency ratios.

In our analysis, which studies the specific effects of alternative immigration and integration levels, we obtain the following results under the specified fertility and mortality conditions (see Table 5.3). The increase in the elderly proportion of the total population (natives plus immigrants) ranges from about 16 percentage points in the case of the low immigration scenario to 10 percentage points in the case of the high immigration scenarios. Two conclusions can be drawn from these findings: (1) the proportion of the population older than 65 will increase

Table 5.3 Proportion of elderly aged 65 years and over in Western Europe (%)

Year	Scenario 1 Low migration, low integration	Scenario 2 Medium migration, low integration	Scenario 3 Medium migration, high integration	Scenario 4 High migration, low integration	Scenario 5 High migration, high integration	Scenario 6 High migration, low integration of offspring
1990	14.4	14.4	14.4	14.4	14.4	14.4
2000	15.5	15.5	15.5	15.4	15.4	15.4
2010	17.1	17.0	17.1	16.4	16.5	16.4
2020	20.1	19.7	19.8	18.3	18.4	18.3
2030	24.6	23.6	23.8	21.3	21.5	21.3
2040	28.7	27.1	27.3	23.9	24.2	23.9
2050	30.3	28.1	28.4	24.5	25.0	24.5

Table 5.4 Proportion of elderly in the non-European immigrant population (%)

Year	Scenario 1 Low migration, low integration	Scenario 2 Medium migration, low integration	Scenario 3 Medium migration, high integration	Scenario 4 High migration, low integration	Scenario 5 High migration, high integration	Scenario 6 High migration, low integration of offspring
1990	2.0	2.0	2.0	2.0	2.0	2.0
2000	2.9	2.9	2.3	2.5	2.0	2.5
2010	5.6	5.0	3.3	3.6	2.2	3.6
2020	13.1	9.1	4.6	5.6	2.7	5.5
2030	29.6	15.6	6.1	9.1	3.6	8.8
2040	54.2	21.8	7.0	13.1	4.7	12.6
2050	73.5	24.0	7.2	16.8	5.7	15.9

significantly under all circumstances, and (2) taking 2050 as a time threshold, immigration to Western Europe tends to lower the proportion of the population above 65.

Within the non-European population in Western Europe there will be even more significant ageing in the future because of the present uneven age distribution. Assuming that the non-Europeans will not leave Europe once they retire, the proportion of men and women above 65 among the non-European subpopulation will increase from a very low 2 per cent at present to at least around 6 per cent by 2050 (see Table 5.4). Under scenario 1 (assuming no immigration from outside Europe after 2000 as well as low integration), the non-European population will eventually die out. By the year 2050 it will have already decreased to around 8 million from 11 million, and an incredible 73 per cent will be above the age of 65.

Under the two scenarios 4 and 6 which will result in the highest numbers of non-Europeans in Western Europe (close to 100 million), about 16 per cent of the non-European subpopulation will be over 65. This is still a significantly lower proportion than in the total population and implies that the non-Europeans will represent a lower than average burden to the pension system.

Population composition by groups

In the initial year of our projections, 1985, 2.4 per cent of the total population of Western Europe was calculated to belong to the group of non-European immigrants. According to scenario 1, which assumes no immigration after the year 2000 and low integration, this proportion will ultimately approach zero and show extreme forms of ageing as described above. In all the other scenarios the proportion of non-Europeans is expected to increase, although at quite different rates depending on the immigration and integration assumptions (Figure 5.3).

In the case of very high immigration and low integration of non-Europeans (scenarios 4 and 6), the proportion of non-Europeans in Europe will increase to about one-fifth of the total population in 2050. This essentially describes a dual society of two groups with little or no interaction. As the comparison with scenario 5 will show, however, this situation is only to a minor extent caused by high migration levels; the more important cause would be the complete lack of integration into the native society, whether this be due to the failure of integration policies or the lack of will to integrate on either side. Scenario 5, for instance, which assumes a 5 per cent and 10 per cent annual integration rate for first- and second-generation non-Europeans, will only result in 7.7 per cent of non-Europeans by 2050 under the same high immigration assumption. Hence, integration makes a big difference under the given model specifications; integration can even be more important than the pure number of immigrants (compare scenarios 5 and 2).

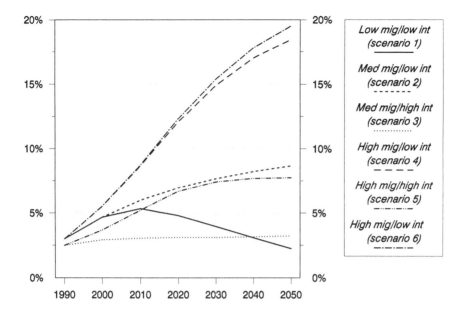

Figure 5.3 Proportion of non-Europeans in Western Europe, 1990–2050, by scenario

Scenario 3, which essentially assumes a continuation of present immigration together with the same high annual integration rates as scenario 5, would only result in an insignificant increase in the proportion of non-Europeans to 3.2 per cent of the total population by 2050, or an absolute total slightly in excess of 13 million (Table 5.5). This is a scenario that should be relatively manageable by society. It would also have many economic advantages stemming from age structural considerations when compared to the low immigration scenario.

Differences in the number of non-Europeans between scenarios are similar to above (see Table 5.5). From around 11 million people in 1990, the number of non-Europeans in Western Europe would increase tenfold under the high immigration and low integration assumptions of scenario 6, while it would reach some 37 million under either high immigration/high integration or medium immigration/low integration assumptions. Medium immigration with high integration would keep the size of this subgroup of the Western European population almost stable.

As for the Eastern European sub-population in Western Europe, Table 5.6 demonstrates the insignificant quantitative impact of this group. Due to lower cumulative numbers of immigrants and the undoubtedly higher integration rate, Eastern Europeans will at no point — even under relatively high East–West migration assumptions during the next three decades — comprise more than 7 million people. This peak is reached in

Table 5.5 Number of non-Europeans in Western Europe (million)

Year	Scenario 1 Low migration, low integration	Scenario 2 Medium migration, low integration	Scenario 3 Medium migration, high integration	Scenario 4 High migration, low integration	Scenario 5 High migration, high integration	Scenario 6 High migration, low integration of offspring
1990	11.4	11.4	9.5	11.4	9.5	11.4
2000	18.6	18.6	11.7	22.1	14.8	22.1
2010	21.7	24.5	12.5	36.9	22.1	37.2
2020	19.5	28.9	12.9	54.4	29.9	55.5
2030	15.8	32.1	13.0	70.3	34.6	72.6
2040	12.0	34.3	13.1	83.4	37.1	87.2
2050	8.4	35.6	13.1	93.5	38.4	99.0

Table 5.6 East Europeans in Western Europe by scenario ('000)

Year	Scenarios 1–3 Immigration until 2000	Scenarios 4, 5 Immigration until 2010	Scenario 6 Immigration until 2010, low integration of offspring
1990	3,417	3,417	3,618
2000	5,118	5,118	5,898
2010	3,187	5,720	6,851
2020	1,119	3,398	4,651
2030	382	1,193	1,916
2040	126	407	763
2050	39	134	297

2010 in the case of scenario 6. Due to an assumed end to significant East–West migration by 2010 and bearing in mind the assumption of high integration, there will be virtually no East European subpopulation left in Western Europe by 2050.

Conclusion

This chapter has described alternative scenario calculations which provide some sensitivity analysis on what alternative levels of immigration and integration into the Western European population would do to total population size, to the relative sizes of the four subpopulations considered (natives, East Europeans, non-Europeans and second-generation non-Europeans), and to the age structure of the population. The main conclusion of these calculations is that the population of Western Europe is heading for significant population ageing no matter what happens with immigration. Even strong immigration (unless it increases indefinitely from year to year) will in the long run hardly affect the ageing trend, for this is mainly influenced by low fertility levels. Apart from this universal trend, the six alternative scenarios considered show considerable differences.

Firstly, with respect to total population size, the 'end to immigration scenario' 1 will result in declining population figures for Western Europe (under the assumed fertility and mortality levels) after the year 2010. Assuming high immigration, total population size could increase by 35 per cent over the next 60 years.

Secondly, the proportion of non-Europeans (first and second genera-tions together) within Western Europe will increase from the present 2.4 per cent under all scenarios. It turns out that the rate of integration into the native population influences the future size of the non-European population to a greater extent than the assumed alternative levels of immigration. The high immigration scenario that assumes annual integration rates of 5 per cent and 10 per cent will result in only 7.7 per cent non-Europeans by the year 2050, whereas the scenarios in which integration is restricted to the second generation result in close to 20 per cent non-Europeans.

Thirdly, in the long term the East Europeans in Western Europe will be quantitatively insignificant because of high assumed integration and a likely decrease of immigration flows after 2010.

Fourthly, the absolute number of annual cases of integration into Western Europe around the year 2000 ranges from 0.75 million in scenario 6 to 1.68 million in scenario 5. The highest assumed annual number of integrations is far below 0.5 per cent of the total population of Western Europe. Even including all cases where newborn babies are assumed to be integrated automatically, the sum of adult and infant integration hardly exceeds 0.5 per cent over the next two decades, and in the distant future never comes close to 1 per cent of the Western European population.

It is difficult to come up with a general statement about the absorptive capacity of the Western European populations, but one may assume that such integration rates could at least theoretically be achieved. Whether they actually will be achieved is a matter of willingness at the individual and political level. This chapter has only attempted to show the quantitative impacts of alternative levels of immigration and integration in Western Europe. Qualitative judgements about the desirability of a society with very large non-integrated non-European groups as opposed to immigration combined with successful integration or a strongly ageing society entirely closed to immigration are left to the reader.

Notes

1. This conceptual approach is discussed at length in Lutz (1991); many of the choices for specific fertility, mortality and migration assumptions are based on the broader discussions in this book. The present chapter is a modification and extension of another recently published study (Lutz and Prinz 1992) that did not distinguish between foreigners of the first and second generation.
2. On this see the discussions in Duchene and Wunsch 1991; Manton 1991.

References

Cliquet, R. (ed.) 1993, *The future of Europe's population: a scenario approach*, Council for Europe, Strasbourg.
Duchene, J. and Wunsch, G., 1991, 'Population aging and the limits to human life', in Lutz, W. (ed.), *Future demographic trends in Europe and North America*, Academic Press, London, 27–40.
Heilig, G., Büttner, T. and Lutz, W., 1990, 'Germany's population: turbulent

past, uncertain future', *Population Bulletin*, 45(4): 1–47.

Lutz, W. (ed.), 1991, *Future demographic trends in Europe and North America*, Academic Press, London.

Lutz, W. and Prinz, C., 1992, 'What difference do alternative immigration and integration levels make to Western Europe?' *European Journal of Population*, 8(4): 341–61.

Lutz, W., Prinz, C., Wils, A.B., Büttner, T. and Heilig, G., 1991, 'Alternative demographic scenarios for Europe and North America', in Lutz, W. (ed.), *Future demographic trends in Europe and North America*, Academic Press, London, 523–60.

Manton, K.G., 1991, 'New biotechnologies and the limits to life expectancy', in Lutz, W. (ed.), *Future demographic trends in Europe and North America*, Academic Press, London, 97–115.

Öberg, S. and Boubnova, H., 1993, 'Ethnicity, nationality and migration potentials in Eastern Europe', in King, R. (ed.), *Mass migrations in Europe: the legacy and the future*, Belhaven, London, 234–56.

Steinmann, G., 1991, 'Immigration as a remedy for birth dearth: the case of West Germany', in Lutz, W. (ed.), *Future demographic trends in Europe and North America*, Academic Press, London, 337–57.

Wils, A.B., 1991, 'Survey of immigration trends and assumptions about future migration', in Lutz, W. (ed.), *Future demographic trends in Europe and North America*, Academic Press, London, 281–99.

Chapter 6

Control in immigration policies: a closed Europe in the making

Grete Brochmann

Spring 1991 witnessed a European nightmare: thousands of Albanian citizens evacuated their chaotic and poverty-stricken home country, trying to enter Western Europe in boatloads. Italy, the gatekeeper in this case, acted resolutely with the dual aim of not letting in the masses and at the same time sending a clear message to all potential migrants in less fortunate areas inside and outside Europe that intrusions like these would not warrant the effort. What was subsequently termed the 'Italian solution' to the immigration problem might prove to be an extreme case of a 'European solution' if the member states of the European Community (EC) succeed in their effort of creating a common immigration policy.

Immigration to Western Europe: a new era?

Immigration issues have risen high on the political agenda as the Single European Market (SEM) takes shape — higher than most politicians expected a few years ago. Developments both inside and outside Europe in the last few years have created a notion that a new era is in the making in relation to migratory movements. The single most important event in this respect was the dismantling of the 'Iron Curtain' in 1989. This new pressure from the 'East' came at a moment when the number of asylum-seekers as well as the quantity of unauthorised (illegal) immigration from poor countries in the 'South' had reached considerable proportions in many of the member countries.

The opening-up of East–West relations, together with the already existing uneasiness over immigration in many EC countries, have disturbed the integration process in the West in many ways, and this has created new conditions for immigrants from the poorest parts of the world. This applies both to the ones who already live within the EC region, and those who knock on the gate.[1]

Protection of national borders and labour markets are not new issues. Border control against citizens of other countries has been a central aspect of the sovereignty of European nation-states. With the establishment of the Single Market in 1993, however, this is no longer solely a national consideration. The promotion of mobility of labour, being one of the pillars of the EC philosophy, may have the side-effect that the preconditions for control of 'third-country nationals' (citizens of countries outside the Community) are fundamentally changed. The open internal frontiers in the Common Market may imply that anyone entering a member country from outside the Community will have free access to all other member states. The 'weakest link in the chain' may consequently, as a port of entry, define the control of the influx. Besides, to prevent the variation in immigration policies (welfare benefits, social status, political rights, possibilities for citizenship, etc.) from making some member countries more attractive for immigrants than others, a harmonisation of these measures will be necessary.

But harmonising immigration policies in Europe has proved to be a more difficult undertaking than might have been expected. Being closely attached to the issue of national sovereignty, immigration control in a broad sense appears to be one of the strongholds of the nation-states in the integration process.

This chapter will focus attention on this key issue of immigration control in Europe. Why is it so difficult both nationally and supranationally? And provided control *is* possible, what are the various costs involved? In attempting to answer these questions, I will pay particular attention to the interplay between internal and external control mechanisms in society.

Immigration control and nation-states

Until the First World War, few political and legislative barriers hindered the international movement of people. It was possible to travel throughout Europe and overseas without a passport. Even the settlement of people in new countries implied few bureaucratic formalities. Immigration from poor countries in the South — be it from colonies or elsewhere — was rarely thought of as a realistic possibility until transport and communication facilities were significantly improved in the beginning of the present century. Immigration control in the modern sense is consequently a fairly recent phenomenon.

It has been common among scholars to view immigration control as virtually an intrinsic part of the development of the modern nation-state: in other words, a state ultimately 'ceases to be a state if it does not control the implantation of foreigners on its soil' (Freeman 1979, p. 209). Immigration control appears to serve a dual function in manifesting sovereignty externally whilst at the same time maintaining the socio-cultural confines internally, thereby sustaining political backing and nation-state integration (Freeman 1979; Zolberg 1983).

Viewed from the perspective of the nation-state, migration can be seen as a disturbing factor in the nation-building process. The state may therefore introduce border control, and control of 'foreigners' in a general sense, to subdue this disturbance. The idea of the nation as historically and culturally distinct, with the state as its 'natural' political and territorial framework, has put emphasis on cultural or ethnic *homogeneity*. Although there is much to be said about the empirical evidence concerning the connection between ethnic homogeneity and successful integration (the United States being the most common example of nation-building in a non-homogeneous society), the ideology has served a function in its own right historically speaking. According to the ideal of the nation-state, people should stay in the country where they were born, provided this was in their 'natural' environment.

One knows from historical experience that profound differences in people's living conditions as well as political conflicts of various kinds make people uproot themselves in search of safer havens and a better standard of living. Bearing in mind the emphasis placed on the cultural homogeneity factor, it is reasonable to expect some kind of regulation or control of potential and actual flows of people in modern nation-states. Apparently, this formal right of border regulation has so far never been rejected by modern states, although many modifications have been accepted in terms of bilateral agreements and international conventions.

Immigration and the welfare state

National integration and boundary control have acquired a new dimension through the development of the modern welfare state. Michael Walzer sees the connection between population and territory as the core element in national identity. He argues that the solution to a series of political problems connected to the distribution of public collective goods presupposes a distinct manageable area in which the population resides, and over which the state has full sovereignty (Walzer 1981). Walzer thus contends that giving up full control of the borders would imply the end of national self-determination in the broadest sense.

Historically the welfare state has developed hand-in-hand with the nation-state, although the 'end result' varies in kind throughout the world. Various civil, political and social rights developed within specific states that granted and protected them. The welfare state evolved basically into a closed system where the individuals who 'agree to share according to need, have to experience a sense of solidarity that comes from common membership in some human community' (Freeman 1986, p. 52). The crucial issue in such a closed system is, of course, citizenship. No similar *international* system provided similar rights and assets. The unequal development of the world is marked by vast differences in power, wealth and welfare for the people. Access to goods and rights for members of the fortunate societies requires the exclusion of 'the others'.

Thus, the welfare state brings a dual dimension into the migration context: on the one hand it becomes pertinent to control the limited goods of the welfare societies, yet on the other hand the welfare aspect makes it more attractive to enter from 'the other side'. As Freeman (1986) expressively puts it: 'Without the welfare state, Germany would lose whatever charm it now holds for unemployed migrants.' The 'collective good' component of income helps explain why the tendency to move from poor to rich countries is often independent of given labour market conditions in the place of destination, why the supply of foreign labour tends always to outrun the demand for it, why many who set out as migrants strive to become immigrants, and especially why, in the final analysis, 'all relatively advanced countries must adopt restrictive immigration policies to protect their advantages' (Zolberg 1983, p. 37).

The discussion on migration and the welfare state is nevertheless not all that simple. It we set aside the fact that even among the fortunate citizens of the 'North', access to benefits is often differentiated, the presence of immigrants in welfare societies may have complex effects. One might argue that the very presence of cheaper labour facilitates the sustenance of many of the welfare provisions (in terms of services) in times of economic recession. It is also frequently argued that immigrant labour provides a net economic benefit to the rich states of the 'North', considering demographic dimensions, taxes, favourable (i.e. downward) effects on inflation, etc. (see e.g. Castles 1986). Freeman argues rather functionalistically that a *mésalliance* is created between employers and indigenous labourers in the welfare societies in letting immigrants take jobs in the lower segments of the labour market, which the citizen-workers do not want. Social benefits facilitate this fussiness, even in periods of unemployment. The employers on their side maintain a cheap supply of labour by omitting social costs. This is in turn the kind of situation which Brox (1991) and others picture as the basic long-term threat to welfare society at large — the disturbance of the regulated labour market, and in consequence the undermining of the political consensus which forms the skeleton of the welfare state.

We will not go any further into this complex discussion for the various cost and benefit calculations tend to be highly complicated and the ideological premises often seem to be chosen to support the argument. The real point here is that the (European) welfare states *act* as if immigration is a threat to society — at least under the current economic and political conditions. Hence the heavy focus on control and regulations.[2]

This brief discussion of the modern welfare state in relation to immigration brings us to the various control mechanisms that are in operation — explicitly or more subtly — to regulate the flows and the pace of integration into the host societies.

External versus internal control

We have so far looked at the formal external control mechanism — the historical development of the context for immigration control undertaken by nation-states. Yet nation-states play an important but not exclusive role concerning today's immigration policies. Unofficial actors within society on different levels and across borders serve, on the one hand, to limit or even derail the effectiveness of control policies; on the other hand, more subtle internal control mechanisms may supplement and even reinforce the course of public policy.

This interplay between external and internal control forces is most interesting from an analytical point of view, as it is here one may find explanations as to why the explicit policy often does not work in practice.

Apart from the internal interaction between state policies and the various societal forces, there is, as the former discussion has indicated, also an interaction between states internationally. There is usually a close connection between national politics and the dynamics of the international context, both in terms of the general migration pressure and connected to other states' immigration policies. I will leave this last intersection aside for the moment, concentrating on the national scene.

Both the internal and the external control complex might be seen as continua. For the sake of clarity and based on Figure 6.1, I will divide each complex into an explicit and an implicit dimension: explicit meaning public policy, and implicit meaning hidden or subdued control mechanisms and more or less systematic malpractices of the public policies. The explicit dimension is by definition open, whereas the implicit might be both concealed and occasionally having public expression. As usual the distinctions are not clear-cut. There are grey areas in between the boxes, as well as important interactions across the spheres.

A relevant question is whether there are causal connections between the kind of external control that is practised and the way internal control is undertaken: for example, whether a lax external control is combined with a strict internal control (in an explicit sense) or the other way round. One might argue that Great Britain has practised a quite strict external control over the last 10–20 years, whereas the internal control has been more lax. Italy, on the other hand, until 1982 put strongest emphasis on the internal control (Sciortino 1991). In Scandanavia Sweden has been characterised (at least until recently) by a fairly lax external scrutiny in terms of rather liberal entry restrictions, whereas the internal supervision has been systematically organised through public control mechanisms.

One might, with Hollifield (1986), see the efficiency of immigration policy to a certain extent as a measure of the strength of the state. In modern welfare states this strength is more a question of ability to supervise the strategic labour market rather than policing the national border.

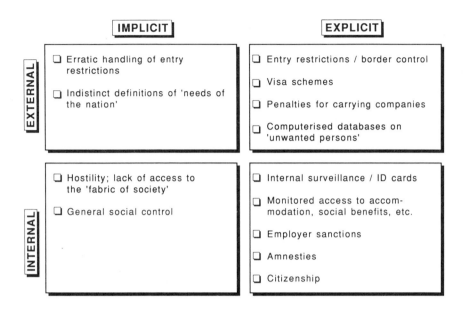

Figure 6.1 A model for immigration control policy

It is manifested by the ability to prevent employers from hiring undocumented workers and the ability to maintain high standards of employment conditions in general. This again may be conditioned by the production structure in the country. It might be easier, as Hollifield points out, to control foreign labour in large manufacturing industries than in small shops.

Networks and 'pull forces'

To trace fully the various control mechanisms of a given country is a complex endeavour, as it involves an analysis of complicated social processes that are not always openly linked to the migration complex. The notion of 'general social control' is unwieldy in itself, as is its causal connection to the migration question. The interactions between explicit policy and the more subtle mechanisms are also difficult to trace empirically. Besides, comparative studies of the control complex of different countries are not meaningfully undertaken unless its interplay with the 'market forces of migration' is taken into consideration.

Potential migrants do not respond to reality like 'atomistic flies', as Robin Cohen (1987) puts it. There are multifaceted networks established over the years between sender and receiver countries, with various institutions involved (kin groups, villages, recruitment agencies, companies, employers' associations, etc.). These networks are directly or indirectly involved in channelling the migrants to specific destinations, and the presence of large communities of foreigners in some of the European countries may serve as a primary promoter of migration. Such networks may act as *buffers* between the individual immigrant and the internal control structures in the receiving country. It is likely that the scope of the networks' field of operations is related to the internal control complex in the first place. If the structural control is extensive, the networks' abilities are more limited. On the other hand, in the countries where the entry of large groups of foreigners has been allowed (or made possible), and the control of the labour market is more lax, the networks may play an extensive role in work intermediation and thereby alleviate some of the central burdens individual migrants face.

The presence of strategic networks consequently serves as a 'multiple' in the migration system, promoting new contingents of illegal (and legal) immigrants, provided there are 'holes in the external fence'. Networks therefore become a central part of the total 'pull package' for potential immigrants. On the other hand, when the networks are not present, possibly as a consequence of a strict internal (and/or external) control system, the attraction is accordingly weak. If a society, therefore, has a 'reputation' internationally for being highly controlled (in various forms) internally, the state might not have to police its borders in the first place.

These added effects and self-reinforcing mechanisms may partly explain why in a relatively homogeneous region like Western Europe there are striking contrasts in the number of applications for asylum, and in the proportions that are approved (see Hovy's chapter in this book).

Western Europe and control policies since the 1970s

European immigration policies since the beginning of the 1970s have been based on the assumption that *control is possible.*

During the 1960s and the beginning of the 1970s different European countries made a conscious migrant recruitment effort in the period of industrial expansion. Labour was in demand, and foreigners became a structural component of labour supply, with immigrants taking over specific categories of low-paying, low-skill jobs in manufacturing, construction and the service sector (Hollifield 1986). The most systematic example in this respect was West Germany where the so-called '*Gastarbeiter* system' was formed. The recession in the early 1970s following the oil crisis caused all the West European countries to introduce an 'immigration stop' to control the influx. After this point the receiving countries have intended to let in only specific people with specific qualifications to fill defined needs in the labour market.

However, the 'stop policy' has not been a success as such in any of the countries in question. A number of unforeseen consequences have appeared. Migrants as a group influenced the recipient countries in ways that were not planned, and which now in turn constitute the basis for policy-making within the European Community.

First and foremost, the recipient countries calculated from the beginning that the influx of foreign workers would be a temporary phenomenon. This proved to be invariably wrong. Migrants who were recruited during the growth period have so far chosen to stay; more than that, they have to a large extent brought their families with them. The registered growth in foreign population after the 'immigration stop' is not constituted by new workers, but by family members of the ones already immigrated, through the rights of 'family unification' or through reproduction (births). This is the case in all Western European countries (King 1993).

Secondly, the restrictions in themselves have implied that immigrants who are already inside the EC would not risk to leave for fear of not being allowed to re-enter.

Thirdly, it seems that the kind of immigration that dominates in each country is to a certain degree a function of the policies that are followed by the authorities. The potential migrant would (if he or she has a choice and access to the relevant information) figure out which queue is most conductive to try.

The costs for the state vary according to type of immigration. The recipient country may consequently be confronted with irrational macro-effects of policies intended to reduce immigration overall. When trying to limit labour migration to a minimum, one may find that the much more expensive asylum-seeker queue is growing. The most inexpensive type of immigration in the short run — temporary labour without dependants — may on the other hand have detrimental effects on society through pressure on wages, social dumping, ethnic tension, etc. This form of immigration could be the most attractive one for some employers, but at the same time untenable for the unions.

In other words, the lessons learnt from the period after the 'immigration stop' in most European countries are that the total number of immigrants has increased substantially and that the composition of the group has changed in favour of family members of original migrants, asylum-seekers and an indistinct group of 'illegals' — huge yet impossible to estimate accurately. The possibilities of entering as asylum-seekers have made the 'stop' policies less effective, and this has in turn made the traditional distinction between the 'economic' migrant and the 'political' migrant more obscure. Information flows to areas that are 'producing' asylum-seekers tell the story that 80 per cent of these migrants are able to stay in Europe even though they have been refused the status of refugees. Legal entrants who have overstayed now constitute the main illegal immigrants in most European countries (Salt 1989). The fairly liberal policies of the Western European countries with respect to asylum-seekers has become a 'pull' factor, a fact which in turn has made the main receiving countries revise their policies towards this category.

The main point to be made here, then, is that the different streams of migrants are connected and influence the actions and movements of each other. After the door was closed for labour migrants in the early 1970s, the only legal entry was through the asylum path. Likewise, having minute odds of succeeding through legal recruitment channels, foreign job-seekers from 'peaceful' countries in the South entered by means of unofficial channels. Control of one gateway may consequently direct the flow on to a new track.

Immigration control and the informal labour market

The labour market plays a key role in relation to illegal immigration. An illegal worker implies an illegal employer. Access to work is a central attraction in relation to the establishment and maintenance of clandestine immigration. As long as there exists work for these migrants when they arrive, the motor in the system will be sustained.

Irregular immigration in itself causes insecurity and lack of stability in the labour market, which again may imply greater difficulties for immigrants already resident when it comes to integration in society. The 'hidden economy' and irregular immigration have a tendency to reinforce each other, at the same time disturbing the labour markets at large.[3]

To make the phenomenon more visible and thereby easier to act upon, the authorities in Spain, Italy and France have several times over recent years introduced co-called 'amnesties' or 'regularisations'. These offers allow illegal migrants to register their presence in the country and consequently become 'regular' without risking penalties.

The amnesties in southern Europe have brought into the open the various segments of the labour market that actually hire the illegal immigrants. Tougher economic conditions often tempt employers to hire illegally: the use of cheap foreign labour has become an important means for small and medium-sized firms to retain some flexibility and lower the costs of production in a competitive situation. The service sector is typical in this respect, although other segments are also involved. In France irregular labour is employed particularly in hotels, cafés and shops, in private households and in the construction and health sectors, whereas in Spain and Italy such labour is concentrated in the tourist sector, private households, catering and in the agricultural sector. Data from these regularisation programmes reveal that the scale of unregistered work undertaken by illegal immigrants is very considerable, and that illegals may stay in the host countries for years.[4]

An important lesson learnt from the migrant amnesties is that it is impossible to control irregular immigration without attacking structural aspects of the labour market. Entry control, ID checks and various sanctions against employers and possible mediators can be only a part of a policy to curtail illegal immigration. Sanctions policies have been tried out in various countries. The overall experience is that sanctions must be carried out with vigour and persistence if they are to be effective. Fines must be significant, otherwise they will simply be calculated by the employer or mediator as part of the regular 'business costs'. Any effective sanctions policy is costly both in terms of finance and manpower.[5]

Yet the structural aspects of the labour market are very complicated to come to grips with. The large-scale presence of unauthorised immigrants points to the fact that there are internal (unofficial) contradictions in the various receiving countries when it comes to influxes of cheap labour. Among groups of employers within the various EC countries, there exists a number of more of less open pressure groups in relation to the question of access to cheap foreign labour. Experiences from Italy reveal that a restrictive legislation can exist together with a *de facto* lenience towards illegal labour in some contexts (Sciortino 1991).

Internal variation and common dilemmas

Today the various EC countries are placed differently as to the economic, political and physical preconditions for handling immigration. The structure of the labour market, the political complexion and the nature and location of the physical borders are all factors that interplay and form a state's posture in this context.

It is here that one is likely to find important conflicts, both between separate EC countries and between various interest groups within each country. Efforts towards harmonisation might as a consequence lead to social and political tensions, as well as a number of practical problems within each EC country, since established national arrangements are challenged and organised interests and power relations are disturbed.

A North–South axis can be depicted in this respect. The rich north European countries are pressuring the southern areas (Spain, Portugal, Greece and Italy) into a more restrictive stance (entry control), whereas powerful business circles in the south have vested interests in a continuing flow of cheap labour from Africa and Asia.[6] Meanwhile the labour market in the northern European countries has undergone structural changes since the 'stop' policy was introduced. This labour market has seen growth in part-time work, extension of subcontracting and the general growth of the informal sector. Demand for foreign labour has continued in these segments, despite growing unemployment.

Physical feasibility of control is an important aspect of immigration regulation. Migrants manage to penetrate most borders, unless the authorities are prepared to militarise them. In the present international climate militarisation can only be regarded as 'an option of last resort'. The extended coastlines of the countries of southern Europe make supervision of the influx particularly difficult.

Against this background, it is not surprising that immigration issues increasingly carry political significance. Immigration is related more or less directly to each country's welfare arrangements and labour market policy. This in turn indicates that the anticipated increased mobility of people after 1992 (both between the different EC countries and from outside) may indirectly increase the pressure to harmonise the welfare systems to prevent what has been called 'social tourism'. This linkage between social benefits and immigration has become more prominent in public discussions as the integration process proceeds. Until now most member states have wanted to minimise the effects of the integration process on their own security policy and ability to control their borders. European immigration dilemmas are beyond the control of any single government, yet each nation-state apparently clings to its sovereignty — none more so that Britain.

So far the discussions and negotiations between the EC countries have been concentrated on better and more coordinated control at the external borders, in anticipation of the Single European Market (SEM). The SEM has itself become a significant factor influencing the internal discussions in the respective member countries. It has made it possible to refer to the detrimental effects for the Community as a whole if a restrictive policy is not followed nationally — as with the case of Italy and Albania, mentioned at the beginning of the chapter — and it has brought pressure on individual countries to step up the pace of reform in order to move towards the goal of a common EC immigration policy (Sciortino 1991).

This is in broad terms the context in which the European Community has to act in order to formulate a common immigration policy for the Single Market. It has transpired that, once immigrants have been admitted, the policy options for the authorities are limited. Measures aimed at limiting entry of family members of the original migrant, or the access of these groups to the labour market, as well as arrangements to facilitate repatriation of immigrants in general, have all failed. These lessons learnt from the policies of the 1960s and 1970s have made the various receiving countries take a restrictive stand, perhaps even beyond what may be desirable from the economic standpoint.

When unintended consequences materialise, the policy-makers tend to go into 'crisis-management mode', which in many ways is counter-productive to solving or even accommodating the problem, as Philip Martin pointed out in Chapter 1 of this book. Public attention is aroused and this then serves to reinforce the crisis perception of the problem. Extreme reactions are whipped up by politicians like Le Pen in France, which again limit the policy-manoeuvring space for the authorities. The frequently used 'Fortress Europe' metaphor reflects the most rigid anticipation of what policies will be like in post-1992 Europe.

Control at what costs?

As with the various dimensions of the control mechanisms, the costs of control can be divided into those which are visible and those which are less visible.

Firstly, the economic cost of a strict control policy has been touched upon already. To the extent that it is possible, the total control of (particularly long and 'untidy') external borders would require equipment and manpower on a huge scale. In few places in Europe has this kind of ultimate control yet been practised (the 'Albanian case' has so far been the exception, as it appeared to be so acute and distinct). Extensive internal control is also costly, depending on the kind of control in question. Intensified police control as well as effectively implemented sanction policies are both economically demanding strategies. Management of the swollen asylum-seeker queue (which is partly a consequence of the 'stop' policy) is obviously also costly.

A counter-argument in this respect is, of course, the alternative costs. Many governments seem to think that the alternative to effective control policies is unlimited flows of immigrants. But perhaps the key point to be made here is that when the control policy is not efficient, it may produce some counter-effects in society that are much more subtle and thus more difficult to come to grips with in the longer run.[7]

The standard argument in favour of a strict control policy on entry is that receiving countries cannot handle further large influxes of immigrants for political and social reasons. Cultural tensions, social unrest, xenophobia and more explicit racism are all existing social expressions relating to immigration in today's Europe. Even though the social sentiments may have other deeper causes, immigration has *de facto* become the public target for the dissent, in turn pushing politicians into a constituency trap. The interplay between the voters and the politicians is intricate in this respect. Being responsive to their voters' expectations, politicians may serve as 'reinforcers' of the hostile tendencies, thus inducing new claims for control.

A more sophisticated argument for a restrictive stance, particularly in relation to asylum-seekers, is that the 'generosity' towards these immigrants has the unintended effect of aggravating the situation for *bona fide* (UN quota) refugees and in turn for the immigrant population as a whole. The EC Commission is also of the opinion that restrictions in the number of asylum-seekers are preconditions for an improved integration policy in the respective member countries.

This brings us to the area of the less visible or implicit interactions between immigration control and public sentiments. It is possible to turn the above hypothesis upside down, claiming that a 'stop' policy contributes to aggravating the climate rather than alleviating the relations between immigrants and 'nationals' (Sciortino 1991).

I have argued that full control is nearly impossible in the Western democracies today, because of the political and economic costs of militarising external borders and policing internal structures. Neither does it seem possible due to the fact that the labour market in itself represents a 'pull' factor in many of the countries, indicating that (sometimes powerful) groups have vested interests in a continued flow. Moreover, the 'half-way' solution that has been practised in many countries in Western Europe might reinforce the perceived problems of immigrants in terms of xenophobic reactions and irregularities in the labour market.

The heavy emphasis on immigration control since the 1970s, in combination with the subsequent increase in number of asylum-seekers as well as illegal immigrants, has made it difficult to avoid a rising hostility towards immigrants in society. After the immigration 'stop' was introduced, ethnically 'visible' immigrants were not supposed to come in at all, apart from a very few traditional *bona fide* refugees. 'Immigrant' has become synonymous with 'unwanted', a fact that feeds back into the attitude towards the already legitimately integrated immigrants. Public opinion becomes 'confused' as to 'who is who'. This public ambiguity is illustrated by the 'amnesties' in southern Europe. Generally new waves of culturally and racially different immigrants are not wanted in the first place, yet when they have managed to get in, they get legal residency. If we leave aside the signals these 'regularisations' send to the potential regions of emigration, the communication to the citizens of the receiving country is quite double-edged: the authorities are 'asserting the right to stay for the already-established immigrant, while identifying the new immigrant as a potential danger' (Sciortino 1991, p. 93).

Likewise, the labour market is detrimentally affected in the sense that a continuous incentive exists to hire illegally as the supply is there. Sciortino argues that in Italy the basic reason behind the ethnic tension is the interaction between the different segments of the labour market — between the official and the 'shadow' market. Concentrations of illegal immigrants are encouraged where 'semi-criminal labour brokering already operates, thus assuring the protection from the authorities' (Sciortino 1991, p. 93). Thus, the matching of cultural stereotypes and individual behaviour has the effect of each reinforcing the other through the labour market.

It can be argued that a similar relationship exists between the welfare state and the immigrants in areas where asylum-seekers are numerically dominant over illegal immigrants. The 'stop' has channelled immigrants into routes and positions that are more costly for the authorities to control and manage, hence producing opinions that they come 'to exploit our welfare state', again leading to increased hostility.

The utmost cost of a distorted control policy might be an undermining of the welfare system for all citizens. As Brox (1991) argues, unless one keeps insisting that the immigrants should have the same standards as the nationals, one risks creating a subproletariat which ultimately may subvert the labour market for everybody.

This points to a central dilemma for the European welfare states at the moment: the norms and values that define the democratic welfare state may become violated by excluding immigrants either at the border or internally by not giving them access to social, economic and political benefits. On the other hand, their inclusion could imply a challenge to people's sense of fairness when it comes to the divisions of burdens and rights among 'those who struggled to construct the collective bargains represented by the welfare state' (Heisler and Heisler 1986).

A tentative conclusion in this highly complicated matter would be a relaxation of the 'immigration stop' in the Western European countries. Germany is bilaterally experimenting in this field at the moment. It remains to be seen, however, whether other countries will follow suit, and whether the supra-national structure is ready for this challenge.

The Single Market and the control of immigrants

Certain basic formal preconditions are still unclear regarding the EC's immigration policies. Whether internal borders in the EC will be open for 'third country' citizens is an important aspect when it comes to possibilities of international diffusion. The Single European Act (1986) implies that measures should be taken by the end of 1992 to permit the freedom of movement of EC nationals. So far it is unclear whether this will apply to non-EC nationals. It is here worth noting that whereas there are 5 million EC migrants, migrants from 'third countries' number at least 8 million among the registered only.

Harmonisation of immigration policies will most likely not succeed as a unilateral directive from above. A complex network of actors with various interests, ventures and conceptions, operating both locally and internationally, will in practical terms try to influence both the direction of the harmonisation policies and their overall implementation. Even after the formal closure of the process at political level, there will probably be room for diverse practices in the different countries, partly due to lack of control, and partly because of unequal national power complexes. Besides, a unilateral policy on immigration within the EC is only a necessary, not a sufficient precondition for stemming unauthorised immigration. The control aspect would still constitute great challenges at least at the outer frontiers, but possible also internally in the Community, a question which again feeds back into the political level.

Notes

1. Immigrants are here defined as refugees (including asylum-seekers), 'guestworkers' and close relatives of the original migrants (immigration through family reunion arrangements), as well as unauthorised immigrants (illegals).
2. The United States, Canada and Australia together represent an interesting contrast when it comes to public attitudes towards immigration. Although these countries are subject to many of the same economic setbacks as Europe, increased (legal) immigration appears to be public policy. For more details, refer back to Chapter 1 of this book.
3. The 'black' labour market has grown over the last two decades in many EC countries. According to some investigations, illegal immigration has in some cases implied that capital increasingly is transferred from the formal to the informal sector of the economy (see, for example, Dell'Aringa and Neri 1987).
4. For a detailed comparative study on regularisation programmes in France, Spain and Italy, see SOPEMI Report 1989, OECD, Paris.
5. Employer sanctions is an old instrument. It was introduced in France as early as 1926 and later in 1946. Most European countries initiated this kind of sanction policy during the 1970s, not primarily in relation to illegal immigration but as a means to control the labour market.
6. Here there is apparently also an internal schism within the Community at the political level: southern Europe might use its comparative advantage in relation to northern Africa to neutralise Germany's favourable disposition towards Eastern Europe.
7. For readers of the Scandinavian languages, I have discussed various scenarios in this respect in Brochmann (1991).

References

Brox, O., 1991, *Jeg er ikke rasist, men . . . Hvordan får vi våre meninger om innvandrere og innvandring*? Gyldendal, Oslo.

Brochmann, G., 1991, *Europeisk intergrasjon og innvandring fra 'tredje land': Relevans Norge*, ISF, Oslo.

Castles, S., 1986, 'The guest-worker in Western Europe: an obituary', *International Migration Review*, 20(4): 761–78.

Cohen, R., 1987, *The new helots: migrants in the international division of labour*, Gower, Aldershot.

Dell'Aringa, G. and Neri, F., 1987, 'Illegal immigrants and the informal economy', *Labour*, 1(2): 107–26.

Freeman, G.P., 1979, *Immigrant labour and racial conflict in industrial societies: the French and British experience 1945–75*, Princeton University Press, Princeton, NJ.

Freeman, G.P., 1986, 'Migration and the political economy of the welfare state', *Annals of the American Academy of Political and Social Science*, 485: 51–63.

Heisler, B.S. and Heisler, M., 1986, 'Transnational migration and the modern democratic state: familiar problems in new form or a new problem?' *Annals of the American Academy of Political and Social Science*, 485: 12–22.

Hollifield, J.F., 1986, 'Immigration policy in France and Germany: outputs versus outcomes', *Annals of the American Academy of Political and Social Science*, 485: 113–28.

King, R., 1993, 'European international migration 1945–90: a statistical and geographical overview', in King, R. (ed.), *Mass migrations in Europe: the legacy and the future*, Belhaven, London, 19–39.

Salt, J., 1989, 'A comparative overview of international trends and types, 1950–80', *International Migration Review*, 23(3): 431–56.

Sciortino, G., 1991, 'Immigration into Europe and public policy: do stops really work?' *New Community*, 18(1): 89–99.

Walzer, M., 1981, 'The distribution of membership', in Brown, P. and Shue, H. (eds), *Boundaries, national autonomy and its limits*, Rowman and Littlefield, Totowa, NJ, 1–35.

Zolberg, A., 1983, 'Contemporary transnational migrations in historical perspective: patterns and dilemmas', in Kritz, M. (ed.), *US immigration and refugee policy*, Heath, Lexington, MA, 15–51.

Chapter 7

Migration, employment and social change in the new Europe

Malcolm Cross

Introduction

Amidst the flurry of economic changes over the last two decades, it has been hard to discern precisely what is happening to the labour market, to the distribution of jobs and to qualitative changes in the kinds of jobs on offer. Aside from a growing interest in the involvement of women in the labour market, there have been few studies on the impact of these changes on particular categories of the population such as immigrants and ethnic minorities (Cross 1992a). Similarly, much has been written about regional effects, particularly in relation to European economic integration, but much less about the social and ethnic implications of economic change at city level.

Meanwhile, a cursory inspection of journalistic and political discourse inevitably produces a different impression. The British *Sunday Times*, for example, carried a major article (7 March 1993) predicting the arrival of an American-style 'underclass' in British cities and followed this up with reports on Moss Side, Manchester, depicting this area as a violent, crime-infested, drug-soaked ghetto. The same source on the same day carried a story on illegal immigrants 'pouring west across the German border' to take advantage of the 'slackening of border controls' in the integrated market. A similar story could be found in most papers in northern Europe during the last two years and it is increasingly clear that these issues are becoming more and more central to political debate (Ford 1992).

There is, in other words, a widespread and growing popular perception that many European cities are changing to contain ethnically identifiable minorities living in poor environmental conditions with high unemployment rates, while at the same time new waves of migration are occurring. Is this not a paradox? If jobs are available for new migrants why are they not taken by those who are unemployed? Moreover, why do problems of persistent long-term unemployment in European cities appear to affect some minorities more than others? The delicacy of these questions, and the ease with which they can be phrased and formulated in ways which could damage minority–majority relations, are perhaps the reasons why they have been so infrequently asked by social scientists.

In this chapter I suggest that there are three separable processes through which many European economies are passing which can point to answers to these questions without blaming minorities for their predicament. Each has to do with the demand for labour. The first involves a change in the ratio between higher- and lower-level skills; the second has to do with pressure to reduce labour costs; and the third involves an analysis of the relationship between internal migration and urban labour markets. After a brief overview of the secondary literature, I shall discuss each of these in turn, drawing data from European sources where possible. The second main section of the chapter looks at a particular case, that of Greater London. Here it is suggested that the three processes identified above are highly relevant for cities, especially those that can be described as 'global' or at the hub of current economic change (Sassen 1991). Finally, I shall offer some reflections on the relationship between the three processes and European economic and social policy.

Migrants and minorities in European cities

The problems of labour market exclusion in conditions of environmental decline have been identified within European cities for at least a decade. In 1981, for example, a report originally prepared for the Council of Europe commented that members of Europe's new minorities who had earlier enjoyed high levels of economic activity as migrant labour were facing progressive exclusion as employment needs changed. The report then made the following predictions:

Changes in [labour market] needs have ensured that the secondary economic role of migrants will become increasingly insecure and characterised by unemployment and underemployment. On the other hand, selective outmigration from Europe's inner cities will interact with economic marginality to produce a concentrating effect of progressive ghettoisation. (Cross 1981, p. 25)

I would argue that the first proposition can now be broadly sustained by the evidence available to us. For example, the first book to look across the board at minorities in European cities (Glebe and O'Loughlin 1987) suggested:

What is clear is that all European immigrant nations must expect to retain a large foreigner population who have all the characteristics of permanence and who have not yet indicated any noticeable movement from their marginal position as a 'permanent underclass' . . . High-rise buildings, small and poorly equipped flats, and inner-city projects become the refuge of the poorest council-tenants, often 'problem families' and, increasingly in Continental Europe, of foreigner households. (O'Loughlin 1987, p. 21)

Studies by social geographers have tended to cast these issues in the form of segregation research (Huttman 1991). This has its value, but it points to only one side of the issue, namely spatial organisation. The critical component which has to be added is economic circumstance. In other words, the question of segregation from the dominant society and concentration in certain areas of major cities would not be so much of an issue were it not accompanied by labour market exclusion and resultant poverty (cf. Peach 1992). Spatial polarisation and social polarisation, taken together, suggest a process of *ghettoisation* (Cross 1992b).

Of course, it has to be recognised that the term 'ghetto' in its modern usage is largely North American (Wilson 1987). It is certainly true that differences in population proportions, when combined with housing policies and income support through the welfare state, will mean that most European nations will avoid the desperate situation of, say, parts of Washington, New York City or the south side of Chicago. However, it would be foolish to ignore processes which are pushing in that direction. Countervailing policies can only be developed if there is a clear understanding of the pressures which generate the issue to which such policies are addressed. It is striking that the European Commission itself has now recognised the significance of both growing impoverishment and growing ethnic minority concentrations in situations of environmental stress:

Many of the cities of Europe display particularly sharp distinctions between rich and poor. This is often related to the concentration of foreign migrants in urban areas. Moreover, differences in income and employment opportunities are often associated with profound physical segregation and are manifest in the quality of housing and public service infrastructures. (Commission of the European Communities 1991, p. 20)

Disqualification and the urban labour market

Describing what appears to be happening in a number of cities throughout Western Europe is not the same as accounting for these patterns. This is the task of the remainder of this chapter. In the introduction it was suggested that three processes were occurring simultaneously. Indeed it is partially because they appear to be happening together that confuses the picture. How can 'new migration' appear to be growing when unemployment is also rising? How can some ethnic minorities appear to experiencing such negative pressures when others, with an apparently similar background, are moving swiftly towards educational and occupational success?

The first line of explanation involves the process of 'disqualification'. People can enter the ranks of the long-term unemployed either because there are insufficient jobs for them or because those that there are demand qualifications and experience which the jobless do not possess.

Those familiar with the literature on racism would be swift to add a third factor, namely the particularistic criteria used at the interface between labour demand and supply. Where unemployment rises swiftly for subgroups of the population, it must either be because demand falls or because it becomes more selective. The latter can be either on the basis of 'legitimate' (e.g. educational) criteria or because of 'illegitimate' (e.g. discriminatory) factors.

Europe's geography of employment is changing as economic restructuring and industrial change tend to concentrate employment in regions of growth. In this sense economic integration promotes labour market exclusion in the periphery as it offers new opportunities at the economic core. The changes associated with economic restructuring are, however, also qualitative. The new jobs that appear in the service industries in the 'global cities' and in the zones of advanced manufacturing, where information control is as important as manual dexterity, have no place for those who do not possess a certified education beyond that required only a decade or so ago. Evidence from Germany, for example, confirms what has already been shown in the United States: that there is a major shift going on in industrial cities as they reorganise their economies to take advantage of advances in technology. In German cities during 1980–4, jobs requiring higher-level qualifications increased by approximately 10 per cent, whereas unskilled and semi-skilled jobs decreased by at least that amount (Kasarda *et al.* 1992).

Where migrants or ethnic minorities, either because of lack of familiarity with dominant languages or because of discrimination, are unable to combine what are normally high occupational aspirations with educational success they will be particularly vulnerable to exclusion from large sectors of the job market. Unemployed foreigners, for example, became an increasing proportion of the unemployed overall in Austria, Belgium, France and The Netherlands during the second half of the 1980s (SOPEMI 1992). This has not led to a tendency for foreigner populations to fall. Indeed, the evidence is that they have stabilised or, if anything, risen as family reunion, youthful populations and relatively high fertility levels impact on growth rates.

An urban underclass?

This analysis is far from new. 'Mismatch' theory has been extensively used in the United States where it is frequently employed to sustain the argument of a growing urban 'underclass'. Is this what is happening in Europe? The issue turns on the definition of 'underclass', a term which has been roundly abused by all shades of political opinion. For the so-called 'new right', eager to sustain the radical economic and social policies of the 1980s, the apparent growth in urban poverty and its powerful association with ethnic minorities is evidence of the deficiencies within such communities themselves (Murray 1990). For those on the other side of the political spectrum, who are anxious to mount a defence on behalf of the poor in general, the problem is not seen as one where 'race' or ethnic origin is particularly relevant (Mann 1991).

My position on this issue is very similar to that of William Julius Wilson (1987; 1989). There is a need to identify processes of social and economic exclusion to which some groups appear to be particularly vulnerable. Painting portraits of those whose lives are blighted by these processes is less important than describing how they occur. Equally, it is so far empirically unproved whether the experience of long-term unemployment in conditions of urban stress has a tendency to reproduce itself. There is a profound danger of confusing cause and effect. Even if, as is maintained by new recruits to the old theory that 'cultures of poverty' help reproduce long-term economic and social exclusion, there was evidence that enforced idleness and welfare dependency undermined the Protestant ethic, it would be bizarre to conclude from this that an appropriate policy prescription lay in reducing welfare support. This would be equivalent to curing the impact of 'acid rain' on the world's forests by chopping down the trees they contain.

It may be that the emotive content of the term 'underclass' is such as to render it worthless (cf. Gans 1990). If that is so we shall have to invent another term. Meanwhile it would certainly help if a definition was applied which made the aetiology clear and which narrowed the focus to concentrate the minds of those concerned on the groups which appear to be most severely effected. One such definition might be: 'those of ethnic minority or recent migrant origin living in an area of severe economic stress who, because of a skills mismatch and negative selection criteria, are precluded from entry to employment.' This definition has the merit of both clarity and general application. It is true that it merges all three of the forces of labour market exclusion identified above but empirically that is probably essential. For example, we may point out particular groups whose educational position is such as to preclude them from gaining the new jobs generated by industrial change, but this only begs the question of why such groups fail to be 'credentialised' to the same extent as others. In other words, particularistic (e.g. racial) criteria may be relevant at an earlier stage in the process.

The deregulation process

Economic integration has generated a process of deregulation in capital markets, the most famous of which is probably the 'Big Bang' which was the City of London's attempt to throw off centuries of stultifying tradition in order to preserve a central role in Europe's burgeoning market for financial services. It is less commonly noted that deregulation has also affected labour markets. This is evident in the incorporation of trade unions as 'social partners' and, elsewhere (notably Britain), in the undermining of trade-union power. The bargain that has been struck in most European member states has not permitted a marked deterioration in labour conditions. Britain is an exception, as the reluctance to sign the Social Chapter in the Maastricht Treaty and the abolition of wages councils makes clear. Where the partnership ideology prevails, however, alternative strategies of labour incorporation have evolved in order to reduce costs to levels which can be competitive at a global level. One such strategy is to reorganise work to permit the incorporation of more married women into part-time employment, while another is a return to a reliance on migration (Gordon and Sassen 1992).

In Europe, the dependence on migrant labour is, of course, nothing new. What is not so well appreciated, however, is that after the general cessation of labour migration in 1974, the inward flow steadied before beginning another upward turn in the mid-1980s. Unlike the earlier moves of migrant workers, from the Iberian peninsula, Greece, and from what was then Yugoslavia, the current pressure is from countries of the East and South. In relation to the latter, the issue is making itself felt in the reversal of migration processes in Italy, Spain and Portugal. From being countries of net out-migration, they have now become the destination for mostly unskilled migrants from North Africa and other former colonial dependencies. What is also different is that these flows are largely of undocumented workers moving into the underground or informal economy. In Chapter 10 of this book King and Rybaczuk argue that migrant flows into the Mediterranean member states are clearly directed into segmented labour markets. On the one hand there is a growing number of professional and managerial people from northern EC countries, while on the other the flows of 'irregulars' into the underground economy will also increase. This is partly because of the build-up of population pressure in North Africa but also because of growing demand for unqualified manpower in the rapidly expanding underground economies of southern Europe. Estimates suggest that the informal sector now accounts for 30 per cent of the Greek GDP and 25 per cent of Italian GDP. However, the importance of the migrant-fed informal economy does not mean that the migrants are well catered for. Quite the reverse: they live and work in the worst conditions.

In some countries of northern Europe the pattern is not significantly different. In The Netherlands, for example, there is currently a debate on the so-called 'illegals' whose numbers have been estimated at up to 150,000 or 22 per cent of the foreign population. These workers are concentrated in the horticulture industry and in hotels, restaurants and catering. Although research on this labour force is both difficult and scarce, it would appear that it consists largely of workers from Eastern Europe (particularly Poland) who arrive on tourist visas, work for three months and return, and Turks and Moroccans who are able to stay for longer by being sheltered by family and friends in existing communities.

The liberal Dutch laws, together with the difficulty of policing 'illegals' and the ambiguous status of workers who are clearly in great demand from employers, means that the estimate of those who are eventually removed is put at only 2 per cent.

In the European Community there is no member state with fertility rates above replacement; in 1989, two-thirds of total population increase was accounted for by net migration. Moreover, applications for refugee or asylum status have dramatically risen in recent times (see Chapter 11 for more details). The official estimates are that in 1991–2 there were about 600,000 new applications for asylum, nearly half of which were made to Germany (SOPEMI 1992). The United Nations High Commissioner for Refugees estimated in August 1992 that refugees from the former Yugoslavia added a further 500,000, while the total from Eastern Europe (including *Aussiedler*) has been put at 800,000 in the same year. It must be stressed that some of these categories overlap so that it would be wrong to add them together to obtain the total picture. In addition, it is hard to be certain how these flows will evolve since they are so dependent upon the policies of member states and the pressures of political persecution in countries of origin. It can be safely concluded, however, that Europe has entered a new phase of immigration from that immediately following the cessation of labour recruitment in 1974.

What is particularly important about this new situation is that it may have important labour market effects. Although only approximately half of new migrants are ostensibly moving for work-related reasons, this does not mean that the remainder will not work. On the contrary, while 'illegals', asylum-seekers and refugees are normally excluded from official participation, their very marginality is a factor in their desirability as workers. Even though our knowledge of this issue is very deficient, it is important to stress the relationship between the powerful pressures towards competitiveness, cost-cutting and flexibility, which represent the hallmark of the new integrated European economy, and the incorporation of new workers. These cannot be regarded as unrelated historical events.

Again the European Commission has noted this process, although tending to focus upon the reluctance of workers themselves to work for lower wages at jobs without a minimal welfare and safety umbrella:

We are witnessing rivalry for unskilled jobs between Europeans, who are less inclined to move and are more demanding as regards wages and social cover, and workers who have come, legally or illegally, from non-Community countries and who are far more mobile. (Commission of the European Communities 1988, p. 22)

The new migrant may be seeking work in a variety of industries including some fishing and agricultural activities. It would be surprising, however, if they did not follow their predecessors into the cheaper zones of industrial cities when it comes to finding a place to live.

An ethnic division of labour

It would be wrong to conclude on the basis of the foregoing that all ethnic minorities and migrants are affected in the same way by these processes. As economies change, particularly at the local level, they open and close doors of opportunity which are closer to some groups than others. Roger Waldinger's work on the United States is perhaps the most important in showing how this occurs.

Waldinger demonstrates that in the case of New York at least two separate processes have been at work. Whites have left the city faster than the jobs they formerly occupied, with the effect of opening up opportunities for non-white labour. In the public sphere some native blacks have been the beneficiaries, but in private business new migrants from South East Asia have gained employment. At the bottom, however, there has been a growth of menial jobs which have largely gone to the remaining new migrants — those from Puerto Rico, Haiti and the Dominican Republic (Waldinger 1992).

Comparing the fortunes of Hispanics, black Americans and 'Asians' (Far Eastern origin) in New York between 1970 and 1986, Waldinger (1992) also shows that blacks were sheltered in the early part of this period by being disproportionately located in the public sector, rather than in manufacturing, but this shelter later kept them out of the sun as other areas took off in employment terms. Moreover, an increasing proportion of blacks were falling by the wayside and remaining among the long-term unemployed. Hispanics, by contrast, show a very different pattern. Although heavily dependent on a declining manufacturing base, their position in this sector actually strengthens over the period because the white exodus is more evident than the decline in jobs overall. The garment industry is an obvious example of this process. Foreign-born Asians experienced the transitions in the labour market in yet another fashion. Although originally concentrated in manufacturing and retail, this group was well placed to exploit the rapid rise in financial and related services. In short it is the *structural* position of minorities which determines their experience of labour market change. These positions are not only influenced by labour demand changes but also by the relative size of minorities, their particular concentration in certain sectors and industries, and their capacity to shift from one sector to another. Cross and Waldinger (1992) have attempted elsewhere to apply these ideas to a comparison of New York and London.

The case of Greater London

London is changing rapidly. As a 'global city' it has been at the forefront of economic restructuring. Manufacturing, other production industries and transport and wholesaling jobs fell by 34.6 per cent between 1971 and 1988 and there was a corresponding rise in the service sector (Fainstein *et al.* 1992). Within the region, the decentralisation process continued with total jobs in Greater London falling by 430,000, and rising by 370,000 in the Outer Metropolitan Area over the same period. Also evident is a gender-related process with a recent shift towards part-time work for women.

By the 1991 census, 20 per cent of the population of Greater London was made up of those 'ethnic minorities' recognised in the census, the greater part (15.8 per cent) being 'black' (i.e. Afro-Caribbean) or South Asian. With the exception of the Bangladeshi community, concentrated in the borough of Tower Hamlets just north of the Thames and to the east of the City of London, the South Asians in Britain are not as concentrated in Greater London as the black population. Amongst the latter, 58 per cent of those of Caribbean origin in Great Britain live in Greater London, which is true also for four out of five black Africans.

The distribution of ethnic minorities within Greater London continues, however, to be very different (Figure 7.1). For example, the nine Inner London boroughs with more than 20 per cent ethnic minority population contain 54 per cent of the black population of Greater London but only 29 per cent of the Asian population. By contrast the six Outer London boroughs with more than 20 per cent ethnic minority population contain 43.3 per cent of the South Asian population but under 20 per cent of the black population. The five inner city boroughs where the black population are more than 15 per cent of the population account for 38 per cent of their numbers in Greater London but the same boroughs contain only 8 per cent of London's Asians.

The 'inner city' boroughs with high black concentrations lead the way in terms of out-migration. The fall for Inner London between 1981 and 1991 was − 11.1 per cent but for three of the five boroughs with black populations of 15 per cent or more the figure was well above that (the other two being average for Inner London as a whole). Previous evidence suggests that this out-migration is unlikely to be black, with the resultant greater separation and concentration of population (Cross 1992b, p. 106).

The fact that different groups occupy different segments of urban space does not necessarily mean that they must also experience the labour market in different ways. Indeed the proposition that there are three separable processes at work indicates that a non-spatial one may be of primary importance. This can be shown in Table 7.1, derived from the 1991 census. These data show the economic position of men aged 16 and over in Inner and Outer London. The table demonstrates quite clearly that not all ethnic minorities are in the same position. Four out of five Indian men economically active in London live in the outer boroughs, where they experience unemployment rates which are almost the same as the white population. The 20 per cent who reside in the inner London boroughs have higher rates of unemployment but again no higher than

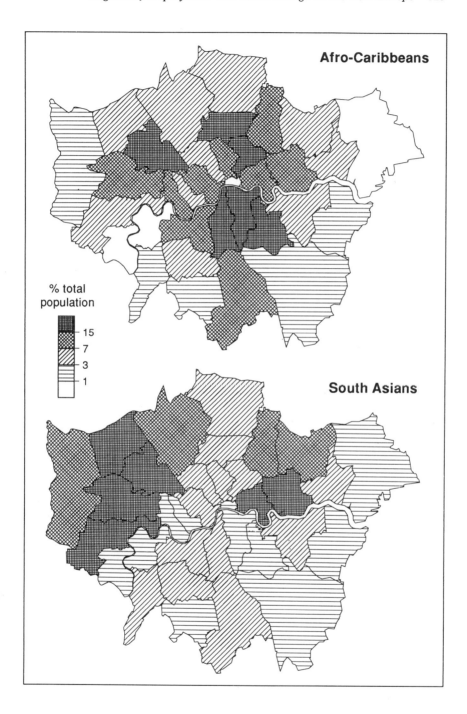

Figure 7.1 Greater London: distribution of Afro-Caribbean and Asian populations by borough, 1991

Table 7.1   Economic status of males aged 16+ in Greater London by ethnic group, 1991 (%)

	White	Black	Indian	Paki-stani	Bangla-deshi	Other	All
Inner London							
Employees, full-time	63.7	54.3	58.1	48.7	46.1	57.8	61.7
Employees, part-time	3.4	5.0	3.5	4.0	3.6	2.5	3.7
Self-employed	15.9	6.9	20.1	16.7	7.5	14.1	14.6
Work scheme	1.0	3.2	2.0	2.8	2.0	0.8	1.4
Unemployed	16.0	30.5	16.3	27.8	40.8	23.5	18.6
Number	551,047	82,493	20,646	7,380	13,100	32,765	707,431
Outer London							
Employees, full-time	69.4	63.4	63.1	55.0	56.7	66.8	68.4
Employees, part-time	3.1	3.7	2.3	3.1	3.0	3.8	3.1
Self-employed	17.2	9.3	22.5	17.6	19.9	13.8	17.1
Work scheme	0.7	2.2	1.2	1.8	1.9	1.8	0.8
Unemployed	9.6	21.4	10.8	22.4	18.4	13.8	10.5
Number	1,015,596	53,939	77,272	14,966	3,576	43,028	1,208,467

Source: Census of Population, 1991.

the white people amongst whom they live. The black population, on the other hand, is not in the same position at all. In the inner areas, where 60 per cent live, their unemployment rate approaches one in three and it remains double the rate for white males in the outer boroughs. In this instance race appears to make a significant difference regardless of space.

This conclusion is further confirmed by looking at the representation of these minorities by socio-economic group (Figure 7.2). In 1981, for example, in all parts of London South Asians were over-represented at the top end of the occupational spectrum when compared with the population as a whole. They were also over-represented in semi-skilled jobs giving a bi-modal distribution. The contrast with the Afro-Caribbean population is very clear. In this case, regardless of where they are resident in the city, the black population is dramatically under-represented at the top of the socio-economic spectrum and heavily over-represented at the bottom. Comparisons over time suggest that the position for Afro-Caribbeans has worsened while for all Asian groups it has improved (Robinson 1990).

In relation to the analysis in the first part of this chapter, the apparent vulnerability of the Caribbean population to unemployment and social exclusion should correlate with low levels of certified educational performance. At a national level this appears to be indisputable. The Youth Cohort Study, a longitudinal sample involving 28,000 young people, shows that just under one in three white young people succeed in attaining four or more 'O' levels or higher grade GCSEs by the age of 18

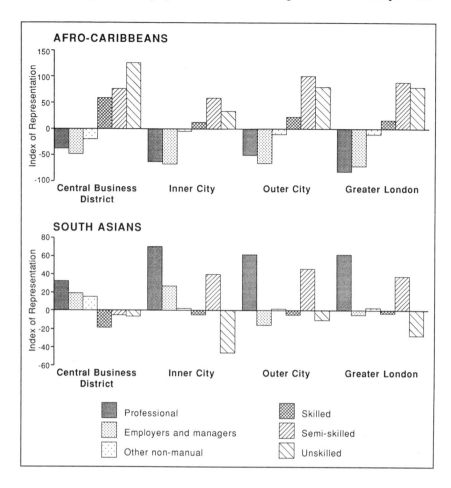

Figure 7.2   Greater London: socio-economic group characteristics of Afro-Caribbean and Asian populations, 1981

Note: The index of representation compares the distribution of the minority group with the average representation in that SEG of the total population. The histogram can be read as deviations from the distribution that would be expected if ethnic minority membership made no difference.

(Drew *et al.* 1992). On this relatively modest yardstick, the British Asian population fare better with 'scores' of 42 per cent and 35 per cent for young men and women respectively. The Caribbean British population, by contrast, do very poorly; only one in five young women and 15 per cent of young men achieve these levels. Broadly the same picture is reflected at the higher standard of two or more 'A' levels. The Asians do half as well again as the whites but only one-third the proportion of

Table 7.2   Proportion of students aged 16+ by ethnic group and gender in Greater London, 1991 (%)

Ethnic group	Inner London		Outer London	
	Male	Female	Male	Female
White	4.1	3.8	3.5	3.2
(Irish-born)	(1.1)	(1.2)	(0.9)	(0.8)
Black — Caribbean	4.8	5.5	4.6	5.25
Black — African	21.5	14.8	17.7	13.7
Black — other	11.9	11.9	11.9	12.3
Indian	10.0	8.5	9.5	8.3
Pakistani	14.4	12.4	13.9	11.2
Bangladeshi	12.9	12.2	13.5	13.0
Chinese	22.5	19.2	16.3	13.3
Other	14.2	12.0	12.3	9.9

Source: Census of Population, 1991.

the Caribbean population achieve the performance of their ethnic minority peers in the Asian community.[1]

These findings are, unsurprisingly, replicated in data for Greater London, except that a powerful social class determinant appears to lower the performance of white pupils and that of some Asians, notably the Bangladeshis. Evidence from the London Borough of Brent, for example, which contains the highest proportion of ethnic minorities in London, shows again that the black population of that borough achieve results at the minimum secondary school leaving age which are well below those for Asians, who in turn achieve higher levels of measured performance than white pupils (Cross *et al.* 1991, p. 153). Data from the 1991 census (Table 7.2) add another dimension to this picture by showing the proportion of those aged 16 and over who are in full-time education. Amongst the ethnic minorities, the Caribbean population is the odd one out with only about 1 in 20 young people remaining in education beyond the minimum age. Of course, these differences are strongly affected by the age distribution of the subpopulations and it is this, together with the inclusion of the Irish-born population, which accounts for the low proportion of 'whites' who are attending school or college beyond the minimum leaving age. The difference between the Caribbean and other ethnic minority groups cannot, however, be accounted for by differences in age profiles.

A lively debate exists in the United Kingdom on the position of Muslim minorities. The Labour Force Survey, for example, has provided support for those who wish to claim that the greater levels of labour market exclusion experienced by those of Pakistani and Bangladeshi origin indicates that a combination of anti-Islamic sentiment and cultural factors account for their particularly poor position (Modood 1991). Such arrangements depend upon aggregate figures on unemployment, based on

Table 7.3 Unemployment rates in London for males 16+ by ethnic group and age

Ethnic group	Inner London			Outer London		
	<25	25+	16+	<25	25+	16+
White	23.7	14.6	16.0	15.8	8.3	9.6
Black	43.3	27.2	30.5	35.1	18.3	21.4
Indian	23.8	15.1	16.3	19.3	9.6	10.8
Pakistani	32.0	26.8	27.8	30.8	20.6	22.4
Bangladeshi	28.4	45.0	40.8	15.7	19.2	18.4
Other	34.2	21.1	23.2	26.4	11.8	13.8
All	27.2	16.9	18.6	17.4	9.2	10.5

Source: Census of Population, 1991.

very small samples, which do indeed show very high rates for Pakistanis and Bangladeshis. These data are, however, very misleading. They rarely control for local labour markets and certainly not for location and age group together.

In fact it is far more probable that it is the later arrival in Britain of minorities from Pakistan and Bangladesh which explains these differences, together with the fact that Muslim minorities in Britain are far more likely than others to live in the north west of the country where downturns in employment have been particularly severe. There are three features in the London data which suggest that this interpretation is correct. First of all, if unemployment levels are disaggregated by age group as well as by city location (Table 7.3), then all 'Asians' under the age of 25 have unemployment rates which are high but not that much higher than the white population in the same age category. For example, in the Inner London boroughs, which include the very poor area of Tower Hamlets with its high concentration of Bangladeshis, young 'Asians' have an unemployment rate of 27.3 per cent compared with the young white male rate of 23.7 per cent. The high Bangladeshi figures for Inner London in Tables 7.1 and 7.3 are the result of older Bangladeshis who often possess very limited education and facility in English.

The second feature of interest in the London data concerns patterns of self-employment. Evidence that Asians in London are strongly represented as entrepreneurs is contained in Table 7.1, which shows that this is particularly so in Outer London. This pattern can also be seen by comparing the 'expected' number of male entrepreneurs, based on the white rate, with the actual number: this calculation is set out in Table 7.4. This table shows that the black population has about half the number of entrepreneurs that it would have if it paralleled the white population regardless of its whereabouts in the city. The Asian population has about the number of entrepreneurs in Inner London that could be predicted from white rates, but in the outer area — where South

Table 7.4   Actual and expected number of male entrepreneurs in London, 1991

	Inner London			Outer London		
	Expected	Actual	Difference (%)	Expected	Actual	Difference (%)
Black	13,116	5,717	− 56.4	9,281	5,002	− 46.1
Asian	6,539	6,358	− 2.3	17,095	20,716	+ 21.2

Note: For explanation of calculations, see text.

Source: Census of Population, 1991.

Asians are concentrated — the numbers are more than 20 per cent higher than expected.

Of course, it cannot be concluded that everyone of these entrepreneurs is on an easy ride towards economic prosperity. Far from it; but neither can it be argued that these differences will be irrelevant in affecting future social mobility options. It is also true that some of these businesses will be 'new' in the sense that they will serve an ethnic market. As other research has shown (Mcleod 1991), however, that is decreasingly true, which adds confirmation to the proposition that Asian entrepreneurs have taken a significant proportion of the opportunities generated by the excess of white out-migration over job loss in Greater London.

The third factor of importance is, of course, educational performance. There is some reason for supposing that some Islamic communities deviate markedly from the high performance levels recorded for South Asians overall. However, this is by no means true for all Muslims and recent evidence on the 'A' level scores achieved for university applicants in 1990 provides compelling evidence that at this level the proper comparison is between South Asians, whose scores are very similar and just below that of whites, and the Afro-Caribbean applicants who are much less likely than others to apply with the 'A' level scores normally necessary to secure admission (Taylor 1992).

The Greater London case shows therefore some but not all of the features anticipated by the discussion in the first part of this chapter. There are grounds for supposing that parts of Inner London, and a small number of areas outside the inner core, are destined to contain stigmatised minorities whose levels of long-term unemployment, particularly amongst the young, are likely to generate disaffection and despair. The descendants of those who came from the Caribbean in the post-war period have been identified as those likely to suffer most from the processes that create this predicament.[2]

There are those who will want to construe from this argument the implication that there is something in the culture of Caribbean minorities that helps sustain this condition. Research on Caribbean societies themselves provides no support for this view. The evidence from studies of educational commitment and occupational aspirations is likewise unhelpful to those who wish to push this argument (Cross *et al.* 1990). A comparative European view is also relevant. In The Netherlands, for example, the plight of Turks and Moroccans in Amsterdam, Rotterdam and The Hague approximates that of Caribbean minorities in London and elsewhere in Britain (Roelandt and Veenman 1992). Caribbean minorities in The Netherlands (Surinamese and Antilleans), by contrast, are more favoured, although — like South Asians in Britain — this is not to say that their condition is not a proper cause of concern.

What Greater London does not yet reveal is the pattern of new migration that is occurring elsewhere in Europe. To be more cautious, we do not yet know whether this is so or not. It would be entirely consonant with the argument presented here if Britain as a whole were not a pioneer in new labour movements. Political intervention in Britain has broken with the broad European consensus and opted for lowering real wages instead. Domestic policy has been paralleled on the European front not merely by opposition to the 'Social Chapter' in the Maastricht Treaty but also by a marked reluctance for Britain to take a proportionate share of refugees, asylum-seekers and Eastern European economic migrants.

Conclusion

The first of the three processes outlined in this chapter is one where the least employable are subjected to growing exclusion from employment in the urban economy. The second is a process of 'deregulation' in which the low-level jobs that are on offer are increasingly made available to those who are prepared to accept wage levels and conditions of employment which are below those assumed by labour market regulations and welfare rules. Finally, I have suggested that the city is a structure in a constant process of spatial sorting. The argument here is that this leads to new opportunities emerging in particular sectors of the urban labour market. Under the right conditions this produces what may be termed an 'ethnic division of labour'.

The central point of linking the three processes outlined above to European economic integration will no doubt now be obvious. The quest for modernisation and the pursuit of efficiency carry with them costs as well as benefits. A growing dependence on post-industrial economic activity will inevitably reduce the number and proportion of unskilled jobs. Where some groups, usually through a combination of discrimination and poor facilities, have been unable to effect a rapid and equivalent transition, they will figure more and more prominently among the workless. Those who have not been able to exploit whatever educational opportunities are on offer are bound to become increasingly excluded from employment as qualifications needs rise. Their 'integration' is thus on the basis of long-term poverty, usually in increasingly separate spatial zones of large cities. This can be referred to as a process of *ghettoisation*.

At first glance, paradoxically, the same imperative towards modernisation generates new low-level jobs, often in the burgeoning service sectors. But the economic gains for the indigenous working class, made possible in part by earlier periods of labour migration and carefully nurtured by corporatist labour policies, make it unlikely (except in deviant cases) that these new jobs will be easily filled locally. The demand for new labour sources at deregulated wages, whether through flexible work patterns or new migration, looks destined to grow.

The massive changes to European cities which are now well under way are unlikely to be an unmitigated disaster for all ethnic minorities. On the contrary, the chances are that new opportunities will open up for some but not others. This will largely depend on whether such groups are able to exploit one or both of the two traditional routes out of economic marginality, namely independent business activity or educational success (often leading to a disproportionate representation in the independent professions). This is the transition being pursued by Asians in Britain, although it is as yet far more evident for some groups within that category of the British population than others.

It would clearly not be possible to provide an adequate assessment here of whether what is being presented as a series of *European* processes are likely to be addressed at a *European* level. Debates on these issues within Europe have so far been confined to what is likely to be the least significant issue: constructing an effective immigration policy for so-called 'third country nationals'. Evidence from the United States and elsewhere would suggest that such ambitions are unlikely to be realised. The real issues perhaps relate to less politically attractive options. For example, will it prove possible to draw upon the numerous European welfare traditions to help ensure that the decline into poverty of significant sections of city-dwellers is halted or reversed? Will the European Commission develop an effective *urban* policy to parallel its long-standing initiatives at the regional level? Will it prove possible to develop a Community-wide response to the existence of discrimination on grounds of ethnic origin or appearance? There are important signs that the Commission itself is very well aware of these issues. The important report *Europe 2000*, for example, argues:

Migration pressures from outside the Community are likely to persist and with them the traditional pattern of residential concentration in particular parts of the major cities. There is a clear case for intensified educational, language and vocational training programmes, especially in those urban areas where high levels of unemployment coincide with shortages of skilled labour . . . . The development of new approaches on the part of cities towards the integration of existing and potentially growing ethnic communities is increasingly required (Commission of the European Communities 1991, pp. 20, 47).

The diagnosis is stronger, however, than the capacity to deliver a cure. Social welfare, urban policy and anti-discrimination are all excluded from the current competence of the Commission. It is only perhaps in the field of vocational training that initiatives are possible and even here the current budgets are very small. It will require a stage beyond Maastricht to address these issues.

Notes

1. The actual figures for the proportions achieving two or more 'A' level passes are 21 per cent for Asian boys and 13 per cent for Asian girls. The proportions for Afro-Caribbean boys and girls are 6 per cent and 4 per cent respectively, and those for white young people 12 per cent and 12 per cent (Drew *et al.* 1992).
2. Although structural position may differ, there is also the possibility that these differences have been mediated by different strategies of exclusion on the part of the majority population. In the conventional language of this discourse, racism would then not be regarded as a unitary phenomenon but rather one with at least two faces. The first is the colonial tradition of biological racism which channels those so stigmatised into unemployment, run-down areas and confrontations with agencies of social control. The second is the exclusion of the culturally different who are subject to abuse, attack and canalising into unwanted occupational niches. Whereas the former helps to generate the spatial ghetto, the latter produces the occupational ghetto.

References

Commission of the European Communities, 1988, *Social Europe: the social dimension of the internal market*, Directorate-General for Employment, Social Affairs and Education, Brussels.

Commission of the European Communities, 1991, *Europe 2000: outlook for the development of the Community's territory*, Directorate-General for Regional Policy, Brussels.

Cross, M., 1981, *Concentration of migrant workers in certain districts within the urban areas of the receiving countries: the situation and its consequences*, Report to the Steering Committee on Intra-European Migration, Council of Europe, Strasbourg.

Cross, M. (ed.), 1992a, *Ethnic minorities and industrial change in Europe and North America*, Cambridge University Press, Cambridge.

Cross, M., 1992b, 'Race and ethnicity', in Thornley, A. (ed.), *The crisis of London*, Routledge, London, 103–18.

Cross, M. and Waldinger, R., 1992, 'Migrants, minorities and the ethnic division of labour', in Fainstein, S.S., Gordon, I. and Harloe, M. (eds), *Divided cities: London and New York in the contemporary world*, Blackwell, Oxford, 151–74.

Cross, M., Brah, H. and Mcleod, M., 1991, *Race equality and the local state*, Centre for Research in Ethnic Relations Monograph Series 1, University of Warwick, Coventry.

Cross, M., Wrench, J. and Barnett, S., 1990, *Ethnic minorities and the careers service: an investigation into processes of assessment and placement*,

Department of Employment Research Paper 73, London.

Drew, D., Gray, J. and Sime, N., 1992, *Against the odds: the education and labour market experiences of young black people*, Department of Employment, Youth Cohort Series 19 and Research and Development Series 68, London.

Fainstein, S.S., Gordon, I. and Harloe, M. (eds), 1992, *Divided cities: London and New York in the contemporary world*, Blackwell, Oxford.

Ford, G., 1992, *The rise of Fascism in Europe*, Pluto, London.

Gans, H., 1990, 'Deconstructing the underclass: the term's danger as a planning concept', *Journal of American Planning Association*, 56: 271–7.

Glebe, G. and O'Loughlin, J. (eds), 1987, *Foreign minorities in continental European cities*, Franz Steiner Verlag, Stuttgart.

Gordon, I. and Sassen, S., 1992, 'Restructuring the urban labour markets', in Fainstein, S.S., Gordon, I. and Harloe, M. (eds), *Divided cities: London and New York in the contemporary world*, Blackwell, Oxford, 105–28.

Huttman, E.D. (ed.), 1991, *Urban housing segregation of minorities in Western Europe and the United States*, Duke University Press, Durham, NC.

Kasarda, J.D., Friedrichs, J. and Ehlers, K., 1992, 'Urban industrial restructuring and minority problems in the US and West Germany', in Cross, M. (ed.), *Ethnic minorities and industrial change in Europe and North America*, Cambridge University Press, Cambridge, 250–77.

Mann, K., 1991, *The making of an English 'underclass'?* Open University Press, Milton Keynes.

Mcleod, M., 1991, *Trading with the inner city*, Centre for Research in Ethnic Relations Monograph Series 3, University of Warwick, Coventry.

Modood, T., 1991, 'The Indian economic success: a challenge to some race relations assumptions', *Policy and Politics*, 19(3): 177–89.

Murray, C., 1990, *The emerging British underclass*, Institute of Economic Affairs, Choices in Welfare Series 21, London.

O'Loughlin, J., 1987, 'Foreign minorities in continental European cities: introduction', in Glebe, G. and O'Loughlin, J. (eds), *Foreign minorities in continental European cities*, Franz Steiner Verlag, Stuttgart, 9–29.

Peach, C., 1992, 'Urban concentration and segregation in Europe since 1945', in Cross, M. (ed.), *Ethnic minorities and industrial change in Europe and North America*, Cambridge University Press, Cambridge, 113–36.

Robinson, V., 1990, 'Roots to mobility: the social mobility of Britain's black population, 1971–87', *Ethnic and Racial Studies*, 13(2): 274–86.

Roelandt, T. and Veenman, J., 1992, 'An emerging underclass in the Netherlands?' *New Community*, 19(1): 129–41.

Sassen, S., 1991, *The global city: New York, London, Tokyo*, Princeton University Press, Princeton, NJ.

SOPEMI, 1992, *Trends in international migration*, OECD, Paris.

Taylor, P., 1992, *Ethnic group data for university entry*, Project report to the CVCP Working Group on Ethnic Data, Centre for Research in Ethnic Relations, University of Warwick, Coventry.

Waldinger, R., 1992, 'Native blacks, new immigrants and the post-industrial transformation in New York, in Cross, M. (ed.), *Ethnic minorities and industrial change in Europe and North America*, Cambridge University Press, Cambridge, 205–25.

Wilson, W.J., 1987, *The truly disadvantaged: the inner city, the underclass, and public policy*, Chicago University Press, Chicago.

Wilson, W.J. (ed.), 1989, *The ghetto underclass: social science perspectives*, Sage, Chicago.

Chapter 8

Mass migration from Eastern Europe: a challenge to the West?

Vladimir Grečić

Introduction

East–West migration has become a controversial topic in the international community. Its importance is indicated on one level by the number of international meetings and conferences devoted to it, and on another level by the fear that it engenders amongst many European people. In the 'West' people are frightened by the prospect of mass migration from the 'East'; in the 'East' people are frightened about their future — by falling living standards and unemployment at home, and by the increased uncertainty about finding employment abroad. However, a proper understanding of the dynamics of East–West migration may help us to shrug off the fear that such movement is beyond control. The aim of this chapter is to analyse the scale of East–West population movements, their forms, causes, patterns of origin and destination, and to consider lessons for the future. It will be seen, amongst other things, that East–West migration is not well defined and is therefore open to a variety of interpretations.

As defined here, the term 'East' includes Central and East European countries and the former USSR. Former 'Eastern Europe' is now Central and Eastern Europe, and the former Soviet Union is now the Commonwealth of Independent States (CIS), the Baltic states (Estonia, Latvia and Lithuania) and Georgia. The countries identified as Central European are Poland, Hungary and the Czech and Slovak republics. Bulgaria and Romania are identified as Eastern Europe. Somewhat more marginal are Albania and the former Yugoslavia. By the characteristics of its internal political and economic system, Albania belongs to the Eastern family; however, by its population growth it is part of the 'South'. Until recently, there were few Albanian emigrants in Western Europe. This situation changed dramatically in March 1991 when, after multi-party elections, many Albanians fled the country. Probably many more wish to leave. Yugoslavia, in its former size, has similarities with the countries of Central and Eastern Europe as identified above, but also differences. It has played a special role in European migration since the early 1960s, since it was the only country of the former socialist bloc which allowed

Table 8.1   Ethnic composition of former Eastern bloc countries, 1989

Country	Population	Ethnic division (%)	
Albania	3,208,000	96.0	Albanians
		4.0	Greeks, Vlachs, Gypsies, Serbs and Bulgarians
Bulgaria	8,972,700	85.3	Bulgarians
		8.5	Turks
		2.6	Gypsies
		2.5	Macedonians
		0.3	Armenians
		0.2	Russians
		0.6	Other
Czechoslovakia	15,658,100	64.3	Czechs
		30.5	Slovaks
		3.8	Hungarians
		0.4	Germans
		0.4	Polish
		0.3	Ukrainians
		0.1	Russians
		0.2	Other (mainly Jewish, Gypsies)
Hungary	10,566,900	96.6	Hungarians
		1.6	Germans
		1.1	Slovaks
		0.3	Southern Slavs
		0.2	Romanians
Poland	38,169,800	98.7	Polish
		0.6	Ukrainians
		0.5	Belorussians
		0.2	Jewish
Romania	23,153,500	89.1	Romanians
		7.8	Hungarians
		1.5	Germans
		1.6	Ukrainians, Serbs, Croats, Russians, Turks and Gypsies
Soviet Union	288,742,300	52.0	Russians
		16.0	Ukrainians
		32.0	from over 100 other ethnic groups
Yugoslavia	23,724,900	36.3	Serbs
		19.7	Croats
		8.9	Muslims
		7.8	Slovenes
		7.7	Albanians
		5.9	Macedonians
		5.4	Yugoslavs
		2.5	Montenegrins
		1.9	Hungarians
		3.9	Other

Source: CIA, 1989.

Table 8.2 Ethnic composition of the Soviet Republics (CIS, Baltic States, Georgia), 1990

Republic	Population	Ethnic division (%)	
Armenia	3,376,000	89.7	Armenians
		5.5	Azerbaijanis
		2.3	Russians
		1.7	Kurds
Azerbaijan	7,137,000	78.1	Azerbaijanis
		7.9	Russians
		7.9	Armenians
Belorussia	10,260,000	79.4	Belorussians
		11.9	Russians
		4.2	Polish
		2.4	Ukrainians
		1.4	Jewish
Kazakhstan	16,793,000	40.8	Russians
		36.0	Kazakhs
		6.1	Ukrainians
		2.1	Tatars
Kirghizia	4,422,000	40.7	Kirghiz
		22.0	Russians
		10.3	Uzbeks
		2.6	Ukrainians
		1.7	Tatars
Moldavia	4,367,000	63.9	Moldavians
		14.2	Ukrainians
		12.8	Russians
		3.5	Gagauzi
		2.0	Jewish
		2.0	Bulgarians
Russia	148,543,000	82.6	Russians
		3.6	Tatars
		2.7	Ukrainians
		1.2	Chuvash
Tajikistan	5,358,000	58.8	Tajiks
		22.9	Uzbeks
		10.4	Russians
		2.1	Tatars
Turkmenistan	3,714,000	68.4	Turkmen
		12.6	Russians
		8.5	Uzbeks
		2.9	Kazakhs

continued

Table 8.2   cont.

Republic	Population	Ethnic division (%)	
Ukraine	51,944,000	73.6	Ukrainians
		21.1	Russians
		1.3	Jewish
		0.8	Belorussians
		0.6	Moldavians
		0.5	Polish
Uzbekistan	20,708,000	68.7	Uzbeks
		10.8	Russians
		4.2	Tatars
		4.0	Kazakhs
		3.9	Tajiks
		1.9	Karakalpaks
Estonia	1,582,000	64.7	Estonians
		27.9	Russians
		2.5	Ukrainians
		1.6	Belorussians
		1.2	Finnish
Latvia	2,681,000	53.7	Latvians
		32.8	Russians
		4.5	Belorussians
		2.7	Ukrainians
		2.5	Polish
Lithuania	3,728,000	80.1	Lithuanians
		8.6	Russians
		7.7	Polish
		1.5	Belorussians
Georgia	5,464,000	68.8	Georgians
		9.0	Armenians
		7.4	Russians
		5.1	Azerbaijanis
		3.3	Ossetians
		1.7	Abkhazians

Notes: Figures do not add up because of rounding and because minor ethnic populations are excluded; many minor (but numerically quite significant) populations are omitted for Russia.

Source: *Current History*, 90 (561), 1991, p. 340.

its people to leave the country without restrictions (Baučić 1973). The flow of migrant workers to Western Europe from the old Yugoslavia reached a peak in the early 1970s and then became sharply reduced after the 'immigration stop' of 1973–4. Recently the tragic ethnic conflicts have caused the breakup of Yugoslavia; the former multinational society has come to an end. Taking into account the ethnic minorities living there (see Table 8.1), migratory movements may well be their reaction to growing nationalistic tendencies on behalf of the majorities. Such confused ethnic situations are not confined to Yugoslavia (see the rest of Table 8.1). The potential for migration induced by ethnic conflict in the former USSR has recently been analysed by Öberg and Boubnova (1993), and can be gauged from an inspection of the data in Table 8.2.

Looking back

The countries of the 'East' have been a traditional source of manpower for the 'West' since the beginning of the present century. When the communists took over at the end of the Second World War, emigration was generally prohibited on political and economic grounds (Bouscaren 1963). For many years a policy of isolation from the West was pursued. Travelling abroad was reduced to officially approved business, cultural and scientific exchange, and sport; individual tourism and family visits were discouraged. The two main instruments used by the communist governments to prevent people from travelling abroad were the strict eligibility criteria for issuing passports and the correspondingly tough rules concerning currencies (Okolski 1992).

Despite the difficulty of emigration, a considerable number of people left the Central-East European countries: between 1948 and 1989 Poland, Czechoslovakia, Hungary, Romania and Bulgaria collectively lost about 5 per cent of their populations due to emigration. Most of these emigrants went to Western Europe, about 75 per cent of them to West Germany (Chesnais 1992). Central and Eastern European countries have been responsible for a large share of the refugees admitted by Western Europe over the past four decades.

East–West movement has dramatically increased in recent years. In many respects 1989 was the watershed year for Central and East European countries; in the histories of these countries it will undoubtedly come to be well remembered. The latest phase of population movement began in earnest on that day in May 1989 when the first Hungarian border guard cut away the first piece of the Iron Curtain. Subsequently important steps were taken towards establishing freedom, including the freedom to leave one's own country and to return. Since late 1989 all Central-East European countries have opened their borders; even the USSR formulated new draft legislation on entry to and exit from the country.[1]

So, hundreds of thousands of people are now moving from the East into the West of Europe. From the early 1970s to the mid-1980s, outflows from the Warsaw Pact states to the West involved less than 100,000 annually. In 1989 more than 1.3 million people emigrated from the East: 80,000 asylum-seekers; 150,000 Jews and other people from the

USSR; and 720,000 Germans, of whom 345,000 were from the German Democratic Republic and the rest from Poland and other Central and Eastern European countries (Widgren 1990). There are several names for the new migrants, corresponding to the various causes of their migration: asylum-seekers, economic refugees, conventional refugees, foreign workers and their families, people fleeing from clear risk or danger, seasonal workers and illegal immigrants. However, the most important groups for the Western countries are:

(i)   clandestine or illegal workers whose entry may or may not be sanctioned by the receiving country's government;
(ii)   asylum-seekers who cross borders and appeal for a more secure status on grounds of political discrimination; and
(iii) refugees as defined by the 1951 United Nations Convention on the Status of Refugees (Appleyard 1991).

Countries of origin and destination

Apart from Yugoslavia, the main countries of origin in East–West migration are Poland, Czechoslovakia, Hungary and Romania; the CIS has up to now been marginal (Table 8.3). The Federal Republic of Germany has accepted about 70 per cent of the total number of East Europeans arriving in the 12 receiving countries listed in the table (Hönekopp 1992). Table 8.4 shows annual inflows of migrants into Germany, 1985–91: key elements of this table are the escalation of immigrant numbers in and after 1989, the important East–West flow within Germany (*Übersiedler*), the growth in numbers of ethnic Germans from other East European countries during 1988–90, and the escalating number of asylum-seekers (Kemper 1993).

There has also been a rapid revival of some of the former migratory movements such as those from Poland to France; from the CIS, Hungary and Poland to North America; and from the CIS to Israel and, to a lesser extent, to Finland and the other Nordic Countries (SOPEMI 1992). The countries of destination for people from former USSR are Israel, Germany, the United States, Canada, Australia, Finland and Greece. As an example, 184,600 Jews left the Soviet Union for Israel in 1990. Migration to Israel is a family-oriented ethnic migration, not a work-oriented economic migration, although obviously the question of employment is by no means unimportant.

The latest phase of population movements, since 1990 in the CIS and since mid-1991 in Yugoslavia, has been marked by the migrations of displaced persons, usually minorities within a given area. There are already more than 1 million 'internal refugees' in the CIS. Given events in Armenia, Azerbaijan, Central Asia, etc., Russian minorities living outside Russia (around 20 million people) and non-Russian minorities

Table 8.3 Foreign residents from former Eastern bloc countries in selected West European countries, 1990–91

	Poland	Czechoslovakia	Hungary	Bulgaria	Romania	Former USSR	Yugoslavia
Belgium	4,689	438	745	–	–	542	5,537
Denmark	4,709	307	294	147	774	399	10,039
Finland	582	128	308	159	83	4,181	75
France	67,189	2,871	3,750	1,122	5,058	–	51,700
Germany (W)	241,300	30,400	25,800	11,400	53,100	8,100	652,500
Germany (E)	51,743	3,218	13,424	4,939	1,162	14,885	2,055
Greece	15,216	994	887	2,582	2,643	3,041	1,892
Italy	3,172	1,026	995	561	1,843	1,104	11,933
Netherlands	3,966	–	1,001	–	1,315	–	13,505
Norway	2,854	186	233	298	276	373	4,242
Sweden	15,672	1,571	3,155	1,103	5,313	2,119	41,053
Switzerland	5,264	5,882	4,722	641	2,404	2,761	141,397

Source: SOPEMI 1992.

Table 8.4   Annual inflows of migrants into Germany, 1985–91 ('000)

	1985	1986	1987	1988	1989	1990	1991
Germans from Central and Eastern Europe (excluding East Germany)	39.0	42.8	78.5	202.7	377.1	397.1	200.0
of which: Poland	22.1	27.2	48.4	140.2	250.3	138.9	
Ex-USSR	0.5	0.8	14.5	47.6	98.1	148.0	
Romania	13.1	14.0	12.9	23.4	111.2		
East Germany	24.9	26.2	19.0	39.8	343.9	381.3	
Asylum-seekers	73.8	99.7	57.4	103.1	121.3	193.1	256.1
Foreign workers (net inflow)	−42.3	30.9	80.9	186.4	211.2		

Source: SOPEMI 1992, p. 19.

living in Russia (also about 20 million) could create insurmountable problems if they were displaced (Öberg and Boubnova 1993). According to data from the UN High Commissioner for Refugees (UNHCR), since Croatia and Slovenia proclaimed independence in 1991, more than 2 million persons have become displaced in the territory of the former Yugoslavia.

Yugoslavia is a country of emigration by tradition (Baučić 1973). The early flows were directed mainly towards West Germany (especially in the 1960s and early 1970s) together with some overseas destinations — the United States, Canada, Australia and New Zealand. Other European countries were also of some importance — France, Austria, Sweden, Switzerland, etc. However, starting in 1989, as we have seen, the former Yugoslavia started to disintegrate, and finally decomposed in 1992. The Federal Republic of Yugoslavia (FR Yugoslavia) was proclaimed on 26 April 1992, consisting of only two republics of the former Yugoslavia — Serbia and Montenegro. According to the 1991 Census the population of the new state is 10.4 million, 42.5 per cent of the total population of former Yugoslavia.[2] The same Census gave 251,000 persons from FR Yugoslavia living and working mainly in West European countries. More important, in late July 1992 UNHCR registered in FR Yugoslavia 431,000 refugees from other republics, and there are some not registered who have found shelter with relatives. A large number of these refugees are trying to settle permanently in FR Yugoslavia. However, due to the war, since 1991 435,000 citizens of former Yugoslavia have escaped abroad as refugees.[3] The majority are young, educated people who are an additional pressure on the West European labour market. Further waves of refugees are being created as the Bosnian crisis unfolds.

Another distinct type of East–West migration which has emerged rather suddenly in the last few years is 'labour tourism' from Poland to the former West Germany. According to Heyden (1991) over 2 million

Poles came to FR Germany on three-month visas, their real purpose being to work — largely on a clandestine basis — in the agricultural sector.

Asylum-seekers represent another important group constantly increasing in size (see Hovy's chapter in this book). Although the number of arrivals from the East rose dramatically during the 1982–92 period, the trend has not been as alarming as some reports have suggested.

Causes of contemporary East–West migration

Contemporary East–West migration involves massive push and pull factors that reflect perceptions (perhaps exaggerated, but generally accurate) of the enormous differences between the politically, economically and socially rich nations of the West and the frustrated expectations of many people in the less privileged nations of the East. There is nothing new in any of this — it is part of the age-old pattern of human migration — except that the scale of the movement is threateningly large. The East–West flow has so far been relatively modest; however, the reality is that it will increase.

According to Okolski (1992) the specifically relevant factors for contemporary East–West migration are as follows. Amongst *push* factors operating in the East, currency exchange regulations, passport regulations, manpower export agencies, unemployment, political discrimination and ethnic minority problems are probably the most important. Amongst *pull* factors, operating especially in the countries of the European Community, inter-governmental agreements, work permits, the existence of earlier-established migrant communities, and the availability of often irregular work in the underground economy are some of the key influences.

The reform era has created a new situation whereby these push and pull forces, previously hypothetical, are now very real. With political democratisation, freeing of travel restrictions and dissemination of mass information, people in the East are fully informed about the parlous social and economic situation in their own countries. They are better able to assess their prospects at home or abroad — and to act on that assessment. For instance, the enormously high purchasing power at home of wages earned in EC or EFTA countries is a very important stimulus for migrant workers from the East to take a temporary job abroad. Öberg and Boubnova (1993, p. 254) point out that a Russian professor could be paid the equivalent of a year's salary in Moscow for a two-hour lecture given in Sweden. Similarly it has been estimated that a Romanian doctor can earn 100 times more abroad than at home, and that in two months' work in Germany a Polish construction worker can pick up what it would take four years to earn in Poland.[4] The specific issue of East–West 'brain drain' migration is dealt with in Chapter 12 of this book.

Other push factors from the East are particularly important in certain countries only. Poor standards of accommodation and housing shortages are key factors in Poland and Romania. Elsewhere ecological disasters (Chernobyl), environmental degradation due to polluting industries, religious tensions and inter-ethnic violence play important roles (Widgren 1990). We have already noted the strong potential for civil war in Yugoslavia to 'create' emigration.

In the receiving countries, meanwhile, there are widespread opportunities to engage in illegal work that is poorly paid by the standards of the West but well paid by the standards of the East. The 'irregular' situations of overstaying tourists and of asylum-seekers who have been refused status provide willing cadres of workers for the abundance of vacant jobs which, because of their low pay, insecurity, bad working conditions etc., are unattractive to resident workers. Hence the increasing clandestine employment of illegal immigrants (Okolski 1992).

From the above it can be seen that East–West migratory trends are primarily fuelled by economic circumstances, which are now allowed to operate by the policies of the West. The engine of this migration is human deprivation on the one hand and an explosion of expectations for a better life on the other.

Prospects for the future of East–West migration

It is impossible to predict the scale and form of future East–West migration flows. Such flows will be the result of many complex political and economic factors rather than the result of a simple matching of labour supply and demand in different parts of Europe. However, in looking to the future the following assumptions may reasonably be made.

First, and most generally, we may assume that the various causes of East–West migration will not only continue to exist but will tend to increase. World Bank projections show that the existing economic gap between East and West within Europe will become wider. In the Central-East European countries the rate of growth of output over the past two decades, and particularly during the 1980s, has been consistently below the average of OECD countries. The evidence of severe environmental degradation and unhealthy working conditions in the former group of countries suggests a further source of reduced living standards.

Second, we may assume that the process of economic and political transition in the countries of the East will continue. This transition from a centrally planned to a market economy will create high unemployment, inducing many to emigrate. Overemployment in agriculture constitutes a particular problem and represents an additional factor in future migration. Most countries (Czechoslovakia being the main exception) have a share of the economically active population working in agriculture of at least 20 per cent.

Table 8.5 Growth in population of working age in some East European countries, 1990–2000

Country	Working-age population ('000) 1990	2000	% increase	Population aged 25–34 ('000) 1990	2000	% increase
Bulgaria	5,745	5,686	– 1.0	1,216	1,253	3.0
Czechoslovakia	9,783	10,549	7.8	2,250	2,276	1.1
Hungary	6,718	6,797	1.2	1,416	1,486	4.9
Poland	23,904	26,015	8.8	6,021	5,302	– 11.9
Romania	14,799	15,407	4.1	3,131	3,844	22.8
Soviet Union	178,220	190,059	6.6	47,503	41,577	– 12.5
Yugoslavia	15,551	16,216	4.3	3,646	3,631	– 4.0

Notes: Working-age populations: males 15–64 years, females 15–59 years. UN medium-variant figures.

Source: United Nations 1989.

Third, demographic factors *per se* are unlikely to play an important role in stimulating movements from the East, since the overall increase in the size of working-age population will be modest, especially after 2000. As Golini *et al.* show in Chapter 4 in this volume, the total fertility rate of the former Eastern bloc countries is around or below the replacement rate of 2.1 children per women. In the short term, however, there will be quite sharp increases in working-age populations, especially in the younger age brackets, as Table 8.5 shows. This table is based on UN medium-variant projections for the period 1990–2000.

Fourth, 'ethnic migration' will probably become more important, if impossible to forecast. Some of the scenarios here are very worrying. If ethnic tensions and secessionist pressures in the CIS erupt into violence, there could be some very large waves of emigration, particularly if accompanied, as seems likely, by increased economic hardship. Sixty million former Soviet citizens live in republics other than their own (Table 8.2). There are about 15 minorities in the CIS with a strong ethnic consciousness and a feeling of belonging to some place outside the CIS; these minorities number some 20 million people (Chesnais 1993). Recent troubles have led to considerable internal migration (see Chapter 9), and future explosions could sweep millions westward across Europe. For the period 1991–3 the likely scale of 'Soviet' emigration has been variously estimated at between 3 and 20 million (Salt 1992). In June 1991 some experts from the Institute of Sociology at the USSR Academy of Sciences predicted that 8–10 million Soviet citizens might leave when the new entry/exit law comes into effect (probably in 1993).

The fifth and final assumption is that skills and qualifications will be an important variable defining the character of future flows. Already East–West migration involves a disproportionate amount of young, well-qualified workers: they have the qualities (including language skills) required by Western employers. Moreover they are part of a wider phenomenon of enhanced intellectual mobility within the whole of Europe, particularly of students, teachers, researchers, technical experts, etc. (see Chapter 12 in this volume).

However, according to the decisions made in Maastricht, immigrants and asylum-seekers will face simpler — and tougher — rules when they try to enter the European Community. East Europeans will have to wait for equal rights in the United Europe until the late 1990s at the earliest. Meanwhile the Conference on Security and Cooperation in Europe has neglected new migratory processes and has only reaffirmed the protection and promotion of the rights of immigrants who are already resident in the immigration countries.

Possible consequences of East–West migration

The effects of East–West migration on sending countries should be seen in relation to the causes of emigration: decrease of unemployment and workers' remittances in convertible currencies. The positive view sees remittances as an effective response to market forces, providing a transition to an otherwise unsustainable development (Keely 1989). There is a general feeling, however, that the net balance of positive and negative consequences may be unfavourable. Instead of East–West labour migration being a step towards a new self-correcting equilibrium and a reduced desire to migrate, the outflow of labour might exacerbate and deepen economic decline, thereby leading to a greater division between the two Europes and even stronger pressures to migrate.

As the only country with reasonably good data on emigration for the 1980s, the case of Poland can be used to examine briefly some of the characteristics of the outflow (Okolski 1992, pp. 94–7). Between 1981 and the end of 1988, 222,000 persons emigrated officially, 58 per cent to FR Germany and 10 per cent to the United States. However, unofficial emigration, defined as those who left as tourists and did not return, was estimated at 533,000 for the same period. By the end of the decade total net emigration — 227,000 in 1988 — exceeded natural increase, causing an overall decline in the Polish population living in the country. In general the educational status of the emigrants was higher than that of the population at large: for instance in 1988, 40 per cent of the official emigrants and 46 per cent of the unofficial emigrants had at least secondary schooling, compared to only 33 per cent of the national population. Very few old people are numbered amongst the emigrant flow, which is mainly made up of young adults. By contrast the return flow contains higher proportions of over-55s and few young people. Quite apart from the normal human disadvantages of emigration (family separation, difficulty in finding a marriage partner, cultural disorientation, hard work in the West, etc.), the outflow from Poland clearly has the makings of a brain drain and threatens demographic distortions.

Negative consequences can also be identified in the presence of the immigrant workers in the shadow economies of the West European countries. The shadow economy and clandestine migration often nourish each other (Golini *et al.* 1991). In fact illegal immigration can function as a mechanism to attract capital from the formal to the informal sector. In addition, migrants from the East who relocate in the EC will be strong competitors, at least in some segments of the labour market, for migrants coming from the Mediterranean region and other less developed countries. The losers in this competition will probably be the migrants from the less developed countries (Grečić 1991). The geographical and cultural closeness of Eastern Europe to Western Europe, and the political responsiveness of the EC and EFTA countries in supporting the 1989–90 revolutions, will probably make both the governments and the populations of West European countries opt for 'Eastern' rather than 'Southern' immigrants — if immigrants there have to be.

Possible solutions

There are two main groups of policy solutions to the problem of mass East–West migration flows: preventive and restrictive measures. These are not necessarily mutually exclusive, however.

First, some authors argue that if the developed countries are really interested in the economic development of the Central-East European countries and the CIS, they should launch policies to accelerate the economic reforms in these countries and encourage productive employment in them rather than immigration. This is the preventive approach. Attention should be given to the remission of debts and the approval of non-repayable grants — a policy of government aid, direct investment in the East, and trade. This implies intensive and coordinated assistance from the 'West'. At the same time, the migrant-receiving countries should make greater efforts to harmonise their policies with regard to potential migrants from the East (and the South).

Turning to the restrictive group of measures, the West European receiving countries have generally had restrictive immigration policies since the early to mid-1970s. Nevertheless, the annual numbers of arrivals from both the East and the South have increased quite sharply in recent years, especially since the late 1980s (King 1993). A policy of 'closed borders' on the part of Western countries will not, in itself, provide a solution (Heyden 1991). Restrictive and exclusive immigration procedures have tended to oblige many would-be migrants to follow the asylum route. Laws on asylum leave little room for the receiving states to debate the weight of the pull factors where persons are refugees. Many are not refugees in the accepted sense, however, having been impelled or encouraged to leave more by the lure of settling in a prosperous and stable environment than by any reason of persecution. While the number of people who are eventually defined as refugees is relatively small, the most telling figure is the 75–85 per cent of failed asylum-seekers who remain in the country of reception.

In finding solutions full account should ideally be taken of the (often conflicting) interests of the countries of origin, the receiving countries, and the migrants themselves. Responses to the complex challenges of East–West migration should take the shape of a combination of systematic efforts in the following fields: action to attack and mitigate the root causes of the refugee crisis through the United Nations or bilaterally; international cooperation to limit as much as possible the generation of sudden mass flows of migrants; increased economic and other assistance so as to lessen the burden of the sending countries; peaceful settlement of regional and ethnic conflicts; halting environmental degradation; and alleviating poverty (Widgren 1989a; 1990). New forms of economic assistance should he higher, in real per capita terms, than post-war Western Europe received under the Marshall Plan. All the countries of the former Eastern bloc have a huge need for investment, but before increasing investments their economies must be stabilised and the economic restructuring process deepened: at the moment the adjustment process is at very different stages in different countries. Official flows of capital are most probably necessary to support the adjustment process and ease the social cost of transition from a centrally planned to a market-oriented economy. Private flows, particularly foreign direct investment that could provide technology transfer, are also needed. Until the reforms gain credibility and output begins to increase, private external flows are unlikely to rise substantially. This is particularly so in the light of the debt situation in some of the countries.

The recent historic changes in the countries of Central and East Europe pose new challenges to their governments and to the international community (Wapenhans 1990). Stabilisation programmes alone will not be sufficient; if anything they will have a short-term negative impact on output and employment. Experience suggests that such programmes fail in the absence of significant reform of the old public enterprise structures and financial institutions. The big challenge here is to develop a modern system of responsibilities and relationships between governments, enterprises and individuals. All Central and East European countries need help, especially infusions of modern technology to raise productivity in all economic sectors.

Ultimately, however, the success of political and economic reforms in the former Eastern bloc states depends largely on the efforts of those countries themselves; Western assistance may be crucial in helping them to overcome certain obstacles but it will not be sufficient in itself. Even this help has to be carefully planned. Transformation strategies will need to be developed and implemented through a structured dialogue within each country and with the assistance of multilateral institutions such as the International Monetary Fund, the World Bank, the UN Economic Commission for Europe, the OECD, the Conference on Security and Cooperation in Europe, the European Community, the Council of Europe, and others.

Within the general policy guidelines set out above, East and West can negotiate transfers of manpower, whether temporary, seasonal or permanent (Heyden 1991). However, any future policy on European East–West migration must be based on the principles of solidarity and joint action by all the countries concerned (Kussbach 1992).

Conclusion

The future size of the waves of East–West migrants will depend on the nature of events taking place in the countries of origin, on their economic trends, and on the policies of the receiving countries regarding visas, asylum, etc. Clearly there are far too many unknowns here to enable any confident predictions. It is difficult enough to get a sense of scale of present movements let alone those of the future. On the basis of a careful analysis of economic factors and past migrations, Layard *et al.* (1992) suggest that East–West migration is likely (in the best of both worlds) to run at about 1 million per year for the next 15 years. This can be regarded as only a guess, but it is as well informed as any.

There are important reasons for considering the very complicated issues related to asylum-seekers, refugees, illegal migrants and legal migrants as a whole (Widgren 1989b). In long-term planning for East–West migration, priority should be given to economic factors, although it would be a grave error to believe that non-economic factors (political explosions, ethnic wars, human rights, etc.) are not of enormous importance. Much more international cooperation in the field of asylum and other forms of population movement is necessary, including the collection and exchange of information on labour market conditions, action to prevent disorderly migration, research programmes and appropriate educational strategies, and technical and economic assistance. There is, however, no 'quick fix', no short-term escape from the huge economic differential between East and West which is the fundamental driving force behind current migration. The best that can be hoped for are policies aimed at creating more 'life chances' for the people of the East through easier access to the Western markets alongside measures to increase the attractiveness of investing in the East (Blazyca 1993). The best response of Western countries is to prevent truly destabilising mass migration before it begins.

Notes

1. The 'Law on the Procedures of Exit from the USSR and Entry into the USSR for Citizens of the USSR' was passed on 20 May 1991. It was due to go into effect in January 1993. This law was later adopted by the Russian Federation which, in the meantime, had also passed a law which stated that Russian citizens had the right to work temporarily abroad.
2. Figures for the province of Kosovo are estimated, since Albanians boycotted the Census.
3. Data from *The Economist*, 25–31 July 1992.
4. *Wall Street Journal*, 8 February 1991.

References

Appleyard, R., 1991, *International migration: challenge for the nineties*, IOM, Geneva.

Baučić, I., 1973, 'Yugoslavia as a country of emigration', *Options Mediterra-néennes*, 5(22): 55–66.

Blazyca, G., 1993, 'A continent minus walls and curtains', *Times Higher Education Supplement*, 19 February 1993: 21.

Bouscaren, A.T., 1963, *International migration since 1945*, Praeger, New York.

Chesnais, J.-C., 1992, 'By way of introduction', in *People on the move: new migration flows in Europe*, Council of Europe Press, Strasbourg, 13–40.

Chesnais, J.-C., 1993, 'Soviet emigration: past, present and future', in *The changing course of international migration*, OECD, Paris, 105–12.

CIA, 1989, *The world factbook*, US Government Printing Office, Washington, DC.

Golini, A., Gesano, G. and Heins, F., 1991, 'South–North migration with special reference to Europe', *International Migration*, 29(2): 253–79.

Grečić, V., 1991, 'East–West migration and its possible influence on South–North migration', *International Migration*, 29(2): 241–52.

Heyden, H., 1991, 'South–North migration', *International Migration*, 29(2): 281–90.

Hönekopp, E., 1992, 'The cases of Germany and Austria', in *People on the move: new migration flows in Europe*, Council of Europe Press, Strasbourg, 117–42.

Keely, C.B., 1989, 'Remittances from labour migration: evaluations, performance and implications', *International Migration Review*, 23(3): 500–25.

Kemper, F.J., 1993, 'New trends in mass migration in Germany', in King, R. (ed.), *Mass migrations in Europe: the legacy and the future*, Belhaven, London, 257–74.

King, R., 1993, 'European international migration 1945–90: a statistical and geographical overview', in King, R. (ed.), *Mass migration in Europe: the legacy and the future*, Belhaven, London, 19–39.

Kussbach, E., 1992, 'European challenge: East–West migration', *International Migration Review*, 26(2): 646–67.

Layard, R., Blanchard, O., Dornbusch, R. and Krugman, P., 1992, *East–West migration: the alternatives*, MIT Press, Cambridge, MA.

Öberg, S. and Boubnova, H., 1993, 'Ethnicity, nationality and migration potentials in Eastern Europe', in King, R. (ed.), *Mass migration in Europe: the legacy and the future*, Belhaven, London, 234–56.

Okolski, M., 1992, 'Migratory movements from countries of Central and Eastern

Europe', in *People on the move: new migration flows in Europe*, Council of Europe Press, Strasbourg, 83–116.

Salt, J., 1992, 'Current and future international migration trends affecting Europe', in *People on the move: new migration flows in Europe*, Council of Europe Press, Strasbourg, 41–81.

SOPEMI, 1992, *Trends in international migration*, OECD, Paris.

United Nations, 1989, *Global estimates and projections of population by sex and age: the 1988 revision*, UN, New York.

Wapenhans, W., 1990, 'The challenge of economic reforms in Eastern Europe', *Finance and Development*, 27(4): 2–5.

Widgren, J., 1989a, 'Asylum-seekers in Europe in the context of South–North movements', *International Migration Review*, 23(3): 599–605.

Widgren, J., 1989b, 'Europe and international migration in the future: the necessity for merging migration, refugee, and development policies', in Loescher, G., (ed.), *Refugees and international relations*, Oxford University Press, New York, 49–61.

Widgren, J., 1990, 'International migration and regional stability', *International Affairs*, 66(4): 749–66.

Chapter 9

Regional migration in the former Soviet Union during the 1980s: the resurgence of European regions

Richard Rowland

Introduction

Recently published data from the 1989 census of the former USSR, as well as oblast-level vital statistics, make it possible for the first time since the mid-1970s to investigate both regional and subregional net migration patterns. Accordingly, the purpose of this chapter is to explore regional and subregional net migration patterns during the intercensal period 1979–89 as well as post-census trends during 1989. Comparisons will also be made with regional net migration trends during the preceding intercensal period, 1970–9. The presentation will follow a three-level discussion of macroregional, regional and subregional trends. In addition, for the first time in more than a decade, urban migration data based on the registration of people moving in and out of cities are available for 1989 and will also be used. Finally, the nationality composition of the major migration trends will be investigated.

Regional framework, data sources and procedures

The regional framework employed here is the economic regions of the former USSR as of 1961 (see Figure 9.1), the comparable regional framework used in other studies by the author (Rowland 1988; 1990). These regions have in turn been amalgamated into larger macroregional frameworks of the dichotomous Western and Eastern USSR and Northern and Southern USSR. Four quadrants will also be investigated: Northern European USSR, European Steppe, Russian East and Non-Slavic South (see Figure 9.1 for the components of the macroregions). Subregional trends for the roughly 150 oblasts and other political units of the former USSR will also be examined.

With respect to data availability, complete natural increase vital statistics are available for all 15 union republics for every year of the 1970–90 period (to be precise, January 1970 to January 1990). Thus complete residual technique net migration data are available for six of

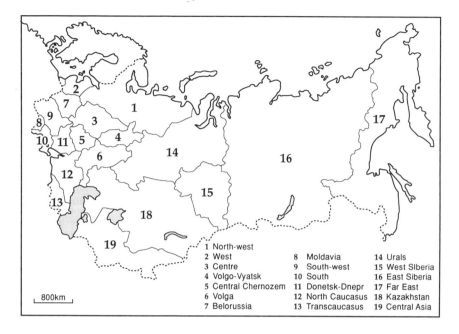

Figure 9.1 Economic and macroregions of USSR as of 1961

Notes: Western USSR = regions 1–13; Eastern USSR = regions 14–19; Northern USSR = regions 1–11, 14–17; Southern USSR = regions 13, 18–19; Northern European USSR = regions 1–7, 9; European Steppe = regions 8, 10–12; Russian East = regions 14–17; Non-Slavic South = regions 13, 18–19.

the 19 regions which consist solely of one republic (Belorussia, Moldavia and Kazakhstan) or of a combination of republics in the West or Baltic region (Latvia, Lithuania and Estonia), the Transcaucasus (Georgia, Azerbaijan and Armenia) and Central Asia (Uzbekistan, Kirghizia, Tajikistan and Turkmenistan). In addition, natural increase data are available for all but one of the roughly 150 oblast subunits in 1989 *per se*, or the year after the census of mid-January 1989. The one exception is, not surprisingly, Nagorno-Karabakh Autonomous Oblast of the Azerbaijan SSR, scene of recent and continuing ethnic friction with Armenians. Thus, with that one exception, complete data are available for all geographical levels in 1989.[1]

It should also be noted that, given some boundary changes, certain oblasts had to be combined in order to provide comparability over the 20-year period under investigation. This problem was exclusively confined to the Southern USSR. For example, Bukhara, Samarkand and Syr-Darya Oblasts of Uzbekistan in Central Asia were aggregated in 1989 to provide comparability with the combination of units with the same names in the past along with Navoy and Dzhizak Oblasts, which were abolished by 1989.

Furthermore, complete vital statistics and thus net migration data have been recently published for the economic regions of the RSFSR, or Russian Republic, and its oblast-level units for both the 1970–9 and 1979–89 periods. For 1970–9, the published average annual net migration rates for the oblast-level units were multiplied by the estimated midpoint population of July 1974 and multiplied by nine to estimate net migration for these units and hence the regions. Similarly, for 1979–89 published net migration rates were multiplied by the midpoint population of January 1984 and multiplied by ten. With respect to the latter, the resulting estimates of net migration were all very close to the published absolute amounts of net migration for 1979–89 based on the *de jure* population. For 1989 *per se*, migration rates were based on the estimated July 1989 populations, which were derived as the average of the January 1989 and January 1990 populations.

The chief problem was to estimate regional net migration patterns for the three economic regions of the Ukrainian Republic and its subregional units, as well as oblast-level units for other regions. Unfortunately, unlike for the Russian Republic, this has not been rectified by the above-mentioned recently published complete data. Therefore, estimating procedures used in a previous study (Rowland 1990) for the regions and oblast-level units based on the inflation of data for only a few years will have to be used here. The validity of these past estimates has been supported by the recently published complete data for the RSFSR, which are very close to previously estimated rates for the RSFSR based on incomplete data. Rates for the Ukraine and other republics are again based upon estimated or actual midpoint populations for July 1974, January 1984 and July 1989.

Urban migration registration data are, as noted, now available for 1989. These data probably accounted for the clear majority of migration in the USSR. Indeed, a sample microcensus of 1985 suggested that roughly three-quarters of the migrations in the USSR involved migration to and from urban centres (Rowland 1988, p. 820). These 1989 registration data take on added significance because they also include the nationality of the migrants.

It should be noted that the 1989 census also includes migration data. However, these have not yet been published.

Macroregional net migration trends

Macroregional migration patterns are shown in Table 9.1. As can be seen, a clear east to west and south to north trend has been occurring in the USSR; thus the basic shift is from the south and east to the European north-west. In particular, during both 1970–9 and 1979–89, there were roughly similar annual rates of net in-migration to the Western USSR (0.7 and 0.5 per thousand respectively) and net out-migration from

Table 9.1 Net migration in the former USSR by macroregion, 1970–89

Region	Total			Annual average			Annual average per thousand population		
	1970–79	1979–89	1989	1970–79	1979–89	1989	1970–79	1979–89	1989
Western USSR	1,086,351	906,271	84,390	120,706	90,627	84,390	0.7	0.5	0.5
Eastern USSR	−939,973	−1,009,897	−369,176	−104,441	−100,990	−369,176	−1.3	−1.1	−3.6
Northern USSR	507,497	2,153,871	129,983	56,389	215,387	129,983	0.3	1.0	0.6
Southern USSR	−361,119	−2,257,497	−414,769	−40,124	−225,750	−414,769	−0.8	−3.8	−6.3
N. European USSR	483,164	1,117,638	130,789	53,685	111,764	130,789	0.5	1.0	1.1
European Steppe	677,544	414,935	74,674	75,283	41,494	74,674	1.7	0.9	1.5
Russian East	−653,211	621,298	−75,480	−72,579	62,130	−75,480	−1.6	1.2	−1.4
Non-Slavic South	−361,119	−2,257,497	−414,769	−40,124	−225,750	−414,769	−0.8	−3.8	−6.3

Sources and procedures: See text and note 1, p. 173.

the Eastern USSR (−1.3 and −1.1 per thousand). However, whilst the rate for the Western USSR remained constant for 1989 (0.5), that for the Eastern USSR deepened sharply to −3.6 per thousand; and whereas net migration to the Western USSR approached 85,000, that for the Eastern USSR approached −370,000.

The decreasing balance between the two regions was almost certainly due to increased emigration from the Western USSR of the Soviet Union. In particular, during 1989 emigration from the USSR ballooned to 234,994, more than half (126,078 or 53.7 per cent) of which occurred from the seven republics wholly (Ukraine, Belorussia, Moldavia, Latvia, Lithuania and Estonia) or partly (RSFSR, where nearly two-thirds of the population resides in the European part) in the north-western or European part of the country (see Öberg and Boubnova 1993). Thus, in this and subsequent discussions it should be kept in mind that the internal north-western migration shift was probably even greater than measured, but was partly dampened by emigration from these areas. During 1989, 40 per cent of the 47,251 emigrants from the RSFSR came from Moscow and Leningrad (now again St Petersburg) cities and oblasts of the European RSFSR. The majority destinations were Israel (44.7 per cent of emigrants), former West Germany (41.8 per cent) and Greece (4.6 per cent). Although nationality data are not given, the movement to Israel, of course, consisted virtually exclusively of Jews, especially from the cities of Moscow, St Petersburg, Kiev and Minsk. The movement to West Germany similarly was by ethnic Germans, although not necessarily from the European RSFSR; in fact they chiefly came from Kazakhstan which, in absolute terms, had the greatest number of emigrants (52,927) of any republic. Kazakhstan had a large 'unassimilated' ethnic German population.

The Southern to Northern USSR shift was even greater than the Eastern to Western USSR shift. Although the south to north shift began during the 1970s, reversing the long-standing north to south migration in the former USSR, it exploded in the 1980s. Table 9.1 shows that during 1979–89 the Northern USSR gained more than 2.1 million people by net in-migration (1.0 per thousand per year), while the Southern USSR lost nearly 2.3 million by net out-migration (−3.8 per thousand per year) over the same ten-year period. For the Southern USSR the net out-migration rate deepened during 1989 to −6.3 per thousand, an absolute net loss of 414,769, although the net in-migration rate to the Northern USSR subsided somewhat to 0.6 per thousand with increased emigration.

This south and east to north-west shift was also evident at the 'quadrant' level. During 1970–9, 1970–89 and 1989, Northern European USSR and the European Steppe both had net in-migration, and the rates for each were roughly equal during the 1980s. In addition, the Non-Slavic South — the same macroregion as the Southern USSR (see Figure 9.1) — had by far the highest rate of net out-migration during the 1980s.

Of particular interest are developments in the Russian East or Siberia.

During 1970–9 as well as 1959–70, it experienced net out-migration, reversing another long-standing migratory movement in Russia and the USSR (Lewis and Rowland 1979, p. 116). However, during 1979–89 it again experienced net in-migration and indeed had the highest such rate of any quadrant. As will be seen later, this was largely due to high net in-migration to the oil- and gas-producing unit of Tyumen' Oblast. But in 1989 it again experienced net out-migration, suggesting that the resurgence of Siberian migration may have been short-lived.

Economic region net migration trends

The south and east to north-west migration shift in the USSR is also apparent at the economic region level, especially in 1989 (Table 9.2 and Figure 9.2). During 1979–89, although the sparsely populated Far East continued to have the highest rate of net in-migration of any of the 19 regions (3.7 per thousand), nearly comparable rates occurred in the three north-western regions of the Centre (3.6), North-west (3.4) and West (3.2), the first two of which reflect high net in-migration to the cities of Moscow and Leningrad, the two largest cities of the USSR. The highest rates of net out-migration during 1979–89 occurred in the southern regions of Kazakhstan (−5.0), the Transcaucasus (−4.2) and Central Asia (−2.9). The high net out-migration from Central Asia was especially significant, for this is the most populous and probably most overpopulated region in the former USSR. Whereas Kazakhstan and the Transcaucasus were already experiencing net out-migration during the 1970s, Central Asia still had net in-migration, but that situation dramatically changed during the 1980s. Indeed, the absolute turnabout was more than 1 million, unmatched by any region, from +192,265 in 1970–9 to −845,661 during 1979–89 (Table 9.2). However, as will be discussed later, recently published nationality data suggest that this large-scale out-migration consisted largely of Russians rather than of indigenous Turkic Muslims.

During 1989 this south and east to north-west shift became even more accentuated (Table 9.2 and Figure 9.2). The highest rates of net in-migration occurred in the north-western regions of the South (4.4), Centre (3.1), West (2.4) and Central Chernozem (2.1). In-migration to the South probably partly reflects a return of Crimean Tatars, a group formerly deported to the east during the Second World War after being accused of collaborating with the Nazis. The fact that the Central Chernozem had net in-migration is very significant, for this region has been a long-term source of high rural out-migration in Russian and Soviet history. The existence of net in-migration reflects the greatly reduced rural to urban migration in the former USSR in recent years with slowing industrialisation plus efforts to increase rural living standards in the European RSFSR (Rowland 1990; 1992). It will also be noticed that in

Table 9.2 Net migration in the former USSR by economic region, 1970–89

Region	Total			Annual average			Annual average per thousand population		
	1970–79	1979–89	1989	1970–79	1979–89	1989	1970–79	1979–89	1989
North-west	549,531	500,347	7,924	61,059	50,035	7,924	4.5	3.4	0.5
West	231,025	246,464	19,268	25,669	24,646	19,268	3.6	3.2	2.4
Centre	694,404	1,020,756	92,582	77,156	102,076	92,582	2.8	3.6	3.1
Volgo-Vyatsk	−344,529	−222,214	−8,858	−38,281	−22,221	−8,858	−4.6	−2.7	−1.0
Central Chernozem	−399,240	−148,881	17,943	−44,360	−14,888	17,943	−5.1	−1.7	2.1
Volga	164,106	−1,479	18,599	18,234	−148	18,599	1.2	−0.0	1.2
Belorussia	−82,937	−6,521	9,030	−9,215	−652	9,030	−1.0	−0.1	0.9
Moldavia	−19,934	−56,521	−21,108	−2,215	−5,652	−21,108	−0.6	−1.4	−4.9
South-west	−329,196	−270,834	−25,699	−36,577	−27,083	−25,699	−1.6	−1.2	−1.1
South	352,460	186,265	33,876	39,162	18,627	33,876	5.8	2.5	4.4
Donetsk-Dnepr	201,549	236,977	36,432	22,394	23,698	36,432	1.2	1.2	1.8
North Caucasus	143,469	48,214	25,474	15,941	4,821	25,474	1.0	0.3	1.5
Transcaucasus	−74,357	−626,302	−121,073	−8,262	−62,630	−121,073	−0.6	−4.2	−7.7
Urals	−560,466	280,256	−32,755	−62,274	28,026	−32,755	−3.0	1.3	−1.4
West Siberia	−417,852	−35,149	−13,862	−46,428	−3,515	−13,862	−4.3	−0.3	−1.2
East Siberia	21,051	134,322	−25,201	2,339	13,432	−25,201	0.3	1.4	−2.5
Far East	304,056	241,869	−3,662	33,784	24,187	−3,662	6.0	3.7	−0.5
Kazakhstan	−479,027	−785,534	−102,981	−53,225	−78,553	−102,981	−3.8	−5.0	−6.2
Central Asia	192,265	−845,661	−190,715	21,363	−84,566	−190,715	0.9	−2.9	−5.7

Source and procedures: See text and note 1.

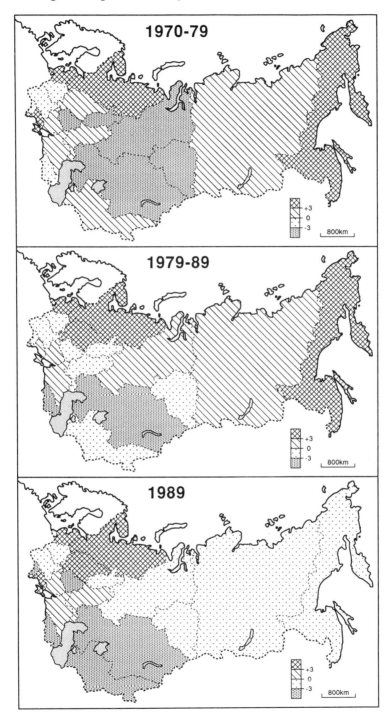

Figure 9.2 Ex-USSR: net annual migration rates per thousand population by economic region

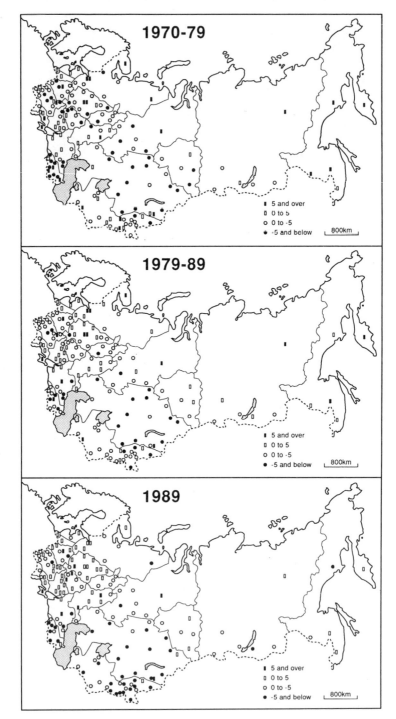

Figure 9.3   Ex-USSR: net annual migration rates per thousand population by subregional units

1989 the Volgo-Vyatsk, another traditional region of high rural net out-migration, had a greatly reduced and relatively low rate of net out-migration.

At the other end of the spectrum, the highest rates of net out-migration for 1989 continued to occur from the three southern regions, all with higher rates than during 1979–89. The Transcaucasus had the highest rate (−7.7 per thousand) followed by Kazakhstan (−6.2) and Central Asia (−5.7). Also of significance is the fact that for the first time *all four* Siberian regions had net out-migration, including East Siberia and the Far East, which had typically had net in-migration prior to 1989.

Net migration trends by oblast

The increased south and east to north-west shift was also apparent on the basis of the roughly 150 oblast-level units (Figure 9.3). During 1970–9, roughly two-thirds of the units had net out-migration, and they were widespread throughout all major regions of the country. The relatively few units with net in-migration generally represented major urban industrial areas with high absolute amounts of net in-migration.

Although these proportions of two-thirds migration loss and one-third gain more or less continued during 1979–89, the geographical patterns changed somewhat. However, as during 1970–9, during 1979–89 some of the highest rates also occurred in relatively remote Siberian areas. By far the highest (34.7 per thousand) was the net migration flow into Tyumen' Oblast in the Urals, a district which accounts for the majority of the oil and natural gas production in the USSR. Indeed, during 1979–89 its net in-migration of 841,476 surpassed that of all *economic* regions, except for the Centre. If it is excluded the Russian East or Siberia, in fact, experienced net out-migration during 1979–89. Relatively high net in-migration rates for 1979–89 also occurred to the remote units of Kamchatka Oblast in the Far East (9.8) and the Yakutsk ASSR in East Siberia (9.7), although absolute numbers were much lower (41,778 and 92,488 respectively). Primorskiy Kray and Khabarovsk Kray (Far East) also had relatively high net in-migration.

However, to repeat the findings of the previous levels of analysis, the greatest number of oblast units with net in-migration during 1979–89 occurred in the north-western USSR, especially in the North-West, West, Centre, South, Donetsk-Dnepr or the Eastern Ukraine, and the Volga. Especially high levels and rates occurred to the highly urbanised units: Moscow City (682,960 and 8.0), Moscow Oblast (324,950 and 5.0), Leningrad City (318,582 and 6.6) and Leningrad Oblast (101,052 and 6.3), as well as Murmansk Oblast in the North-west (74,480 and 7.0).

Unlike 1970–9, when units with net out-migration were widespread, during 1979–89 most of the units with net out-migration were located in southern regions — Central Asia, Kazakhstan and the Transcaucasus (Figure 9.3). Indeed, the only southern units to have net in-migration were republic capitals. Thus, net out-migration was widespread throughout the Southern USSR. Especially high net out-migration was again characteristic of Kazakhstan; the majority of its units (10 out of 17) had net out-migration rates of − 5.0 and below. Two, in fact, had rates exceeding − 10.0 (Kyzl-Orda Oblast, − 10.5, and Taldy-Kargan Oblast, − 10.1). However, the highest rate of net out-migration in the USSR was found in another southern region, the area outside of the city of Yerevan in Armenia (− 16.1). In addition, Issyk-Kul Oblast in Kirghizia, Central Asia also had a double-digit rate (− 10.9), as did Dagestan ASSR in the North Caucasus (− 12.0), a predominantly Muslim unit which borders on the Southern USSR.

However, net out-migration was still quite widespread throughout more traditional rural regions in the north-western USSR, specifically the Central Chernozem, Volgo-Vyatsk and South-west. Indeed, the Volgo-Vyatsk was the only region where all component units had net out-migration.

During 1989, this south and east to north-west pattern also became accentuated at the oblast level. However, this time high net in-migration was especially characteristic of rural-oriented rather than urban-oriented units of the north-western USSR. Notable was the fact that numerous units of the Centre and Central Chernozem, which had traditionally had high rates of net out-migration, now had net in-migration. Indeed, it will be noticed that whereas most units of the Centre had net out-migration during the 1970s, most had net in-migration during 1989 (Figure 9.3; compare the top and bottom maps). Especially notable in this regard was Kostroma Oblast in the north-eastern Centre. During 1970–9 it had the second highest rate of net out-migration of any unit in the USSR (− 10.5 per thousand), but in 1989 it had a net in-migration rate of 1.3. The 'turnaround' of 11.8 points was the second greatest for any Soviet unit. Similarly, half the units of the Central Chernozem also had net in-migration and two had rates in excess of 5.0 per thousand: Orel (5.9) and Belgorod (5.7). Tyumen' Oblast, the clear national leader during 1979–89, saw its rate drop from 34.7 to 6.3 per thousand, due to declining oil production (Sagers 1991, pp. 252–63).

At the other end of the spectrum, the southern regions had almost ubiquitous net out-migration during 1989 and typically high net out-migration. Especially notable was the fact that more than half of the units of Central Asia (13 out of 24) now had net out-migration rates of − 5.0 and below. Moreover, the clear majority of units in Kazakhstan (12 out of 17) and the Transcaucasus (6 out of 9) also had net out-migration rates of − 5.0 and below. By far the highest net out-migration in the USSR was experienced by the Adzhar ASSR in Georgia in the Transcaucasus (− 40.0 per thousand), and the Armenian republic in the Transcaucasus had a rate of − 13.5. Overall, of the 50 units for which data

Table 9.3 Ex-USSR: urban migration by macroregion, 1989

Region	In-migration	Out-migration	Net migration	Per thousand population In	Per thousand population Out	Per thousand population Net
Western USSR	5,020,572	4,056,021	964,551	39.2	31.6	7.6
Eastern USSR	2,839,246	2,635,027	204,219	46.1	42.8	3.3
Northern USSR	6,628,542	5,492,255	1,136,287	42.0	34.8	7.2
Southern USSR	1,231,276	1,198,793	32,483	38.8	37.7	1.1
Northern European USSR	3,313,361	2,628,513	684,848	38.7	30.7	8.0
European Steppe	1,418,524	1,166,252	252,272	42.4	34.8	7.6
Russian East	1,896,657	1,697,490	199,167	48.8	43.7	5.1
Non-Slavic South	1,231,276	1,198,793	32,483	38.8	37.7	1.1
Total USSR	7,859,818	6,691,048	1,168,770	41.4	35.3	6.1

Sources: See note 1.

are available in the Southern USSR, the clear majority (31) had rates of net out-migration of −5.0 and below. In comparison, there were only 17 such units in both 1970–9 and 1979–89. In addition, these 31 southern units with high net out-migration in 1989 accounted for most (79.5 per cent) of all such units in the USSR.

Despite the near-universal high net out-migration from the Southern USSR during 1989, the Northern USSR also had some units with significant net out-migration. The highest rate occurred from a north-eastern unit, Magadan Oblast in the Far East, with −17.4 per thousand. In contrast, as recently as 1970–9, this remote unit had one of the highest net in-migration rates in the USSR, 17.2 per thousand. Thus, the 'turnaround' here was −34.6 points, which is symbolic of the retreat from the extreme eastern regions of the USSR.

Urban migration registration data for 1989

Urban registration data for 1989 also indicate a north-western or European shift (Tables 9.3 and 9.4). It should be kept in mind that these regional data include migration to and from areas within the region (unfortunately, urban migration within and from outside the region cannot be disaggregated for the data published for the 19 economic regions of 1961). Table 9.3 shows that the Western USSR had an urban net in-migration rate which was more than twice that of the Eastern USSR (7.6 as against 3.3 per thousand). Of the 'quadrant' regions, the Northern European USSR and European Steppe clearly had the highest rates of urban net in-migration (8.0 and 7.6, respectively), while the Non-

Table 9.4   Ex-USSR: urban migration by economic region, 1989

Region	In-migration	Out-migration	Net migration	Per thousand population		
				In	Out	Net
North-west	515,708	451,727	63,981	41.0	35.9	5.1
West	202,282	171,345	30,937	36.3	30.8	5.5
Centre	769,638	589,963	179,675	31.3	24.0	7.3
Volgo-Vyatsk	235,245	187,123	48,122	40.2	32.0	8.2
Central Chernozem	206,238	149,832	56,406	39.3	28.6	10.7
Volga	488,732	396,202	92,530	41.0	33.2	7.8
Belorussia	330,735	243,140	87,595	49.1	36.1	13.0
Moldavia	99,421	83,877	15,544	48.4	40.9	7.5
South-west	564,783	439,181	125,602	43.1	33.5	9.6
South	230,955	187,016	43,939	45.2	36.6	8.6
Donetsk-Dnepr	658,377	560,980	97,397	39.8	34.0	5.8
North Caucasus	429,771	334,379	95,392	43.9	34.2	9.7
Transcaucasus	288,687	261,256	27,431	31.7	28.7	3.0
Urals	777,251	687,234	90,017	44.2	39.1	5.1
West Siberia	388,910	347,524	41,386	45.2	40.4	4.8
East Siberia	416,721	386,061	30,660	56.8	52.6	4.2
Far East	313,775	276,671	37,104	58.8	51.8	7.0
Kazakhstan	482,710	445,189	37,521	50.7	46.7	4.0
Central Asia	459,879	492,348	− 32,469	35.0	37.5	− 2.5
Total USSR	7,859,818	6,691,048	1,168,770	41.4	35.3	6.1

Sources: See note 1.

Slavic South barely had urban net in-migration (1.1). It should be noted that the Russian East had the highest rate of urban in-migration (48.8), but also had by far the highest rate of urban out-migration (43.7), resulting in a below-average rate of urban net in-migration (5.1).

Table 9.4 demonstrates that the highest rates of urban net in-migration at the economic region level also occurred in the north-western or European USSR. These included Belorussia (13.0 per thousand), the Central Chernozem (10.7), the North Caucasus (9.7), the South-west (9.6), the South (8.6) and the Volgo-Vyatsk (8.2). At the other end of the spectrum, Central Asia actually had urban net out-migration in 1989!

At the oblast level, the vast majority of regions with urban net in-migration rates in excess of 10 per thousand in 1989 were also in the north-western or European USSR. In fact, 32 of the 40 such oblast units were in European regions. The highest were found in Belorussia (Brest, 24, and Grodno, 19), although the troubled Nagorno-Karabakh had a rate of 22. At the other end of the spectrum some oblasts of Central Asia had high urban net out-migration rates, specifically Fergana in Uzbekistan (− 20) and Khatlon in Tajikistan (− 14).

Although urban migration to and from beyond the region for each of the 19 economic regions of 1961 could not be isolated out, it could be for the 20 economic regions for the Soviet Union in the late 1980s. These

Table 9.5   Ex-USSR: urban migration beyond the economic region, by macroregion, 1989

Region	In-migration	Out-migration	Net migration	Per thousand population In	Out	Net
Western USSR	2,533,673	2,093,093	440,580	19.8	16.3	3.5
Eastern USSR	1,243,552	1,287,061	− 43,509	20.2	20.9	− 0.7
Northern USSR	3,351,029	2,805,897	545,132	21.2	17.8	3.4
Southern USSR	426,196	574,257	− 148,061	13.4	18.1	− 4.7
Northern European USSR	1,674,290	1,345,914	328,376	19.7	15.8	3.9
European Steppe	770,666	616,197	154,469	22.6	18.1	4.5
Russian East	906,073	843,786	62,287	23.3	21.7	1.6
Non-Slavic South	426,196	574,257	− 148,061 .	13.4	18.1	− 4.7
Total USSR	3,777,225	3,380,154	397,071	19.9	17.8	2.1

Sources: See note 1.

regions differ little from the 19 regions of 1961. The chief difference is that the former North-west was subdivided into two new regions, the North and North-west. Otherwise, only minor oblast-level adjustments are involved. Results are shown in Tables 9.5 and 9.6.

As can be seen, the geographical patterns are generally similar to those of the 19 regions. In particular, the Western and Northern USSR each had net urban in-migration (3.5 and 3.4 per thousand respectively), while the Eastern and Southern USSR each had net urban out-migration (− 0.7 and − 4.7 per thousand respectively). In addition, the two European quadrants of the European Steppe and Northern European USSR had the highest rates of net urban in-migration (4.5 and 3.9, respectively), while urban centres of the Russian East had only slight net in-migration (1.6) and the Non-Slavic South — equivalent to the Southern USSR — had net out-migration (− 4.7).

Likewise, among the 20 economic regions (Table 9.6), the highest rates of urban net in-migration from beyond the region at hand were also in the north-western or European regions. These included the North Caucasus (6.1 per thousand), the South (5.7), the Centre (5.3) and the Central Chernozem (5.1). In contrast, urban net out-migration occurred from all three southern regions: Central Asia (− 5.7), the Transcaucasus (− 4.6) and Kazakhstan (− 3.3).

Table 9.6   Ex-USSR: urban migration beyond the economic region, by economic region, 1989

Region	In-migration	Out-migration	Net migration	Per thousand population In	Out	Net
North	126,082	124,614	1,468	26.8	26.5	0.3
North-west	164,371	137,712	26,659	22.9	19.2	3.7
West or Baltic	100,764	82,844	17,920	16.1	13.2	2.9
Centre	466,146	332,628	133,518	18.5	13.2	5.3
Volgo-Vyatsk	107,908	90,200	17,708	18.4	15.4	3.0
Central Chernozem	95,348	71,402	23,946	20.3	15.2	5.1
Volga	261,481	209,742	51,739	21.7	17.4	4.3
Belorussia	131,222	103,997	27,225	19.5	15.4	4.1
Moldavia	40,238	39,638	600	19.6	19.3	0.3
South-west	220,968	192,775	28,193	17.9	15.6	2.3
South	140,026	110,770	29,256	27.4	21.7	5.7
Donetsk-Dnepr	367,889	302,305	65,584	21.3	17.5	3.8
North Caucasus	222,513	163,484	59,029	23.1	17.0	6.1
Transcaucasus	88,717	130,982	−42,265	9.8	14.4	−4.6
Urals	281,831	268,623	13,208	18.5	17.7	0.8
West Siberia	280,526	246,102	34,424	25.6	22.4	3.2
East Siberia	155,623	156,392	−769	23.5	23.6	−0.1
Far East	188,093	172,669	15,424	31.0	28.5	2.5
Kazakhstan	171,607	202,613	−31,006	18.0	21.3	−3.3
Central Asia	165,872	240,662	−74,790	12.6	18.3	−5.7
Total USSR	3,777,225	3,380,154	397,071	19.9	17.8	2.1

Sources: See note 1.

Nationality composition

The south to north migration trend within the former USSR in the 1980s was not unexpected; fifteen years ago Lewis and Rowland (1979) predicted that such a migration would occur in the 1980s and 1990s. This forecast was based on the presence of emerging labour surpluses among the high-fertility, rapidly-growing, predominantly Turkic Muslim nationalities of the less-developed southern regions, especially Central Asia, and chronic labour shortages amongst the low-fertility, predominantly European nationalities of the more developed northern regions, especially the RSFSR. Such a migration would not be unique, but would follow past and existing south to north migrations: blacks to northern cities of the United States, Puerto Ricans to New York City, Mexicans to the South-western United States, peoples of the Mediterranean Basin to Western Europe, and Indians, Pakistanis and West Indians to Great Britain.

However, recently published nationality data suggest that at this stage Russians and not Turkic Muslims have been the chief participants in this migration. Unfortunately, the nationality data are only available for the

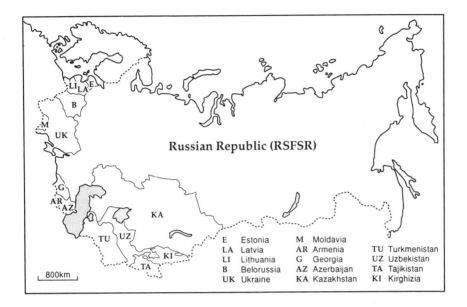

E	Estonia	M	Moldavia
LA	Latvia	AR	Armenia
LI	Lithuania	G	Georgia
B	Belorussia	AZ	Azerbaijan
UK	Ukraine	KA	Kazakhstan

TU	Turkmenistan
UZ	Uzbekistan
TA	Tajikistan
KI	Kirghizia

Figure 9.4 Ex-USSR: union republics

former union republics, and thus a breakdown of migration to the European and Asian or Siberian components of the RSFSR cannot yet be discerned (Figure 9.4). However, given the net out-migration from Siberia during 1989 as well as the 1989 urban registration data discussed above, it can probably be assumed that the greater share of the south to north Russian migration shift has been to the European RSFSR.

Two procedures were used to estimate the nationality composition of the migration. First, based upon nationality data by ethnic units from the 1979 and 1989 censuses, net migration for a nationality was estimated by applying the union-wide growth rate for that nationality between 1979 and 1989 to each unit, a technique also used by Anderson and Silver (1989). Since there was little emigration from the USSR during this period, it was assumed that the growth rate was equivalent to the natural increase rate for that nationality. This 'natural increase' rate was then applied to each relevant unit and used to project the 1979 population to 1989. If the projected 1989 population exceeded the actual 1989 population of that nationality in that unit, an estimated net out-migration was assumed to have occurred. If it was lower, net in-migration was assumed. The second source of data was explicitly published data on the nationality composition of migration in and out of urban centres from the urban registration data of 1989.

The results of the investigation suggest that, at this stage (1979–89), the south to north migration consisted mainly of Russians rather than the

Table 9.7   Estimated net migration of Russians and other selected nationalities, 1979–89

Region	Russians	Trans-caucasus	Kazakhs	Central Asians	Tatars
Northern USSR	484,399	379,731	1,098	101,760	94,073
Southern USSR	− 504,175	− 382,488	235	− 105,002	− 91,002
North plus South	− 19,776	− 2,757	1,333	− 3,242	3,071
RSFSR	− 71,941	305,026	− 6,829	74,603	59,121
Transcaucasus	− 186,061	− 361,868	2,295	− 776	− 7,123
Kazakhstan	− 100,312	3,507	− 32,161	− 20,461	− 11,885
Central Asia	− 217,802	− 24,077	30,101	− 83,766	− 71,993

Notes: Transcaucasus = Georgians, Armenians, Azerbaijanis.
Central Asians = Uzbeks, Kirghiz, Tajiks, Turkmen.

Sources and procedures: See text and note 1.

indigenous southern nationalities.[2] Tables 9.7, 9.8 and 9.9 provide the raw data for this overall conclusion. Based on the 'natural increase' or first procedure, the combined net out-migration of the eight major indigenous nationalities of the Southern USSR (− 578,257) was only slightly higher than that of Russians (− 504,175), despite the fact that the indigenous population exceeded the Russian population of the southern USSR by many times (Table 9.7). Furthermore, the bulk of the indigenous net out-migration came from the Transcaucasus (− 382,488); only − 105,002 came from the much more populous Central Asia. Net out-migration of the four Central Asian nationalities from Central Asia was only − 83,766, whereas the estimated net out-migration of Russians was − 217,802. Russian net out-migration was also considerable from both Kazakhstan and the Transcaucasus. It should be added that, except for Tatars, a non-indigenous Turkic Muslim nationality, no other nationalities in the Southern USSR were found to have substantial net out-migration. The estimated net out-migration of Tatars from the Southern USSR amounted to − 91,002 with by far the greatest amount, − 71,993, occurring from Central Asia (Table 9.7).

It should also be added that the Russian net out-migration from the predominantly Muslim south was not confined to the republics outside the RSFSR. Apparently it has also been occurring from the seven titularly non-Russian units of the North Caucasus region, which are chiefly Muslim and primarily on the southern fringes of the region, adjacent to the Transcaucasus region (Figure 9.1). Using the same projection estimating method employed above, it can be concluded that Russian net out-migration from these seven units was − 142,479; reflecting this, it will also be noticed from Figure 9.3 that the oblast units of the southern North Caucasus had consistent net out-migration. Combined with the

Table 9.8 Ethnic composition of urban migration from Southern to Northern USSR, 1989

	Total	Russians		Southerners		Tatars	
		No.	%	No.	%	No.	%
Out-migration, Southern to Northern	343,613	157,375	45.8	84,615	24.6	38,526	11.2
In-migration, Northern to Southern	214,164	104,675	48.9	58,515	27.3	11,096	5.2
Net, Southern to Northern	−129,449	−52,700	40.7	−26,100	20.2	−27,430	21.2
In-migration, Northern from Southern	334,306	149,991	44.9	105,114	31.4	17,365	5.2
Out-migration, Northern to Southern	222,490	95,103	42.7	80,598	36.2	8,117	3.6
Net, Northern from Southern	111,816	54,888	49.1	24,516	21.9	9,248	8.3

Note: Southerners = Georgians, Armenians, Azerbaijanis, Kazakhs, Uzbeks, Kirghiz, Tajiks, Turkmen.

Sources and procedures: See text and note 1.

Table 9.9 Ethnic composition of urban migration from Central Asia to the RSFSR, 1989

	Total	Russians		Central Asians		Tatars	
		No.	%	No.	%	No.	%
Out-migration, Central Asia to RSFSR	98,355	53,599	54.5	13,378	13.6	10,182	10.4
In-migration, RSFSR to Central Asia	61,757	31,596	51.2	12,964	21.0	5,678	9.2
Net, Central Asia to RSFSR	−36,598	−22,003	60.1	−414	1.1	−4,504	12.3
In-migration, RSFSR from Central Asia	86,287	42,084	48.8	22,635	26.2	7,035	8.2
Out-migration, RSFSR to Central Asia	63,858	27,101	42.4	22,314	34.9	4,322	6.8
Net, RSFSR from Central Asia	22,429	14,983	66.8	321	1.4	2,713	12.1

Note: Central Asians = Uzbeks, Kirghiz, Tajiks, Turkmen.

Sources and procedures: See text and note 1.

estimated Russian net out-migration of − 504,175 from the Southern USSR (Table 9.7), this means that the Russian net out-migration from the southern units was nearly − 650,000.

Registration data for urban areas in 1989 also tend to suggest that net out-migration from the Southern USSR and Central Asia is not largely indigenous in nature but instead is, to a great extent, Russian. According to these data, Russians alone comprised nearly one-half (45.8 per cent) of the urban out-migrants from urban areas of the Southern USSR to Northern USSR (see the top half of Table 9.8). Russians also accounted for nearly one-half (40.7 per cent) of the total net out-migrants from southern cities to the Northern USSR. In contrast, the eight major indigenous nationalities of the Southern USSR combined accounted for much lower shares in all regards, generally one-fifth to one-quarter. For example, they accounted for only 24.6 per cent of the out-migrants from cities of the Southern USSR to the Northern USSR, a proportion only about one-half that of Russians. Tatars alone accounted for more than one-tenth (11.2 per cent) of the out-migrants; and, moreover, Tatars actually comprised a higher share of the net out-migrants than did the eight major nationalities combined (21.2 versus 20.2 per cent).

One problem with this perspective is that relatively large shares of indigenous southern nationalities, especially those of Central Asia, are possibly not counted, because they reside in and would originate from rural areas rather than from urban areas. Fortunately, registration data allow for some hints about indigenous rural-origin, south to north migration. Namely, from the available perspective of migration in and out of northern cities, migrants of both urban and rural origins and destinations would be included. However, these data also do not suggest much southern indigenous northward migration (Table 9.8, bottom half). In particular, of the in-migrants to urban areas of the Northern USSR from the Southern USSR, Russians again comprised nearly half (44.9 per cent). They also comprised nearly half of the net in-migrants in this regard (49.1 per cent). These proportions were all clearly higher than corresponding ones for the eight southern nationalities combined.

A narrower focus on migration between Central Asia and the RSFSR further suggests a Russian rather than indigenous nature of the south to north flow. Table 9.9 (top half) shows that Russians comprised more than half (54.5 per cent) of the urban out-migrants from Central Asia to the RSFSR, four times as much as that for the four major Central Asian nationalities combined (13.6 per cent). Moreover, Russians loomed especially large in net out-migration, accounting for three-fifths (60.1 per cent) of this net out-migration, as compared to only 1.1 per cent for the four Central Asian nationalities.

From the perspective of movements in and out of cities of the RSFSR, Russians rather than indigenous Central Asians again dominated the Central Asian to RSFSR flow (see Table 9.9, bottom half). For example, Russians clearly dominated the net in-migration to RSFSR urban areas from Central Asia, accounting, in fact, for two-thirds, with the indigenous Central Asians accounting for only a miniscule share (1.4 per cent).

In short, projection-residual technique data and urban migration registration data suggest that the emergent south to north migration flow in the USSR during the 1980s chiefly consisted of Russians rather than the indigenous, predominantly Muslim nationalities of the Southern USSR. This Russian out-migration, indeed retreat, from the Southern USSR is most likely largely due to the fact that although Russians previously moved to the Southern USSR, especially Central Asia and Kazakhstan, in a colonial-type fashion, that situation has been changing as educational levels have increased among the Muslim nationalities, who are now better able to provide more educated and skilled labour, reducing the need for Russians. In addition, the forces of nationalism released by glasnost have unleashed anti-Russian sentiments and movements in the southern regions (Smith 1990, pp. 316–17).

Concluding summary

Recently published data have allowed for a geographically detailed investigation of recent regional and subregional migration patterns in the former USSR. Results reveal a major reversal of the long-standing west to east and north to south trends. Consequently, there has emerged a shift from the south and east of the USSR to the north-west. At the macroregional level, during the 1980s, both the Eastern USSR and Southern USSR had net out-migration, while the Western USSR and Northern USSR had net in-migration. Similarly, net out-migration occurred from the Non-Slavic South, while the Northern European USSR and the European Steppe had net in-migration.

Among economic regions, the highest rates of net in-migration generally occurred to the extreme north-western regions of the Centre, North-west and West, as well as to the South of the Ukraine. Conversely, the highest rates of net out-migration occurred from the extreme southern regions of Kazakhstan, the Transcaucasus and Central Asia. In addition, in 1989, net in-migration took place for the first time to the Central Chernozem region. Also in 1989, for the first time, all four regions of Siberia experienced net out-migration.

At the oblast or subregional level, although the oil and gas unit of Tyumen' Oblast of Siberia had the highest rate of net in-migration during 1979–89, units with net in-migration were largely found in the north-western regions, especially during 1989. Indeed, many units with traditionally chronic net out-migration in the Non-Chernozem Zone and Central Chernozem region had net in-migration in the 1980s, especially in 1989.

Conversely, units with net out-migration were increasingly found in southern and eastern units. Indeed, during 1989 most of the oblasts with high rates of net out-migration were found in the three southern regions, where most units had net out-migration. In 1989, the majority of oblasts in Siberia had net out-migration.

Urban migration registration data for 1989 also suggested a north-western shift. The highest urban net in-migration rates occurred in the Northern European USSR and the European Steppe, especially Belo-russia and the Central Chernozem. Urban net out-migration actually occurred from Central Asia. Generally similar patterns occurred even when urban migration to and from beyond the region was investigated.

Thus, it is clear from all regional levels that there is an increased south and east to north-west shift in Soviet migration patterns. This is not surprising. During the Gorbachev period it was clear that the established north-western industrial regions were the ones most favoured for invest-ment, since it was (and still is) here that the quickest return on invest-ment could occur. In addition, there has been a major recent programme to increase investment and improve living standards in rural areas of the Non-Chernozem Zone of European Russia in order to stem rural depopulation. The results of this policy were reflected in the fact that, by the end of the 1980s, net in-migration was actually occurring to many units here, although this rural inflow also partly reflects slowing industrial growth and declining urban in-migration.

Net out-migration from the east and south is also not surprising. Except for Tyumen' Oblast, the Soviets had difficulty for years trying to settle Siberia, even though higher wages were used as incentives. However, recent nationality and urban registration data for 1989 suggest that at this stage Russians and not the indigenous nationalities are the major participants in this south to north shift, partly due to the increased anti-Russian feelings in the non-Russian areas.

With respect to the future, we can very probably expect a further Russian retreat from the southern regions to European Russia, especially with anti-Russian sentiments in the south and the collapse of the former USSR. However, such a movement could be impeded by the economic crisis and increased unemployment in Russia.

The forces for a potential south to north indigenous out-migration are still great, especially as unemployment increases here too. However, there are now numerous additional impediments to such a migration. First, with increased economic turmoil in the north the demand for labour from other areas is diminished with the increased unemployment among the indigenous Russians. In addition, as we are currently still in the process of witnessing the outcome of the relationships between the members of the Commonwealth of Independent States, it remains to be seen what will be the nature of migration and labour movements between the states. In other words, even if indigenous southern Turkic Muslims wanted to migrate to Russia, would they ever be allowed to do so? Thus it will be of interest to see if the northern states, especially Russia, impose legal restrictions on the 'immigration' of non-Russians from the south. In short, it is possible to anticipate that many of the controversies involving the issues of legal and illegal immigration in the United States and Western Europe will be repeated in the realm of the former USSR.

In addition, a continued Russian migration from Asiatic Siberia to European Russia can also be anticipated, especially as wage incentives in Siberia will probably diminish with the demise of a centrally planned Soviet economy. Moreover, pressures for a leapfrog (over Eastern Europe) emigration from the former Soviet Union to Western Europe will also increase (on this see Grečić 1991; Layard *et al.* 1992; Öberg and Boubnova 1993; Shevtsova 1992). Indeed, the number of emigrants from the former Soviet Union nearly doubled from an already relatively high 234,994 in 1989 to 452,262 in 1990. Undoubtedly, a relatively large share again probably went not only to Israel but also to Western Europe. Many of the Jews emigrating to Israel were destined ultimately for the USA (Öberg and Boubnova 1993). During 1989–90 the number of emigrants from the European regions more than doubled; by 1990 they accounted for nearly three-fifths (58.3 per cent) of the total emigrants, with the RSFSR having the most emigrants of any republic (103,609).

Given the past difficulties of forecasting migration trends in the relatively stable 'old' USSR, a prediction of future migration in the highly unstable region of the ex-USSR is absolutely fraught with uncertainties. Furthermore, the future publication of systematic migration data for the region as a whole is also very uncertain.

Notes

1. A detailed note on sources for the analyses described in this chapter, including the maps and tables, is in order here. All the following sources are in Russian. USSR Central Statistical Administration, *National economy of the USSR 1973 and 1974*, Statistics Publishing House, Moscow, 1974 and 1975 respectively; RSFSR State Statistical Committee (1990), *Number, composition and movement of the population in the RSFSR*, Republican Information and Publishing Centre, Moscow; plus the following USSR State Statistical Committee publications, all printed by the Finance and Statistics Publishing House, Moscow: *Population of the USSR 1988; National composition of the population 1989; Demographic annual 1989; National economy of the USSR in 1989; USSR in figures in 1990.* The last-named of these sources is also available in English.
2. The indigenous southern nationalities consist of six Turkic Muslim groups plus the Christian Georgians and Armenians. The six Muslim nationalities consist of the Azerbaijanis, the Kazakhs and the four Central Asian groups — Uzbeks, Kirgiz, Tajiks and Turkmen.

References

Anderson, B.A. and Silver, B.D., 1989, 'Demographic sources of the changing ethnic composition of the Soviet Union', *Population and Development Review*, 15(4): 609–56.

Gretić, V., 1991, 'East–West migration and its possible influence on North–South migration', *International Migration*, 29(2): 241–52.

Layard, R., Blanchard, O., Dornbusch, R. and Krugman, P., 1992, *East–West migration: the alternatives*, MIT Press, Cambridge, MA.

Lewis, R.A. and Rowland, R.H., 1979, *Population redistribution in the USSR: its impact on society, 1897–1977*, Praeger, New York.

Öberg, S. and Boubnova, H., 1993, 'Ethnicity, nationality and migration potentials in Eastern Europe', in King, R. (ed.), *Mass migrations in Europe: the legacy and the future*, Belhaven, London, 234–56.

Rowland, R.H., 1988, 'Union republic migration trends in the USSR during the 1980s', *Soviet Geography*, 29(9): 809–29.

Rowland, R.H., 1990, 'Economic region net migration patterns in the USSR: 1979–89', *Soviet Geography*, 31(9): 657–78.

Rowland, R.H., 1992, 'Urban settlement size trends in the USSR, 1970–1989', *Soviet Geography*, 33(1): 34–48.

Sagers, M.J., 1991, 'Review of the Soviet energy industry in 1990', *Soviet Geography*, 32(4): 251–90.

Shevtsova, L., 1992, 'Post-Soviet emigration today and tomorrow', *International Migration Review*, 26(2): 241–57.

Smith, H., 1990, *The new Russians*, Random House, New York.

Chapter 10

Southern Europe and the international division of labour: from emigration to immigration

Russell King and Krysia Rybaczuk

This chapter examines the remarkable change in status of southern Europe during the 1970s from a region of mass emigration to one of mass immigration. Four countries will be considered: Italy, Greece, Spain and Portugal. The analysis will be structured in the following way. In the next section the reversal in migration trends will be contextualised by brief reference to some summary data covering the period between the end of the war and the late 1980s. Then we shall put forward and discuss hypothesised causes for this turnaround in external migration to mass immigration: (i) ease of entry; (ii) geographical and cultural proximity; (iii) divergent standards of living; (iv) demographic push pressures; and, perhaps most importantly, (v) economic restructuring and the emergence of new forms of labour market organisation in southern Europe — in particular the segmentation and casualisation of labour demand and the consequent need for cheap, flexible immigrant labour, part of which has fuelled the expansion of the black economy in the four countries under consideration. The succeeding sections of the chapter will then make a descriptive analysis of immigration trends in each of the four countries, particular attention being given to the Italian and Spanish cases where immigration is most highly developed and where there has been a good deal of relevant recent literature. The conclusion stresses the complexity and diversity of the migration trends under observation, and the problems these trends pose for European migration policy now and in the future.

The background context

During the period between the 1950s and the mid-1970s the industrial countries of Western Europe were the focus of the most remarkable and large-scale international migration of labour the modern world has ever seen. Estimates vary as to the number of workers involved (e.g. because of a considerable amount of clandestine movement and the high number of migrants who were 'rotated' on short-term work contracts), but there were clearly many millions, perhaps around 10 million, plus their dependants who became an increasingly important element in the total migration flows of the 1970s. Fielding (1993) has described this huge migration of 'mass collective workers' as Fordist in the sense that their recruitment was for the mass production of standardised products for mass markets: mass migration was thus a corollary to mass production, mass consumption, mass culture and mass society. The geography of the rapid evolution (and decline) of this mass labour migration system was described in detail by Salt (1976) and Salt and Clout (1976): it involved a movement of migrants mainly from southern Europe (Portugal, Spain, Italy, Yugoslavia, Greece and Turkey) to central and northern Europe (France, Switzerland, West Germany, the Benelux countries). Further embellishments to this basically south to north pattern involved Maghreb emigration, chiefly to France, Irish emigration to Britain, Finnish emigration to Sweden, and a series of 'colonial' emigrations of former French West Africans to France, Surinamese to The Netherlands, and Caribbeans and South Asians to Britain.

A few figures, drawn from SOPEMI[1] and various national sources, give an idea of the importance and scale of emigration during this period from the four southern European countries which are the focus of this chapter. The gross emigration flows involved 6.9 million Italians between 1946 and 1970, 1.2 million Greeks between 1951 and 1972, 1.8 million Portuguese between 1951 and 1975, and 2.2 million Spaniards between 1960 and 1971. The different years involved in measuring these national totals reflect partly the slightly different periods of mass migration. For instance, in Italy post-war emigration started and finished earlier than in the other countries; Spain's migration did not get under way as a mass phenomenon until after the 1959 Plan de Estabilización. In the case of Italy, Greece and Portugal there was an initial orientation overseas (to North America and the Portuguese colonies) but after 1958 European destinations predominated, accounting for at least two-thirds of the total outflow. Peak periods of gross emigration were 1960–2 for Italy (an average of 380,000 emigrants per year), 1961–5 for Greece (93,000 emigrants per year), 1966–70 for Portugal (126,000 emigrants per year), and 1964–5 for Spain (200,000 per year). By 1974 about 2.7 million foreign workers from Italy, Spain, Portugal and Greece were resident in France and West Germany, the two major destination countries. By the end of the 1980s, however, this figure had dropped to 2.3 million, indicating substantial return migration. In fact Italy had a positive migratory balance (i.e. returnees outnumbering emigrants) for the first time in 1972, Spain and Greece turned positive in 1975 following the recruitment stop by the main destination countries, and Portugal in 1981 (Montanari and Cortese 1993a).

Soon after the switch to a net positive migratory balance by the excess of returns over departures another important migratory process started: the arrival in the four southern European countries of increasing numbers of immigrants from economically less developed countries in Africa, Asia and Latin America. The sudden surge of immigrants was unexpected and exposed the unpreparedness of the administrative structures and cultural mentalities of the recipient countries which had turned from being major exporters to major importers of migrant labour within about a decade (Penninx 1986). One of the reasons for unpreparedness was the lack of quantitative information on the new immigrants. Official entry records and work permit data gave only sketchy underestimates, firstly because much of the entry was (and remains) clandestine, and secondly because official work permit statistics do not distinguish between permits issued to new arrivals and those which are changes or renewals of permits for workers already living in the country.

Whatever the shortcomings of the available statistical data on this new immigration (some figures will be presented later in this chapter), it is now clear that, aside from Germany, southern Europe has, since the early 1980s, been the major focus for new immigration into Western Europe from outside the region. At a simple geographical level, Europe's 'migration frontier' shifted suddenly southwards during the 1970s. In the 1960s it ran along the north coast of Spain, followed the Pyrenees and the south coast of France, cut diagonally across northern Italy to pass north of the regions of Veneto and Friuli-Venezia Giulia, and then continued to the north of Yugoslavia and Greece to the Black Sea. Now the line between immigration and emigration runs east–west through the Mediterranean from Gibraltar to the Bosphorus, passing south of Sicily and Crete (King 1991).

However, the simple concepts of migration 'turnaround' (from a net negative to a net positive balance) and of the spatial shift southwards of the migration frontier hide the more complex reality that the southern European countries have functioned simultaneously as emigration and immigration countries. In other words, emigration continued for some time after the arrival of the new immigrant flows. During the 1980s gross emigration flows persisted, albeit at a declining rate, from Italy and Spain (mainly from the poorer, more rural parts of these countries). Emigration from Portugal remained steady during the 1980s, and that from Greece to Germany increased slightly after 1988 as the transition period for Greek 'free movement' within the EC came to an end (Salt 1992, p. 56).[2]

The increasingly blurred distinction between northern European countries of immigration and southern countries of emigration was noted in SOPEMI Reports for the first time in 1978. The 1978 Report (p. 2) referred to 'a changing reality which is becoming more and more difficult to grasp in statistical and quantitative terms'. For the first time, Italy and Greece were referred to as countries of immigration as well as of emigration; Spain was also seen as a country of increasingly significant immigration. This reconceptualisation of the pattern of international migration affecting Europe saw some convergence in migration policy matters between northern and southern countries which, until then, had been seen as opposite poles in the international transfer of labour. The shift in migration status was most marked in Italy, was also evident in Greece and Spain, applied less to Portugal and not at all to Yugoslavia and Turkey. SOPEMI Reports in the late 1970s and early 1980s referred repeatedly to the growing number of foreigners' work permits issued in Italy, Spain and Greece, and noted that considerable numbers of migrants were entering and subsequently working in these countries illegally. Thus, for instance, the 1978 Report (pp. 38–9) noted that whilst official Italian Ministry of the Interior figures for 1975 gave 74,000 foreign workers in Italy (55 per cent of them Europeans, 21 per cent from the southern Mediterranean and Arab countries, 4 per cent from Africa, 4 per cent from Asia and 14 per cent from North and South America), an estimate based on data from a variety of sources (private research organisations, trade unions, etc.) yielded a figure of 250,000 for 1977, and with a rather different make-up (23 per cent Europeans, 24 per cent from Mediterranean and Arab states, 40 per cent Africans, 8 per cent Asians and 4 per cent Americans). The clear tendency, which has been continued ever since, as we shall see, has been to under-record Third World immigrant workers living clandestinely in the country. By 1979 SOPEMI was reporting a figure of 500,000 foreign workers in Italy (1979 Report, p. 1), and the 1985 Report (p. 8) referred to repeated incidents of racial violence against foreigners in Italy.

Most recent estimates of the total number of immigrants in the four countries under consideration give figures around 2 million (of which about one-half were in Italy) for the late 1980s. Heyden (1991, p. 287) quotes a figure of 2.7–3.0 million for the total foreign population of the same countries, half of whom are illegal immigrants. According to the same source (a survey by the ISOPLAN organisation, Saarbrucken), the foreign population will increase to about 5 million by 2000, including approximately 2 million regular migrants from developing countries and at least 2 million irregular immigrants.

Causes of immigration to Southern European countries

If the influx of large numbers of immigrants into southern Europe was so unexpected, how can it be explained? Several factors seem to have played a role.

The first factor is largely pragmatic: ease of entry. At a time when the traditional destination countries — Germany, France, Switzerland, Great Britain — were making entry more difficult to Third World immigrants, access remained relatively easy via the 'soft underbelly' of Europe, just a boat trip away from some of the main sending countries. Italy and Greece especially have long coastlines, many islands and a multiplicity of entry points. All four countries have major tourist industries which make it relatively easy for immigrants to come in on tourist or student visas and then stay on. Tightening controls at ports and airports would undoubtedly jeopardise the mass inflows of tourists which are so vital to the economies of the four countries. Aside from the regular entry points at airports, ports and road crossings, many illegal immigrants from Africa and beyond are landed clandestinely by boat in places like Sicily, whilst immigrants from Eastern Europe and points further east are smuggled across the Italian border in the vicinity of Trieste.[3] This ease of entry reflects the lack of a proper immigration policy which might lay down rules for entry and for the rights and duties of immigrants. It also explains, of course, the difficulty of establishing numbers, since the 'hidden' part of the immigration is so large a proportion of the total phenomenon. From the mid-1980s Spain and Italy took steps to control illegal immigration; they were pressurised into doing this partly by the growing tide of adverse public opinion in their own countries, and also by the attitude of the other EC states which were anxious to control immigration inflows and were worried about the excessive permeability of the Community's southern border in the run-up to the Single Market and the removal of internal frontiers for population movement (Montanari and Cortese 1993a).

The second factor is also pragmatic — geographical or cultural proximity. Physical closeness partly accounts for the movement of Moroccans into Spain or Tunisians into Sicily. In the case of Portugal and Spain colonial and linguistic ties explain part of the migrations from Latin America and from Portuguese ex-colonies in Africa. Religion may also be a factor, especially if it expresses itself in the form of the development of 'connecting institutions' such as the Catholic Church's role in assisting the recruitment, transfer and pastoral care of female migrants from the Philippines to Italy and Spain.

Thirdly, there is the economic factor of divergent standards of living and wage levels. Thirty years ago southern European countries had wage rates which were a fraction of those in northern Europe: individual migrants could thus earn four or five times as much working in Germany or Switzerland as they could at home, especially if the move involved an employment shift from farm labour to industrial work. Although some of the intra-European north–south gap remains, the differential has narrowed considerably as EC membership (amongst other factors) has brought Italian and Spanish (and, less so, Greek and Portuguese) wages up to 'European' levels. Now the big income gap is between southern European countries on the one hand, and southern Mediterranean states (and other less developed countries) on the other. The first part of Table 10.1 shows the generally much higher economic growth rates of southern European (or northern Mediterranean) countries in comparison to both northern European EC states and south-east Mediterranean countries. Thus whereas in 1960 the per capita GDP of the richest southern European country (Italy) was 6.5 times that of the poorest North African

Table 10.1   Economic and demographic trends for selected groups of countries

	GDP per capita (US$ 1980 prices)			Economically active population		
	1960	1985	% change	1960 (millions)	1990	% change 1990–2000
Northern EC						
Belgium	4,379	9,717	+ 121.9	3.5	4.2	+ 1.0
Denmark	5,490	10,884	+ 98.3	2.1	2.9	0.0
France	4,473	9,918	+ 121.7	19.7	25.4	+ 4.3
Germany (West)	5,217	10,708	+ 105.3	26.2	29.3	− 6.4
Ireland	2,545	5,205	+ 104.5	1.1	1.5	+ 16.3
Netherlands	4,690	9,092	+ 93.9	4.1	6.2	+ 2.6
UK	4,970	8,665	+ 74.3	24.3	27.8	+ 1.1
Southern EC						
Greece	1,474	4,464	+ 202.8	3.4	3.9	+ 2.5
Italy	3,233	7,425	+ 129.7	20.7	23.3	− 0.1
Portugal	1,429	3,729	+ 161.0	3.4	4.7	+ 8.2
Spain	2,425	6,437	+ 165.4	11.6	14.5	+ 7.5
Southern Mediterranean and North Africa						
Algeria	1,302	2,142	+ 64.5	2.9	5.8	+ 44.0
Egypt	496	1,188	+ 139.5	7.5	14.6	+ 31.2
Morocco	542	1,221	+ 125.3	3.3	7.8	+ 34.2
Sudan	667	540	− 19.0	3.9	8.1	+ 36.4
Syria	1,234	2,900	+ 135.0	1.3	3.1	+ 49.9
Tunisia	852	2,050	+ 140.6	1.2	2.6	+ 30.2
Turkey	1,255	2,533	+ 101.8	14.0	23.7	+ 21.3

Source: Golini *et al*. 1991, pp. 278–9.

country (Egypt), by 1985 the ratio between the richest and the poorest (Sudan) had doubled to 13.75.

The economic differences referred to above express themselves in terms of differential incomes, wage rates, unemployment rates and rates of annual growth. Whilst these parameters provide the structural context for the international migration of labour, there is often much debate as to whether the dominant influences are 'demand pull' or 'supply push'. Venturini (1988) has set out the nature of this debate amongst labour economists. Those supporting the dominance of the pull effect believe that present-day immigration into southern Europe is caused by unsatisfied labour demand in the destination countries; the immigrants thus play a complementary role *vis-à-vis* local workers. Certainly this was the case with the earlier generation of labour migrants who moved from southern European and colonial countries to France, Britain, West Germany, etc. in the 1950s and 1960s; indeed much of this labour was specifically recruited via bilateral agreements between the governments of the receiving countries and those of the labour suppliers. In the more recent immigration into southern Europe there is an element of demand since these countries' expanding economies have increased their need for unskilled manpower. As well as the availability of jobs (of a certain kind), social welfare systems and liberal, democratic structures also exert a pull for immigrants coming from countries where these things are lacking. However, most authorities (e.g. Ghosh 1991; Golini *et al.* 1991; Salt 1992) agree that the migrations of the 1980s and 1990s are driven much more by push pressures than by demand pulls. The push rationale — that labour will move into a prosperous country from a poor country regardless of the situation of labour demand in the host country — leads to the notion that there will be competition in the labour market of the recipient country between local and immigrant labour. This too is an oversimplification because it assumes homogeneity and interchangeability in the labour market. In reality European, and especially southern European, labour markets have become highly segmented, so that direct competition between immigrant and local workers is reduced. We shall explore this and related points about the changing nature of labour markets a little later.

Behind 'push pressures', differential unemployment rates and slow GDP per capita growth lies the momentum of demographic increase, the fourth factor in our list. Across the Mediterranean Sea, two entirely different demographic regimes confront each other (Montanari and Cortese 1993a). Astride this sharp demographic gradient lie two different economic and cultural systems, reinforcing the interwoven nature of economic, demographic and cultural factors in 'explaining' migration trends. There is a further economic/demographic parallel to draw between the rapid economic growth of the southern European countries since the 1960s and the transformation of their demographies. Italy now claims the lowest birth rate in the world (a total fertility rate of less than 1.3 children per woman) and has a declining population, immigrants excluded (King 1993). Spanish fertility has fallen faster than any other country in Europe and is, at about 1.4, well below the replacement level of 2.1. Portuguese and Greek population trends are following the same trajectory, if less spectacularly. Put simply, the average woman in southern Europe has one or two children, the average woman in North Africa five or six. Thus 43 per cent of the total population of North African countries are under 15 years of age. With static and rapidly ageing populations in southern Europe (where life expectancy is set to overtake north European figures), the economically active populations and, even more, the flow of new young entrants to the labour market will soon diminish. The term 'demographic timebomb' is often used to refer to the effects of the downturn in new labour market entrants in the 1990s and beyond.[4] The second part of Table 10.1 shows that the trends in the economically active populations of the southern and the northern EC countries are quite similar, both for 1960–90 and for

1990–2000 (only Ireland has a projected high rate of increase). By contrast Turkey, Syria and the North African states have rates of growth of the economically active populations which range between 21 per cent and 50 per cent for the decade 1900–2000. Further rapid population growth in these potential migrant-sending countries is unavoidable. According to the United Nations' medium-variant projection (summarised in Montanari and Cortese 1993a), the 15–64 age-bracket population in the African Mediterranean countries is predicted to increase by 31.3 million during 1985–2000 and by a further 52.4 million during 2000–2020; the respective figures for the Asian Mediterranean countries (dominated by Turkey) are 18.9 million and 28.2 million. The combined increase in the non-European Mediterranean region, then, is more than 52 million during 1985–2000 (3.5 million working-age people per year) and 81 million during 2000–2020 (4 million per year). There is no way that new employment opportunities in these high-population growth countries will come anywhere near absorbing these huge numbers of extra workers: south–north migration will be necessary to solve the problem of excessive manpower (Venturini 1988). And of course if demographic trends for other less-developed countries in Africa and Asia which have migratory links to southern Europe are considered (countries such as Senegal, Cape Verde, Ethiopia, India, the Philippines), the figures pertaining to 'migration potential' become much larger.

The final, fifth, factor in which the changing character and pattern of southern European migration has to be embedded consists of the complex processes of post-1970s economic restructuring and the impact that these processes have had on the international division of labour. In a nutshell, restructuring has involved a sectoral shift from heavy manufacturing industry to high-technology production and to services, an organisational shift from mass production along Fordist lines to more flexible and small-scale output, and a shift from rigid to flexible labour markets. Of the four countries, Italy has followed these trends most faithfully. In Spain, Portugal and Greece, industrial employment has held up, or even increased; the growth in service sector employment being matched by the large number of workers leaving farming. Italy's industrial employment decline dates from the 1970s, by which time the bulk of the labour outflow from farming had already taken place. More generally characteristic of the southern European labour market has been the growth of marginal and precarious employment — casual, seasonal and temporary jobs which are part of the increased variety of labour practices produced by the restructuring of production and work regimes.

Let us explore the relationship between economic restructuring, the labour market and migration in southern Europe a little more closely. Fielding (1993) argues that the post-1970s decline of Fordist forms of productive organisation in Europe and their replacement by post-Fordist regimes of 'flexible specialisation' has led to reduced demand for immigrant workers: he writes, *'the most significant feature of mass migration under post-Fordist forms of productive organisation is its absence!'* (author's original italics and emphasis). This is broadly true, but only up to a point. Especially in southern Europe (more so, in fact, than in any other part of Europe), the rise of flexible forms of production and labour market organisation has created all sorts of niches for which 'marginal' forms of inexpensive and flexible labour (such as women, part-time workers and immigrants) are ideally suited. Since many of these forms of labour specialisation are 'hidden' (e.g. in small industrial workshops or in domestic households) or 'mobile' (e.g. semi-itinerant harvesting gangs in agriculture), they are not so immediately visible as the mass concentrations of migrant workers in the Fordist factories of industrial Europe; nevertheless in terms of the overall numbers involved and their presence as a permanent (if floating) structural element of the labour market, we can speak of a mass phenomenon, thereby contradicting Fielding's statement.

Whilst most writers are at pains to point out the differences between the post-industrial migrations of the past decade or so into southern Europe and the mass 'Fordist' emigrations from southern Europe into the industrial districts of the north in the 1960s, there are some historical parallels to be drawn. During the 1950s and 1960s there was much disorganised and clandestine migration from Spain and Portugal into France, particularly of harvest migrants and later of construction labourers. Indeed probably the majority of the migrants entering France at this time were doing so illegally (McDonald 1969). Another intriguing historical parallel can be pointed out between the Senegalese street-hawkers who ply their trade on the pavements of big Italian cities today and the Italian street musicians and itinerant vendors who sold ice-cream, hot chestnuts and religious trinkets on the streets of London, Paris and New York at the end of the last century (Sponza 1988).

The employment of most of the new immigrants in southern Europe tends to be around the margins of the formal or primary labour market or, even worse, in the parallel or secondary labour markets which are by definition uncontrolled. Hence there is no union representation, no fixed minimum wages, and no social security (since most workers in the secondary labour market are illegals and do not have the residence qualifications to receive state benefits). Such workers are prone to exploitation by their employers, and their poor conditions of work are usually replicated by bad housing and living conditions (Salt 1992, p. 67). In big cities like Rome and Barcelona the underground economy consists of a labyrinth of low-skilled, low-paid and informal work opportunities into which immigrant workers are slotted via a range of loose personal contacts. In its own way the system is often quite well organised, especially as regards ethnic recruitment and support networks. In Italy, Dell'Aringa and Neri (1987) have argued that the immigrants have been one of the main causes of the expansion of the underground economy, attracting in not only further waves of immigrants but also capital and labour from the 'legal' economy.

Illegality of migration and of migrants' status can be seen as a product of two contradictory trends: the internationalisation of the labour market, and the increasing restrictions on the entry of migrants from Third World countries into Western Europe. This leads on to a second relationship: that between illegal or irregular migratory status and illegal or irregular work. Migrants who are, by virtue of their illegal status, vulnerable to exploitation, tend naturally to be found in the most precarious, marginal, unprotected, unrewarding and menial jobs. Typical examples would be seasonal agricultural work, fishing, construction work, street-hawking, wiping windscreens at traffic-lights, domestic service, and low-grade cleaning work in hospitals, hotels and offices. Some of these jobs are gender- and nationality-specific: Moroccan farm labourers in Spain, Senegalese male street-hawkers in Italy, female domestic helpers in Italy and Spain.

The apparent paradox of southern European countries attracting immigrants at the same time as there was persistent if modest emigration and high rates of unemployment, especially youth unemployment, is resolved by the fact that most immigrants have established themselves in sectors of the labour market which are relatively uncontested by local workers (Golini *et al.* 1991, p. 257). Several interconnected phenomena are at work here. First, there has been a significant increase in the educational qualifications of local young people; this has led to a certain amount of intellectual unemployment since the academic qualifications acquired (law, teaching, philosophy, etc.) are often unrelated to the more pragmatic technical and commercial needs of the labour market. The rapid rise in household incomes, together with improved social security systems, has cushioned this unemployment in the sense that many young people prefer to remain unemployed (often as semi-perpetual students) well into their late 20s rather than take on 'undesirable' jobs in industry, farming or petty services; and their indulgent and increasingly well-off parents have not forced them to take low-grade jobs that would reflect badly on the prestige of the family. These low-status jobs thus become available to immigrant workers — who may, incidentally, also have good educational qualifications for which they cannot find employment in their countries of origin.

Italy

As the leading country economically in southern Europe and located at the heart of the Mediterranean Basin, Italy has been the pioneer for the migration phenomenon discussed in this chapter. The origins of foreign labour migration into Italy can probably be traced to two trends which started in the late 1960s at opposite ends of the country: in northern Italy labour shortages in industry stimulated an influx of Yugoslavian migrants, whilst in Western Sicily Tunisians started to replace local rural labour which had fled the area in the aftermath of the 1968 earthquake (King 1984, p. 156).

Figures on the early quantitative development of the immigrant worker community were reported in the introduction to this chapter. It would appear that numbers grew exceptionally rapidly in the late 1970s and early 1980s. Various estimates made by the Rome-based CENSIS organisation give figures of about 350,000 in 1977, 500,000 in 1979, and 800,000 in 1982 (SOPEMI Reports for 1980, pp. 113–14; 1982, p. 119). This doubling of numbers in the space of the five years to 1982 (when the government took the first steps to stop uncontrolled immigration) confirmed Italy's status as a country of mass immigration. By 1982 foreign workers made up 3.5 per cent of the labour force. Data on residence permits issued in 1980 give an approximate indication of the major source countries of Third World migrants at this time: Ethiopia 4,367, the Philippines 3,501, Egypt 2,927, Cape Verde 2,004, Tunisia 1,425, Morocco 791, and Algeria 736. However, much of the in-movement took place outside the permit system. Already marked regional employment specialisms for the migrant workers were evident: domestic servants, cleaning and catering in the large cities (Rome, Milan, Turin, Genoa, Naples, Bari), agriculture and fishing in Sicily, small and medium industry in Emilia-Romagna and other parts of north-central Italy, and the construction industry in Friuli-Venezia Giulia.

These jobs give clear indication of the relevance of the 'segmented labour market hypothesis' outlined in the previous section. In spite of the fact that Italy had 2 million unemployed in the early 1980s (60 per cent of them under the age of 25), the wage rate differentials between Italy and the sending countries (four times higher than Tunisia and seven times higher than Morocco, for instance) meant that North African and Philippine migrants were willing to work for wages that would be totally unacceptable to unemployed Italians. Amongst the army of Italy's young educated unemployed, the shame of manual labour means that almost nobody accepts unskilled work: hence the opportunities, and need, for immigrant workers.

Aside from this labour market factor, the attractiveness of Italy also derives from the ease of entering the country. Part of the problem here is the inherent conflict between Italy's desire to be as 'open' as possible to incoming tourists and the fact that entry as a tourist is one of the easiest paths for potential illegal workers to come in and find work (Ascoli 1986, p. 203). The country's geographical position makes it a transit area between Europe and Africa (and also, if to a lesser extent, Asia). This 'accessibility' is also illustrated by Italy's wide range of international relations and the importance of Rome Airport as southern Europe's major air node in terms of connections to African and Asian countries.

Montanari and Cortese (1993b) provide an overview of more recent data on the evolution of the foreign immigrant communities in Italy, up to the regularisation programme of 1990. Parenthetically they note the extraordinary upsurge in both media and scholarly interest in the immigration issue since 1976, the year they identify as the time when immigration into Italy reached a point where it was regarded as a national 'problem'. Between 1976 and 1990 no fewer than 624 academic studies (books, articles, etc.) were published on foreign immigration — far too many to refer to in our bibliography here![5] By the early 1980s immigration had increased to such an extent that in 1982 the Italian Parliament blocked the issue of new work permits for foreign citizens; at the same time those who had arrived in Italy before the end of 1981 were given the chance to regularise their position. Numbers continued to grow, however, and in 1987 it was estimated by Natale (1988) that there were somewhere between a minimum of 700,000 and a maximum of 1.1 million foreigners in Italy. Of these 570,000 had a residence permit (*permesso di soggiorno*).

A law passed at the end of 1986 granted an amnesty to all foreigners living in Italy and encouraged them to legalise their status. Although the deadline for regularisation was postponed several times, by September 1988 only 118,700 had acted, a considerable disappointment since it was known that the true quantity of 'hidden' immigrants was much greater. In February 1990 another indemnity was launched for illegal immigrants to regularise their position — the famous Martelli Law. This one was more successful, with 217,000 foreign citizens taking advantage of the procedure within four months of the amnesty date (Montanari and Cortese 1993b). The greater success of this amnesty was corroborated by ISTAT (Italian National Institute of Statistics) data for 1989–90. At the end of 1989 ISTAT estimated a total foreign population of 1,144,000 (930,000 from non-EC countries), of whom only 489,500 had a *permesso di soggiorno*. One year later, on 31 December 1990, there were 780,100 permit-holders, indicating a drop in 'hidden' immigration of nearly 300,000.

The census of October 1991, which was widely expected to shed further light on the quantity and distribution of immigrants in Italy, was rather disappointing in this regard (King 1993). The preliminary results, published in March 1992, recorded only 502,000 foreigners, about half of those thought to be living in the country. The immigrants were more or less equally divided between those who were 'resident' (231,200) and those who were merely 'present' (270,570). Acquisition of full resident status implies a more formal registration (with the local municipal authorities) than the *permesso di soggiorno*. Figure 10.1 shows the regional distribution of the immigrants according to the census. In both absolute and relative terms they are concentrated in the northern half of the country. Four regions — Lombardy, Latium, Veneto and Tuscany — account for 53 per cent of the migrants. It also appears that the immigrants are more stably settled (as evidenced by the higher proportions who are 'resident' as opposed to 'present') in northern regions like

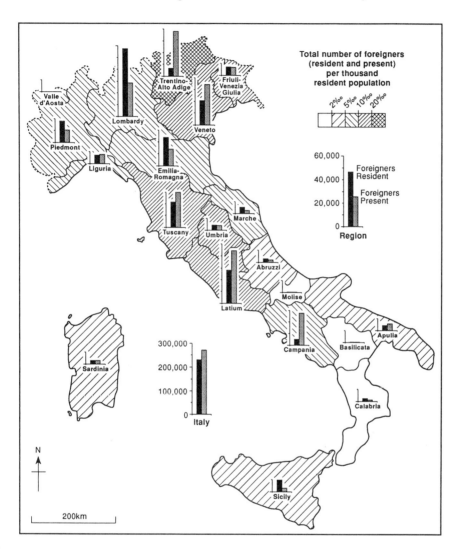

Figure 10.1   Distribution of foreigners in Italy by region, 1991 census

Piedmont, Lombardy and Emilia-Romagna; whereas in Campania, the main southern region to attract large numbers of immigrants, the foreigners are mainly 'present' rather than 'resident'. However, the likelihood is that there is a greater degree of underestimation of the numbers of immigrants in the south, where they are more strongly linked to the semi-illegal underground economy.

More detailed mapping of the immigrant population has been carried out by Montanari and Cortese (1993b) based on provincial and municipal data. Figure 10.2 shows the provincial immigration index for Third

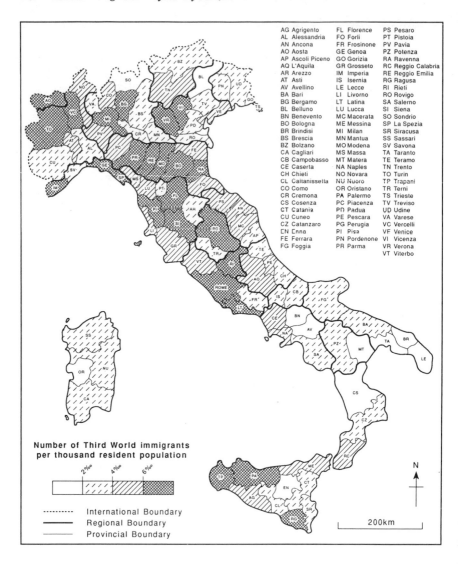

Figure 10.2   Distribution of Third World immigrants in Italy by province, 31 December 1990

Source: Montanari and Cortese 1993b, p. 288.

World migrants only, based on residence permit data for 31 December 1990. This has the effect of screening out the approximately one-quarter of foreigners who are from the advanced countries (USA, Germany, France, UK etc.) and who are probably not true labour migrants. This map shows that, although there are relatively high concentrations of immigrants around the traditional economic strong-points of northern

Table 10.2   Foreigners in Italy according to *permesso di soggiorno* data, 31 December 1991

	No.	%
USA and Western Europe		
USA	59,669	7.0
Germany	39,340	4.6
Great Britain	27,605	3.2
France	24,789	2.9
Switzerland	18,057	2.1
Greece	17,246	2.0
Spain	14,366	1.7
Eastern Europe		
Yugoslavia	33,663	3.9
Albania	26,191	3.0
Poland	18,860	2.2
Rumania	13,407	1.6
Latin America		
Brazil	17,246	2.0
Argentina	16,267	1.9
Africa		
Morocco	88,665	10.3
Tunisia	46,276	5.4
Senegal	27,036	3.1
Egypt	22,373	2.6
Ghana	12,782	1.5
Ethiopia	12,548	1.4
Somalia	11,842	1.4
Asia		
Philippines	40,611	4.7
China	20,597	2.4
Sri Lanka	14,473	1.7
Iran	12,605	1.5
India	12,064	1.4
Total (including countries not listed above)	859,571	100.0

Source: Ministry of the Interior data published in *Servizio Migranti 1992/3*, Rome.

Italy (Turin, Milan, Genoa), there is a much more extensive belt of high index values following the axis from Verona and Vicenza in the Veneto down through Emilia (provinces of Parma, Reggio, Modena, Bologna and Ravenna) and thence via Florence, Pisa and Perugia to Rome. This is the main axis of small and medium industry which has been the backbone of Italian economic dynamism since the 1970s: a model based not only on small-scale enterprise but also, and above all, on flexible work practices into which immigrants have clearly been recruited in large numbers. The importance of western Sicily is also much more clearly evident on Figure 10.2 than Figure 10.1. The Tunisian fishing community at Mazara del Vallo and the importance of North African labour in the vineyards of Trapani and Marsala are the key elements here.

The residence permit data can be used to shed further light on the geographical character of the migrant communities. Table 10.2 shows the most recent figures, for 31 December 1991, by country of origin. Only countries with more than 10,000 presences are included on this table. This leaves out many quite sizeable and distinct communities, including some which are significant because of the small size of the sending country (Cape Verde 5,230, Mauritius 6,008, Dominican Republic 5,416), as well as much larger countries (Algeria 4,373, Nigeria 6,578, Pakistan 7,070, Bangladesh 5,237, Colombia 6,359, Peru 6,358). Although the Moroccans and Tunisians are the most numerous groups, the impressive feature of Table 10.2 is the wide spread of origins, including many countries (Ethiopia, Senegal, the Philippines) which have no real history of mass migration to Europe.

The various communities mentioned in Table 10.2 and in the previous paragraph have been formed over somewhat differing periods of time. Leaving aside long-established, high-status communities such as those from the United States or France, the earliest to arrive (late 1960s) were, as noted before, the Yugoslavs in the north and the Tunisians and Moroccans in Sicily. A second wave, starting in the 1970s, was made up largely of female migrants from the Cape Verde Islands, Ethiopia (Eritrea) and the Philippines who found jobs as domestic cleaners and maids. The 1980s witnessed a sharp increase in the number of immigrants from sub-Saharan Africa (Senegal, Ghana, Nigeria) and from Southern Asia (India, Pakistan, Sri Lanka) and China. The Bangladeshis are amongst the most recent arrivals, drawn in partly by the amnesty of 1990.

The *permesso di soggiorno* data also show the overwhelmingly urban location of the immigrants, 45 per cent of whom live in six major cities — Rome (30 per cent), Milan (9 per cent) and Turin, Genoa, Florence and Palermo (1–2 per cent each). Sizeable communities (of around 1,000–7,000) are found in 20 other Italian towns and cities (from north to south Bolzano, Trieste, Venice, Padua, Verona, Brescia, Varese, Parma, Reggio Emilia, Modena, Bologna, Ravenna, Rimini, Ancona, Perugia, Naples, Bari, Messina, Mazara del Vallo and Cagliari), As befits a country still at the relatively early stages of mass immigration, most of the migrants are young adults in the first third or half of their working lives; there are few children or old people. Striking differences are observable in the gender balance between nationalities: 87.5 per cent of Cape Verdians and 69.7 per cent of Filipinos are females, whereas 90.6 per cent of Moroccans, 89.0 per cent of Tunisians and 96.9 per cent of Senegalese are males. These differences are related to occupational and cultural factors. Immigrants from Cape Verde and the Philippines work in domestic service, often living with their employers' families. Thus their safety is (in most cases) guaranteed, and their migration is also often arranged and monitored by Catholic organisations. The North Africans and the Senegalese work mainly in traditionally male tasks such as fishing and street-trading and come from Moslem societies where the independent emigration of females is virtually banned.

In order to categorise the various *types* of migration with regard to length of stay, occupation, migrant behaviour, etc., a more qualitative approach is necessary. *Frontier* migrants are limited to the Slovenes and Croats who come over the border into Trieste and adjacent areas of north-east Italy to work in domestic service (females) or as agricultural, industrial or construction workers (males). Many are daily commuters who drive across or are ferried over the border in fleets of buses in the early morning. *Seasonal* migrants come mainly from North Africa and are found predominantly in southern Italy in those areas where specialised agriculture (as distinct from residual peasant farming) creates high seasonal demands for labour. Typical areas are western and south-eastern Sicily (vines), Apulia (vines and other specialised tree crops), and the Neapolitan Plains (tomatoes, tobacco and market gardening). These workers are often able to integrate seasonal harvest labour in Italy with other agricultural work back home.

Temporary migrants represent a more diverse and complicated set of people and circumstances. The two unifying factors are the desire to accumulate capital as fast as possible, and the strong link to home. The black African street-sellers or '*vu cumprà*' ('you-buys' — a mocking reference to their pidgin Italian) are a good example of this type of migrant. Driven to migrate to Italy by poverty and their absolute or virtual lack of employment at home, they become adept at hawking (bags, belts, sunglasses, fake Lacoste tee-shirts, etc.), using networks of friends and contacts, and creating a livelihood for themselves out of virtually nothing. With their Islamic background and their strong cultural identity as black Africans, their desire (or possibility) for social integration in Italy is minimal. Female migrants who come from the Philippines as domestics are also temporary migrants, at least at the outset. These migrants are strongly linked to family networks at home (indeed many may be married, but leave their husbands and children behind — for their husbands might be migrant workers in the Gulf) and, once again, the object is to save and remit as much cash as possible to these home-based families. However, there are certain influences at work which tend to prolong their stay in Italy. First is the relative security of their employment, mainly in family homes. Second, they clearly achieve a greater degree of contact with Italian society: although there remains the barrier of ethnicity and the employer–employee relationship (which some commentators have likened to one of virtual slavery), in other respects they get uniquely intimate insights into Italian life. Therefore, in some cases, and tempted by the high standard of living in Italy in comparison to the economic chaos of the Philippines in recent years, these female migrants decide to try to unite their families in Italy, in the hope that their husbands (who, meantime, may have lost their jobs in the Gulf) may find work, perhaps in the catering sector.

Finally there is the *semi-permanent* migration of groups who have achieved a more solid position in the Italian economy, perhaps as traders or other kinds of entrepreneurs. The best example of these are the Chinese *restaurateurs* in Rome who form a remarkably successful, cohesive and well-established community. In the case of the Iranians who came initially as refugees and students and who are now mainly involved in trading Persian carpets, there is an increasing tendency to marry Italians – a clear sign of permanent settlement. These early trends towards family reunification or family formation in Italy will eventually lead to more balanced age and sex structures, which for most groups remain for the time being highly assymetric. Such trends will also cause the immigrant stock to increase, even if the supply of primary labour migrants is reduced by policies of discouragement or exclusion.

Greece

Compared to Italy, information on immigration to Greece is extremely scanty. The phenomenon can be dated to the early 1970s, possibly earlier. Nikolinakos (1973) was one of the first to draw attention to the presence of African immigrants in Greece, attracted there by a combination of excessive Greek emigration and booming industrial, construction, tourism and marine sectors. These contradictory trends of Greek capitalist development — i.e. continuing emigration together with rapid, employment-creating growth leading to labour shortages in certain key sectors of the economy — have led to opportunities for Africans as replacement migrants. Nikolinakos described the district of Chaidari as the Harlem of Athens, a run-down area already inhabited 20 years ago by thousands of Africans from the Sudan, Ethiopia, Egypt, Nigeria, etc. The immigrants worked in the Piraeus shipyards, in hotels and as private servants to the city's bourgeoisie.

The statistical record on foreign immigration into Greece is very weak — hardly surprising considering that departures and entries of *Greek* migrants have not been recorded in official statistics since 1977. Some indications are given by SOPEMI. The 1980 Report stated curtly (p. 109) 'It is thought that there are large numbers of foreigners working in Greece without permits'; by the 1987 Report (p. 37) the number of illegal workers was estimated at 50,000–60,000. The 1988 Report (p. 31) issued more concrete estimates of foreign workers in Greece: 28,300 regular foreign workers in possession of work permits; 76,400 illegal foreign workers; and 12,400 political refugees, of whom 9,300 were awaiting visas to emigrate onwards to Canada, the United States or Australia. Meanwhile the 1981 census recorded 180,595 persons with foreign citizenship (but amongst these were 33,708 foreign citizens from Albania and Turkey of Greek ethnic origin, leaving 146,887 'true' foreigners). Data on residence permit-holders issued by the Ministry of Public Order give a figure of 61,357 for the stock of foreign population in 1988, compared to only 2,126 in 1973. The increase to 1988 is partly explained by Greece's entry to the European Community in 1981, which led to a large number of persons moving to Greece who were the staff of foreign and multinational firms.

The 1989 SOPEMI Report (p. 41) notes four factors which make the enumeration of foreign residents and workers in Greece a difficult task: (i) the free circulation of workers within the EC10, i.e. including Greece, after 1988 (a facility to be extended to Spain and Portugal in 1993); (ii) the already acknowledged existence of a large number of undocumented workers; (iii) the key importance for the Greek economy of the tourist and shipping industries, which are obvious channels by which illegal migrants enter Greece; and (iv) the fact that returning Greek emigrants with dual nationality often register as foreigners upon their return to their mother country. The whole problem is exacerbated by the fact that Greece, even less than Italy, has not yet adapted to its new status as an immigration country. Greece is a relative newcomer to the club of receiving countries and cannot be put on the same footing as Italy and Spain which have larger-scale economies and a greater infrastructural capacity for absorbing foreign workers.

The real problem of numbers surrounds the presence of illegal workers in Greece, whose very clandestine status makes them impossible to estimate with any degree of confidence. In fact, the estimates vary enormously. For instance, whilst the Ministry of Public Order estimated 'at least 105,000' in 1990, the Ministry of Labour figure for the same year was only 30,000 undocumented foreign workers (see SOPEMI Report 1990, p. 51). However, more recent newspaper reports have given figures of 300,000 and even 400,000 for the population of illegal foreign workers. These figures may well be 'over the top'. In a Report to the Athens office of the United Nations High Commission for Refugees (UNHCR), Mestheneos (1989) estimates that anything up to 40,000 foreign workers may be employed in the Greek shipping industry and gives the following numbers for individual nationalities in Greece: 30,000 from Poland, 20,000 from Egypt, 10,000–12,000 from the Philippines and 5,000–6,000 from Pakistan. This report also claims that there are about 150,000 foreign spouses of Greek citizens living in Greece who do not qualify for Greek nationality (many of these would be American or European). By contrast, the Greek government estimates that as many as 150,000 Albanians crossed the border in search of work during 1991, with some 71,000 being deported (Black 1992, p. 4). Another important immigrant group, of greater legal status, are the Pontian Greeks from the ex-Soviet Union. Being of Greek ethnic origin, they qualify for Greek citizenship. By 1989, 10,000 had arrived for resettlement in Greece, and the number is anticipated to be around 12,000–15,000 per year for the early 1990s. Perhaps 40,000–50,000 have arrived to date (SOPEMI Report 1990, pp. 52–3).

Political refugees are the final element in the rapid growth of foreign arrivals in Greece in recent years, although unlike many other European refugee-receiving countries, their numbers coming to Greece have been decreasing (7,930 in 1988, 6,474 in 1989, 4,200 in 1990, 3,808 in 1991). Ethiopia, Iraq, Iran, Poland and Albania have been the main source countries. Most of the Albanian arrivals are ethnic Greeks. According to the Greek Liaison Mission of the International Organisation for Migration, the refugee 'caseload' stood at 13,681 on 31 August 1990. The most significant element of Greece's refugee policy is that the country is designed not as a final asylum destination but mainly as a temporary asylum for refugees in transit, principally to the United States, Canada and Australia (Black 1992).

The quantitative importance of clandestine workers in Greece's foreign worker population means that there are virtually no data on their employment or geographical distribution. The importance of the underground economy and the seasonal demands and short-term informal contracts of the tourist and shipping industries mean that most illegal workers are found in marginal occupations. The geographical configuration of Greece — many islands, importance of marine activities, etc. — allow a division of foreign workers, both documented and undocumented, into two principal categories of 'land' and 'sea' workers. Land workers are concentrated in farming (harvest workers, agricultural labourers), manufacturing, building, hotel work, etc; sea workers in shipping, fishing, trading, etc. Official employment data are only available for documented (work permit-holding) foreign workers whose number stood at 23,919 on 31 March 1990. Of these, 15,888 were males and 8,031 females; 13,073 originated from Europe (9,095 from EC countries), 5,250 from Asia, 2,058 from Africa, and 2,052 from the Americas. However, it must be pointed out that 3,614 of these registered foreign workers are Greek descendants with foreign citizenship who came particularly from Albania, Turkey and Cyprus. Of the total documented foreign workforce, 33.5 per cent work in industry and 31.2 per cent in trade, hotels and restaurants. Work permits are renewed for up to five years depending mainly on the conditions of the Greek labour market; recently rising unemployment has made their renewal less automatic (SOPEMI Report 1990, p. 51).

Spain

Three main sources of data exist on foreign immigrants in Spain. Firstly, there is the Spanish census, but the most recent published material (1981) is sadly out of date. Secondly, there are the annual statistics provided by the Ministry of the Interior giving the number of people in possession of residence and temporary stay permits. Finally, there are the statistics provided by the Ministry of Labour on the number of permits available for issue per annum (Muñoz-Pérez and Izquierdo 1989). Although of little use in retrospective studies, 1991 saw the setting up of the Directorate General for Migration within the Ministry of Labour and Social Services which may in the future be a source of data relating to immigration.

The number of legal foreign residents in Spain increased from 160,000 in 1970 to 406,374 in 1989, the latter figure constituting just over 1 per cent of the total Spanish population. If recent rates of increase (14.2 per cent in 1987 and 8.6 per cent in 1988) continue irrespective of tighter legislation, then the 'new' migrant population could well become an important segment of the Spanish labour force and Spanish society within the next decade. Furthermore, as it is estimated that the number of legal foreign residents only contributes about 69 per cent of the total quantity of immigrants (Gonzálvez-Pérez 1990, p. 18), Spain is heading towards being a country of immigration a lot faster than officially anticipated. Despite steady increases in the total number of legal residents in Spain, the number of work permits handed out has remained fairly constant at around 50,000 per annum over the period 1980–90. Most work permits are issued to the retailing, hotel and building trades (SOPEMI Report 1990, p. 65).

Table 10.3 Legal foreign residents in Spain, 1987 and 1989

Country of origin	1987	1989	% change
UK	55,318	73,535	+ 33.0
Germany	39,066	44,220	+ 13.2
Portugal	31,012	32,936	+ 6.2
France	23,599	27,737	+ 17.5
USA	15,550	18,192	+ 17.0
Argentina	13,500	16,165	+ 19.7
Morocco	11,152	14,471	+ 30.0
Philippines	8,262	6,379	− 22.8
Venezuela	7,850	9,020	+ 15.0
Total (including countries not listed above)	334,935	398,147	+ 18.5

Source: Bel Adell 1989, p. 25; SOPEMI Report 1990, p. 63.

The origins of those immigrants who are legalised are shown in detail in Table 10.3 for both 1987 and 1989. Unlike Portugal, two-thirds of the foreigners in Spain are nationals of European states, 90 per cent of them from EC countries, with the United Kingdom, Germany, Portugal and France being most strongly represented. However, this conceals the growing importance of the African and Asian sectors of the immigrant community. From 1980 to 1988 the African share increased from 2.4 per cent to 5.6 per cent of the total legal foreign population (an absolute change from 4,900 residents in 1980 to 20,500 in 1988), whilst the Asian share increased from 6.6 per cent to 8 per cent (from 13,240 to 28,750 residents). This indicates a new wave of migrants originating in the Third World who before the 1980s were relatively unimportant compared with Latin Americans and Europeans. The African and Asian contingents are respectively dominated by two countries — Morocco and the Philippines — whilst the Latin Americans (65,000 in 1987) consist of a wide range of nationalities.

The lure of Spain as an immigration country is multi-faceted. For the North Europeans (especially the British), Spain has long been a favourite destination for holiday-makers appreciating the warm Mediterranean climate, the sandy beaches and the lower cost of living. Over the past two decades this has led many such visitors to consider permanent residence in Spain, either at the onset of retirement or to participate in the service sector that supports the tourist industry itself. This has resulted both in the implantation of British enclaves in Spain and in the 'Costa del Sol' becoming assimilated into British culture.[6]

For the Portuguese, Spain has provided a nearby source of better-paid employment. Given the similarity in language and culture between the two countries and the relative ease with which cross-border travel can be made between two EC states, Spain offers attractive opportunities for the generally less well-off Portuguese to engage in seasonal work. The Moroccans also find themselves close to Spain geographically and have found the country useful as a source of seasonal work. There have been two waves of Moroccan migration to Spain, one prior to 1986 and one that has occurred more recently. The latter was due in part to a switch from France to Spain as a destination when the French authorities began to demand visas from Maghreb visitors in the late 1980s; Spain only imposed such a sanction in 1991. An interesting aspect of this second phase is the increase in the number of female Moroccan migrants. Migrants from the Maghreb have traditionally been males heading for jobs in the service sector or construction industry, but now women are starting to migrate without the traditional accompaniment of men. This implies that the women who have recently arrived in Spain have attained a reasonable level of education and broken free of the traditional submissiveness of Moslem women. It also indicates a response to the market for domestic labour in Spain which naturally favours women (Colectivo Ioé 1991).

The Filipinos have come to be regarded, along with other Asians in Spain, as 'new' migrants, since they hardly featured at all before the 1980s except as students. The presence of an increasing number of Third World migrants in Spain can be seen as a response partly to the political instability associated with South America, Equatorial Guinea and certain Asian countries, and partly to the general situation of dependency and poverty in the Third World. The Filipino inflow can be directly linked to the crisis of the Marcos regime. The choice of Spain in particular is associated with the comparatively looser immigration controls as compared with northern Europe, and Spain along with Portugal is seen as a stepping-stone to more developed areas such as Australia, Canada or the United States to which such migrants do not have direct access. Most Third World migrants enter clandestinely as tourists who never return. Methods have included entry via Portugal (either clandestinely or with Portuguese visas), via the Balaerics as tourists or as part of an organised group coming from countries in central Europe (Colectivo Ioé 1991).

The distribution of foreign migrants has tended to be determined by their origins and intentions, with certain groups being concentrated in specific areas. In broad terms migrants tend to be found in the major cities and the major tourist areas. Madrid plays host to the largest foreign community with 75,056 official foreign residents in 1989. Other provinces with large urban centres such as Catalonia and Valencia also have large foreign communities — 63,522 and 46,201 legal residents respectively. The major tourist areas also figure highly with Andalusia accounting for 67,410 residents, the Canaries 39,133, and the Balearics 31,225 (Bel Adell 1989).

Most migrant groups are represented in Madrid and Barcelona, but this is especially so with Latin Americans and Filipinos. Some 30 per cent of the Latin American immigrant population are to be found in Madrid, with a further 22 per cent in Barcelona (Gonzálvez-Pérez 1990). Similarly, 52 per cent of Filipinos live in the Madrid region and 18 per cent in Barcelona. This implies attraction to service sector employment found within major urban centres. The English, French and Moroccans tend to congregate around the coastal areas such as Alicante and Malaga and the islands as well as Madrid, also implying service sector employment, but geared more towards tourism. The Portuguese are also found in the major cities, but in addition there is a significant concentration within areas such as Pontevedra and Orense in Galicia. In 1987 the total number of foreign residents in Galicia totalled 12,362 (Bell Adell 1989), the majority of whom were Portuguese. As Galicia borders the poorer areas of the Minho and Tras os Montes in Portugal, and also speaks a dialect of Spanish very similar to that found in northern Portugal, the region is an easily accessible destination for Portuguese immigrants.

As is the case with most southern Mediterranean immigrants to northern Europe, the majority of migrants coming to Spain tend to fill jobs in the service sector, although, given the diversity of nationals to be found in Spain, this is by no means restricted to the most poorly paid or socially undesirable jobs. For the most part, however, immigrant employment includes hotel work, catering, retailing and domestic service, with those not in the service sector working in building and construction (SOPEMI Report 1988, p. 37). Third World migrants and the Portuguese are especially prevalent in the tertiary sector, which in 1988 employed 80 per cent of all foreign workers including more than 90 per cent of all Asians and 56 per cent of all Africans. Even more striking was the position of Filipino women, 70 per cent of whom enter domestic service upon arrival in Spain (Weinert 1991). An in-depth study of the domestic sector of the labour force undertaken by Colectivo Ioé in Madrid in 1991 emphasised this situation. They found the majority of the workers in domestic service to be young females originating mainly from the Philippines, Portugal, Morocco and Dominica. Other sectors in which migrants have found employment include the construction industry, farming and mining. In 1988, 20 per cent of legal Portuguese workers were engaged in farming and a further 20 per cent in building and construction. Although the construction industry was the second most important employer after services for most Africans, notable exceptions included the 67 per cent of Gambians in agriculture and 38 per cent of Cape Verdeans in mining (SOPEMI Report 1989, p. 50). The prevalence of Third World migrants in such low-grade employment can be attributed in part to their lack of fluency in Spanish, but also to their poor educational background. Exceptions to this rule include Latin Americans and East Europeans. Most of the East European women who arrive in Spain seeking domestic work are highly qualified; 40 per cent of those working in the Madrid area have attended university (Colectivo Ioé 1991). Many well-educated Latin Americans fleeing political persecution have taken up jobs in professions such as teaching, medicine and entertainment. In addition, as Spain is a retirement destination, a large number of Spain's foreign residents do not work (SOPEMI Report 1989, p. 49).

So far the discussion has centred around the legalised component of Spain's foreign residents and workers. It is estimated that a large number of those living and working in Spain do so illegally having gained access to the country through clandestine means or having become 'irregular' after arrival. This may come about through a variety of ways. For example, they may have joined family members already present and not bothered to apply for permits, they may not have renewed expired permits, they may be working in unauthorised sectors of the economy, or they may continue to work and reside in Spain after finishing authorised studies. Estimates of the numbers of 'irregular' or illegal immigrants naturally vary: 250,000 for 1988 (Gonzálvez-Pérez 1990) seems a plausible figure, if perhaps a little on the high side, whilst Colectivo Ioé (1991) suggest that 60 per cent of Third World migrants in Spain are 'illegals'.

In an effort to try and reduce this large number of illegals Spain has launched two regularisation programmes. The first programme was undertaken in July 1985. The campaign was heavily advertised amongst employers and included a general amnesty with no penalty for illegal aliens. Applicants were judged on the amount of time they had spent in Spain and the nature of their relationship with Spanish nationals. Anyone who could prove residency and employment in Spain as of 24 July 1985 could apply. The programme resulted in the legalisation of 58,204 illegal migrants, fewer than anticipated. Moroccans — 20 per cent of the total — were the single largest group to regularise. Many migrants found it difficult to obtain proof of employment once employers realised that this was to form part of a petition for regularisation. This was especially true of Moroccans, many of whom regularised their situation by applying for temporary residence permits only which did not require proof of employment. It became apparent that some employers preferred irregular migrants. Should these apply for regularisation, employers no longer wished to employ them and looked for new irregulars instead (SOPEMI Report 1989, p. 76).

The second regularisation campaign was launched in 1991 and ran from June to December. A total of 133,000 applications were received. Figures based on the analysis of the first 100,000 successful applications indicate that 60 per cent of permits were granted for the service sector, 67 per cent to males, 40 per cent to Moroccans, 7 per cent to Argentines, and 2–5 per cent each to Peruvians, Dominicans, Poles, Algerians and Filipinos (SOPEMI Report 1992, p. 76). This serves to assert the Moroccans as the largest Third World migrant group in Spain, and also to confirm the suspicion that they were by far the largest illegal group. As anticipated, the majority of applications originated in the large urban centres and major tourist areas with 40,683 from Catalonia, 39,600 from Madrid, 14,979 from Andalusia and 10,616 from Valencia. Despite a larger response rate than the first campaign, it is recognised that regularisation cannot be seen as the only tool in reducing the number of illegal migrants once and for all. Other measures such as tighter controls at entry points and sanctions against offending employers are also required if the number of illegal migrants is to be controlled.

In addition to applications for regularisation, there has also been an increased number of applications for political asylum and refugee status. During the mid-1980s there were 2,000–2,500 requests for asylum per year on average; by 1990 the number of asylum-seekers had increased to 8,600 of whom 40 per cent were Poles (SOPEMI Reports for 1989, p. 3; 1992, p. 76). Although Spain (along with Portugal) has one of the lowest number of asylum petitions in Europe, it is regarded as having less rigid controls than north European and OECD countries. Spain's looser controls and lengthy application procedures mean that the applicants can reside within the state whilst waiting for the outcome of the petition, thus allowing them to work and in many cases strengthening their case for remaining.

Portugal

There are very few statistics on immigration (legal or otherwise) to Portugal (SOPEMI Report 1990, p. 24). What data do exist on foreign residents are in the form of estimates from the Aliens Department at the Ministry of the Interior and foreign embassy estimates for their own nationals. Additional information on refugees and applications for political asylum is available through the Foreigners and Frontiers Department at the Ministry of the Interior, the Advisory Committee for Refugees and the UN High Commission for Refugees.

During the mid-1970s Portugal had its first experience of mass immigration in the form of returning colonists from Angola and Mozambique who were fleeing civil war and political turmoil (Lewis and Williams 1985). The majority of these *retornados* were first-, second- or third-generation Portuguese and as such did not really constitute foreign immigrants. Furthermore, the enforced return of colonists from Africa was an isolated phenomenon. Since that time, although Portugal can by no means be considered solely as an immigration country, the number of immigrants has shown a consistently upward trend, with a large proportion from the former colonies. In 1980 the number of official foreign nationals resident in Portugal was put at 56,000 by the Ministry of the Interior with half of them originating from the former colonies. By 1985 this figure had risen to 79,594 and in 1990 it was 107,767, although the percentage of Portuguese-speaking Africans had decreased to just over 40 per cent (SOPEMI Report 1992, p. 75). However, despite sharing a common geographical zone of origin with the *retornado* migrants of the 1970s, these African migrants of the 1980s and 1990s constitute a new trend no longer made up of ex-colonists, but rather of young males seeing Portugal as a place to work and perhaps as a stepping-stone to the more industrialised countries of Northern Europe.

The largest group of foreign residents originates from the Cape Verde Islands (28 per cent). The predominance of the Cape Verdeans is in part explained by the fact that, along with Brazilians, Spaniards and British, they generally do not require work permits, and also that in the past (along with other former colonial countries) they have had a right to Portuguese citizenship, although they were not necessarily guaranteed it. The Cape Verdean migrants mostly undertake jobs at the lower end of the socio-economic ladder such as construction, public works and domestic work. In many respects they have a similar profile to the first wave of Portuguese migrants to northern Europe and it has been suggested that they are filling in the gap left in the labour market by these emigrants (Cavaco 1993). As most service sector jobs tend to be found in the urban areas along the coastal regions, the distribution of the African migrants tends to favour the *Litorral*, especially coastal Algarve and the large cities of Lisbon, Oporto and Setúbal.

Although Africans account for almost half of the foreign residents,

Europe and the Americas share the other half almost equally between them (28.6 per cent and 24.5 per cent respectively in 1989). The important European groups are the British (7.7 per cent), the Spaniards (7.2 per cent), the Germans (4.4 per cent) and the French (3 per cent), whilst the Brazilians dominate as the most important group from the Americas due to obvious linkages of culture, social ties and language (SOPEMI Report 1990, p. 62).

The English have historically had a reasonably large community in Portugal, primarily associated with the Port wine trade in Oporto and with commerce in Lisbon. However, in the past decade this has been augmented by a growing British community in the Algarve. Like the Spanish Costa del Sol, this has taken the form of permanent residents who are retired, as well as a large number of workers servicing and supporting the Anglicisation of tourism in the Algarve. There is also a growing artisan and 'Bohemian' European community in the Algarve interior.

As with the other countries dealt with in this chapter, statistics dealing with legal residents can provide only an indication of the number of immigrants Portugal is receiving and retaining. There is no current estimate of the number of illegally resident immigrants in Portugal, but it would be safe to assume that the true number of foreign residents considerably exceeds that implied by the officially available statistics. Furthermore, figures relating to the number of foreign residents give no indication as to the approved length of stay and therefore the potential seasonality of the foreign population. For example, three types of residence permit exist: unlimited, five-year validity and one-year validity.

Another issue is the number of foreign residents that are actually part of the labour force. As residence permits are only granted on the production of a contract of employment, it would seem reasonable to assume that the legal foreign labour force in possession of work permits are a subset of those in possession of residence permits. An alternative source of data is the number of work permits issued each year. However, these are difficult to obtain and do not include several groups who are part of the labour market. For example, Brazilians, Spaniards, Cape Verdeans, Guineans and Britons applying for residence permits often have the work permit condition waived. Seasonal tourist workers often slip through the net and if they are EC nationals different rules apply again. These and other problems mean that the Portuguese authorities have a weak statistical 'hold' over the immigrant population.

Conclusion

The countries of southern Europe have come late to the group of European labour-importing countries. As late arrivals they are tending to imitate the migration needs of other post-industrial European countries of today rather than replicating those countries' immigration experiences of the 1950s and 1960s, when the southern European countries themselves were the main suppliers of migrant workers. The economies of Italy and Spain (less so Greece and Portugal) are now high-tech and post-industrial; for this they require broadly the same high-level skills as their northern neighbours. But the comparison stops there. Southern Europe has a thriving underground economy, chiefly in fragmented petty services, and this area is rife with marginalised immigrant labour.

The previous four sections on the countries of southern Europe have described, within the limitations of the available data, a diversity of flows from lands which are mostly rather distant culturally if not physically. The flows have changed through time and generally diversified, with an increasing proportion of immigrants originating from Africa and Asia. Thus, in each of the southern European destination countries, the national compositions of the immigrant population have been constantly changing, and will probably continue to change as a proportion of the regularised and asylum-seeking migrants move to other countries of the European Community, perhaps to be replaced by new inflows from elsewhere.

The previous pages have also shown that the occupational structure of Third World immigrants in southern Europe is very complex, varying from country to country and from region to region within each country. This diversity of origins and of employment niches makes it virtually impossible to generalise from the experience of one ethnic group to another. The general context, however, is relevant to all situations: the enlargement of the secondary labour market, the segmentation and casualisation of labour demand, the increasing role of the informal and underground economies, minimal social integration, little coherent policy on the part of the receiving countries towards immigration and the already present immigrants, and the decreasing accuracy of official employment and unemployment figures. Some of the most difficult problems are being encountered in the housing sector. Most migrants in the four countries live in conditions of overcrowding and degradation: in shanty-towns both on the urban periphery and in pockets near the city centre (in the case of Lisbon); in inner-city tenements and slums where people may live at a density of five or even ten people to a room; in disused factories such as the Pantanella in Rome or the Cascina Rossa in Milan; and in rural barns and barracks (in the case of agricultural workers).

It is, of course, impossible to predict how many hundreds of thousands (or millions) of immigrants will be coming to seek work in the countries of southern Europe over the next few years. The pressure for migration is obviously there and, whatever barriers are put in the way, they will probably only be partially effective in stemming the flow, since desperate migrants will increasingly resort to illegal means of entry. Shorter and more temporary periods of migration may become more common, especially if big transport infrastructures like the new bridges near Istanbul (already completed) and the projected bridges between Sicily and Calabria and near Gibraltar are realised. These links will clearly facilitate movement between Europe on the one hand and Asia and Africa on the other (Montanari and Cortese 1993a). By contrast, the opening up of Eastern Europe to emigration over the past three years may retard flows from the South because of the West's preference for immigrants who are racially and culturally similar and more highly qualified (Grečić 1991). Already there are considerable numbers of Poles working in northern Italy.

The twin, and related, problems of illegal immigration and asylum-seeking pose tough challenges for policy-makers in the four countries and in the wider Community. Whilst regularisation programmes can help, they can, in one sense, be counterproductive since as soon as they are advertised they may attract sudden inflows of migrants looking for a quick legal foothold in Europe. The Asian community in Italy was greatly boosted by this mechanism in the late 1980s and early 1990s. An unknown but probably considerable proportion of these recent arrivals intend ultimately to resettle elsewhere in Europe, so their stay in southern Europe may prove to be only temporary. Those who do not manage to regularise their situation become a 'shadow' population, about whom little quantitative information is known.

There is little doubt that immigration has become a highly charged political issue in southern Europe and the wider Community in the last few years. According to Montanari and Cortese (1993a) migration has replaced the Cold War as the main source of tension dividing the West from the East and the South. As other chapters in this book have stressed, new thinking is needed about the role of immigration and asylum policy in the Europe of the Single Market, and about specific forms of control over entry, exit and internal mobility. Some elements of a 'ring-fence' or 'fortress Europe' have taken root, whilst the Schengen agreement, signed by the original Six, is creating a new set of guidelines for internal, cross-border movement. The freedom of movement of non-Europeans remains a sticking point, however. An Appendix to the Single Act states: 'Nothing in these provisions shall affect the right of Member States to take measures as they consider necessary for controlling immigration from third countries, and to combat terrorism, crime, the traffic of drugs and illicit trading in works of art and antiques.' Quite apart from the prejudiced juxtaposition of immigrants with crime, terrorism and drugs, this declaration appears to give any member state the freedom to pass national laws on immigration irrespective of whether this new legislation conflicts with Community law or not (Matheson 1991, p. 58). New, and generally tougher, visa regimes have been introduced and several countries have instituted carrier liability legislation. However, since studies have shown that a high proportion of illegal immigrants are 'overstayers', a system of control based on stricter visa regimes may not be appropriate (Salt 1992, pp. 44, 62).

The difficulties faced by policy-makers in grappling with new forms of migration have a parallel in the need for new forms of conceptual understanding about present-day migration into Europe through the southern gateways. The historicisation of migration theory — in which more attention is paid to the changing realities of time and space which surround individual migration waves — implies that concepts and emphases must be modified in the light of changing social realities (Zolberg 1989). The waves of migration entering southern Europe now and in the recent past do, it is true, have some historical parallels, but the search for historical analogy should not obscure the essentially new and specific context of the model of emigration into southern Europe: to repeat, and to conclude, these immigrants are post-industrial (although their backgrounds may be pre-industrial), they come mainly from Third World countries, are propelled more by push forces than attracted by pulls, and they are taking on new roles in an increasingly segmented local labour market.

Notes

1. SOPEMI, the OECD's continuous reporting system on migration, has issued valuable annual reports since 1973. These reports will be referred to frequently in the course of this chapter. Until 1992 these reports were produced in mimeographed form and only circulated informally or upon request. The 1992 Report is the first one to be properly published and sold through OECD outlets.
2. However, the Greek experience, like the Italian experience of the 1960s (when more Italians migrated to non-EC Switzerland than to France or Germany), suggests that there will be no major upturn in emigration from Spain and Portugal after the end of their transition period on 1 January 1993, when full freedom of movement provisions will come into force.
3. A distinction should perhaps be drawn between migrants who enter illegally — e.g. by clandestinely crossing a land border at night or by landing by boat on a deserted piece of shoreline (such immigrants may possess no papers) — and those who arrive legally with passports and visas but who fail to return at the end of their officially permitted stay.
4. For the time being this threat seems more apparent than real for there are extremely high youth unemployment rates in southern Europe. In 1988 the proportion of under 25 year olds out of work was 33.8 per cent in Spain, 32.1 per cent in Italy and 26.1 per cent in Greece. In Portugal unemployment rates are much lower.
5. Here we will simply cite a few recent books on the subject: Barsotti (1988), Calvanese and Pugliese (1991), CENSIS (1991), Cocchi (1990), Dell'Atti (1990), Maccheroni and Mauri (1989), Macioti and Pugliese (1990), Moretti and Cortese (1990), Natale (1988), Sergi and Carchedi (1991).
6. Even a new British TV soap opera (which would normally be expected to centre around established 'regionalised' communities in Britain) has used the Costa del Sol as a base.

References

Ascoli, U., 1986, 'Migration of workers and the labour market: is Italy becoming a country of immigration?' in Rogers, R. (ed.), *Guests come to stay*, Westview, Boulder, CO, 185–206.

Barsotti, O. (ed.), 1988, *La presenza straniera in Italia: il caso della Toscana*, Angeli, Milan.

Bel Adell, C., 1989, 'Extranjeros en España', *Papeles de Geografía*, 15: 21–32.

Black, R., 1992, *Livelihood and vulnerability of foreign refugees in Greece*, King's College, London, Department of Geography, Occasional Paper 33.

Calvanese, F. and Pugliese, E., (eds), 1991, *La presenza straniera in Italia: il caso della Campania*, Angeli, Milan.

Cavaco, C., 1993, 'A place in the sun: return migration and rural change in Portugal', in King, R. (ed.), *Mass migrations in Europe: the legacy and the future*, Belhaven, London, 174–92.

CENSIS, 1991, *Immigrazione e società italiana*, Editalia/CNEL, Rome.

Cocchi, G. (ed.), 1990, *Stranieri in Italia*, Istituto Cattaneo, Bologna.

Colectivo Ioé, 1991, *Foreign women in domestic service in Madrid, Spain*, ILO World Employment Programme, Working Paper 51, Geneva.

Dell'Aringa, C. and Neri, F., 1987, 'Illegal immigrants and the informal economy in Italy', *Labour*, 2(2): 107–26.

Dell'Atti, A. (ed.), 1990, *La presenza straniera in Italia: il caso della Puglia*, Angeli, Milan.

Fielding, A.J., 1993, 'Mass migration and economic restructuring', in King, R. (ed.), *Mass migrations in Europe: the legacy and the future*, Belhaven, London, 7–18.

Ghosh, B., 1991, 'Trends in world migration: the European perspective', *The Courier*, 129: 46–51.

Golini, A., Gesano, G. and Heins, F., 1991, 'South–North migration with special reference to Europe', *International Migration*, 29(2): 253–77.

Gonzálvez-Pérez, V., 1990, 'El reciente incremento de la población extranjera en España y su incìdencia laboral', *Investigaciones Geográficas*, 8: 7–36.

Grečić, V., 1991, 'East–West migration and its possible influence on South–North migration', *International Migration*, 29(2): 241–52.

Heyden, H., 1991, 'South–North migration', *International Migration*, 29(2): 281–90.

King, R.L., 1984, 'Population mobility: emigration, return migration and internal migration', in Williams, A.M. (ed.), *Southern Europe transformed*, Harper and Row, London, 143–78.

King, R.L., 1991, 'Europe's metamorphic demographic map', *Town and Country Planning*, 60(4): 111–13.

King, R.L., 1993, 'Italy reaches zero population growth', *Geography*, 78(1): 63–9.

Lewis, J.R. and Williams, A.M., 1985, 'Portugal's *retornados*: reintegration or rejection?' *Iberian Studies*, 14(1–2): 11–23.

Maccheroni, C. and Mauri, A. (eds), 1989, *Le migrazioni dell'Africa mediterranea verso l'Italia*, Giuffrè, Milan.

McDonald, J.R., 1969, 'Labor immigration in France', *Annals, Association of American Geographers*, 59(1): 116–34.

Macioti, M.I. and Pugliese, E. (eds), 1990, *Gli immigrati in Italia*, Laterza, Bari.

Matheson, J.H.E., 1991, 'The immigration issue in the Community: an ACP view', *The Courier*, 129: 56–9.

Mestheneos, E., 1989, *The protection of human rights of refugees and foreigners in Greece*, Report prepared for the Athens branch of the UNHCR, Athens.

Montanari, A. and Cortese, A., 1993a, 'South to North migration in a Mediterranean perspective', in King, R. (ed.), *Mass migrations in Europe: the legacy and the future*, Belhaven, London, 212–33.

Montanari, A. and Cortese, A., 1993b, 'Third World immigrants in Italy', in King, R. (ed.), *Mass migrations in Europe: the legacy and the future*, Belhaven, London, 275–92.

Moretti, E. and Cortese, A. (eds), 1990, *La presenza straniera in Italia: il caso delle Marche*, Angeli, Milan.

Muñoz-Pérez, F. and Izquierdo, A., 1989, 'Espagne, pays d'immigration', *Population*, 44(2): 257–84.

Natale, M., 1988, *La presenza straniera in Italia*, IRP, Rome.

Nikolinakos, M., 1973, 'The contradictions of capitalist development in Greece: labour shortages and emigration', *Studi Emigrazione*, 10(30): 222–35.

Penninx, R., 1986, 'International migration in Western Europe since 1973: developments, mechanisms and controls', *International Migration Review*, 20(4): 951–72.

Salt, J., 1976, 'International labour migration: the geographical pattern of demand', in Salt, J. and Clout, H.D. (eds), *Migration in post-war Europe: geographical essays*, Oxford University Press, London, 80–125.

Salt, J., 1992, 'Current and future international migration trends affecting Europe', in *People on the move: new migration flows in Europe*, Council of Europe Press, Strasbourg, 41–81.

Salt, J. and Clout, H.D., 1976, 'International labour migration: the sources of supply', in Salt, J. and Clout, H.D. (eds), *Migration in post-war Europe: geographical essays*, Oxford University Press, London, 126–67.

Sergi, N. and Carchedi, F. (eds), 1991, *L'immigrazione straniera in Italia: il tempo dell'integrazione*, Edizioni Lavoro, Rome.

Sponza, L., 1988, *Italian immigrants in nineteenth-century Britain: realities and images*, Leicester University Press, Leicester.

Venturini, A., 1988, 'An interpretation of Mediterranean migration', *Labour*, 2(1): 125–54.

Weinert, P., 1991, *Foreign female domestic workers: help wanted!* ILO World Employment Programme, Working Paper 50, Geneva.

Zolberg, A., 1989, 'The next waves: migration theory for a changing world', *International Migration Review*, 23(3): 403–30.

Chapter 11

Asylum migration in Europe: patterns, determinants and the role of East–West movements

Bela Hovy[1]

Introduction

During the 1980s and early 1990s, the number of asylum applicants in Europe rose significantly, from about 75,000 in 1983 to more than half a million in 1991. At the same time, the proportion of asylum-seekers granted refugee status decreased rapidly, indicating that more asylum applicants had come to Europe with motives other than 'a well-founded fear of being persecuted for reasons of race, religion, nationality, membership of a particular social group or political opinion' — the refugee definition established by the 1951 United Nations Convention relating to the Status of Refugees and its 1967 Protocol and incorporated in the asylum laws of many European countries.[2]

Increasingly, asylum-seekers in Europe have been considered as migrants who seek economic improvement rather than political refuge. Indeed, the increase in the number of asylum-seekers comes at a time when most European countries lack channels for the legal admission of migrants from economically less advanced countries seeking to improve their standard of living. As is well known, most governments in Western Europe abandoned the official recruitment of cheap foreign labour from southern Europe, North Africa and Turkey during the economic downturn of the early 1970s.

However the general ban on labour recruitment, while halting the migration of unskilled and semi-skilled labour, did not bar all forms of migration to Western Europe. Thus, the inflow of highly specialised workers, of foreigners with needed skills and of employees of multi-national companies based in the developed world became the predominant form of economically motivated migration to Europe (Salt 1993). Neither did the 'recruitment stop' affect the migration flows of Europeans between member states of the European Community (EC): the free movement of labour provision of the Treaty of Rome permits EC citizens to seek employment within the territory of the Community without the need to apply for a work permit. In addition, family reunification grew after 1973 as many 'guestworkers' decided to remain in Western Europe and were joined by their close family members (King 1993).

Although the number of economically motivated asylum-seekers is likely to have increased in recent years, it should be stressed that not all those whose refugee claims are rejected on the basis of the 1951 refugee definition are indeed economic migrants (Frelick 1992). Many of today's asylum-seekers are fleeing situations that are considered genuine grounds for refugee protection in various parts of the world but which do not form part of the 1951 Convention. Thus, the 1969 Organization of African Unity (OAU) Convention Governing the Specific Aspects of Refugee Problems in Africa extended the 1951 United Nations refugee definition to those who flee external aggression, occupation, foreign domination, or events seriously disturbing the public order, while the Cartagena Declaration of Refugees, adopted by the Organization of American States (OAS) in 1985, considers as refugees, aside from Convention refugees, those who have escaped generalised violence, foreign aggression, internal conflicts, massive violations of human rights and circumstances which have seriously disturbed public order (Goodwin-Gill 1987).

The mandate of the United Nations High Commissioner for Refugees has evolved to reflect the new developments in refugee protection. In Africa and Central America, the UNHCR's role has been extended to include those who fall under the OAS and OAU definitions. The role of UNHCR in protecting refugees goes beyond these groups, however. In a series of resolutions, the United Nations General Assembly has endorsed UNHCR's involvement on behalf of persons who do not strictly fall under the 1951 United Nations Convention or under one of the regional arrangements, but who are in need of international protection or assistance (Goodwin-Gill 1989; McNamara 1988).

At the same time, however, governments in the West, faced with a steep rise in the arrival of persons seeking asylum, have adhered to a strict application of the 1951 United Nations refugee definition. The divergence in the interpretation of what constitutes a refugee is one of the main reasons for the increase in Western countries in *de facto* refugees or persons in 'refugee-like' conditions who are often granted temporary protection but who are denied official refugee status. In the late 1980s, the number of persons that failed to qualify for Convention status but were allowed to stay for humanitarian reasons outnumbered Convention refugees in Sweden, Switzerland and the United Kingdom.

Data quality and limitations

The number of applications for asylum, while providing an indication of the flow of asylum-seekers, cannot be equalled to that for several reasons. First, a growing number of asylum countries require asylum-seekers to submit their application at a consulate or embassy in their country of origin ('in-country processing') or in a third country. Once the asylum claim is considered *bona fide*, the asylum applicant is allowed to enter the country of asylum. In-country processing not only obscures actual migration flows, it also runs counter to the notion, laid down in Article 1A(2) of the 1951 United Nations Convention, of a refugee as someone who is outside his or her country of nationality of habitual residence (Inzunza 1990).

A second, and probably more important reason why applications for asylum should not be equalled to international migration flows is that persons may apply for asylum after having established residence in a country. For instance, a person who has entered and resided in a foreign country for the purpose of study may request asylum when human rights conditions in his or her country of origin have deteriorated or simply when the person fails to qualify for an extension of the normal student visa.[3]

In addition, it is far from clear who are actually counted in the asylum statistics. First, a distinction must be made between the number of persons seeking asylum and the number of applications submitted. In France, for example, a dossier is opened for every asylum applicant aged 16 and above. Second, some asylum-seekers allegedly submit duplicate asylum applications in one country or in different countries. European countries have increasingly resorted to the centralisation and computerisation of information regarding asylum claimants to avoid this practice.

A further reason for the discrepancy between asylum applications and actual arrivals is that asylum-seekers do not necessarily request asylum in the country where he or she has been granted first asylum. Thus, in Italy it is reported that a substantial number of asylum-seekers decline officially to submit an asylum application with the Italian authorities because it would jeopardise their chances to be granted asylum in the country of their preference, usually Australia, Canada or the United States.[4]

The statistics presented here are mostly based on the applications for asylum submitted between 1983 and 1991 to countries in Europe which are party to the 1951 United Nations Convention and the 1967 Protocol relating to the Status of Refugees and who report to UNHCR. Because governments tend to report only when the numbers are becoming significant, some statistics on the earlier years are not available, as is the case for the Nordic countries. Data for Hungary are available since 1989, the year when the country granted asylum to a large number of Romanians and when it acceded to the international instruments of refugee protection. The so-called 'quota' or 'invited' refugees, who are accepted in close cooperation with UNHCR, are generally not included in these statistics.

The 'old' names of USSR and Yugoslavia have been used, because the data refer to the period prior to the breakup of both states. While the name Germany has been used, the statistical data refer to the former Federal Republic of Germany only. In following the official United Nations classification, Turkey has been considered part of Asia.

General trends and policies

Table 11.1, presenting the annual number of asylum applications by country of asylum, shows that between 1983 and 1991 close to 2.3 million asylum applications were received in the 18 European countries that reported to UNHCR. Three out of every four asylum applications were lodged in the member states of the European Community, while the Nordic countries accounted for about 11 per cent of the asylum requests.

Germany has been by far the largest recipient of asylum applications in Europe. In 1983–91, the country received 42 per cent of all asylum applications that were lodged in Europe, while by 1991 this proportion had increased to close to 50 per cent. In 1992, the German government expected to receive another 470,000 asylum claims, almost double the 1991 figure. Unlike other leading European countries of asylum, including France and Sweden, Germany has had little success in curbing the number of asylum applications. In January 1991, a new Aliens Act came into effect in Germany that shifted the authority to grant asylum and to remove asylum-seekers who have failed to qualify for refugee status from the state to the federal level. In addition, the law abolished the right to appeal for 'manifestly unfounded' claims and allowed asylum-seekers with certain professions to work (US Committee for Refugees 1992). However, the recent political debate has focused on Article 16 of the German Constitution which states that 'persons persecuted on political grounds shall enjoy the right of asylum'. Germany's concept of asylum differs from that of most other refugee-receiving countries who, in accordance to Article 14 of the 1948 Universal Declaration of Human Rights, recognise a person's right to *seek* and enjoy asylum. Aside from changing the Constitutional right to asylum, the German government favours a common European approach to address refugee and asylum issues.

The annual number of asylum applications submitted in the United Kingdom, probably the second largest recipient of asylum-seekers in 1991, has shown a remarkable trend. While during 1983–8 the UK government managed to keep the increase in the number of new asylum applications well below the European average, the country experienced a tenfold increase between 1988 and 1991. In July 1991, the British government responded to this development by announcing changes in the country's asylum law: these changes should speed up the adjudication process, reform the legal aid system and discourage the abuse of the asylum system. Among other things, the fine on airlines bringing in improperly documented asylum-seekers was doubled to £2,000.

In France, the number of asylum applications peaked at almost 60,000 in 1989 and has since shown a significant decline (Table 11.1). The recent trend in asylum applications in France coincided with a number of legislative measures aimed at curbing illegal immigration, promoting the integration of foreigners and streamlining the asylum adjudication

Table 11.1 Number of asylum applications submitted in Europe, 1983–91 ('000)

Country	1983	1984	1985	1986	1987	1988	1989	1990	1991	Total	Annual average
Germany	19.7	35.3	73.8	99.6	57.4	103.1	121.3	193.0	256.1	959.4	106.6
France	22.3	15.9	25.8	23.4	24.8	31.6	58.8	56.0	46.3	304.9	33.9
Sweden	3.0	12.0	14.5	14.6	18.1	19.6	30.4	29.0	26.5	167.6	18.6
Switzerland	7.9	7.4	9.7	8.5	10.9	16.7	24.4	36.0	41.6	163.2	18.1
United Kingdom	3.6	3.3	5.4	4.8	4.5	5.3	15.5	30.0	57.7	130.2	14.5
Austria	5.9	7.2	6.7	8.6	11.4	15.8	21.9	22.8	27.3	127.6	14.2
Netherlands	2.0	2.6	5.6	5.9	13.5	7.5	13.9	21.2	21.6	93.8	10.4
Belgium	2.9	3.6	5.3	7.6	6.0	5.1	8.1	13.0	15.2	66.9	7.4
Italy	3.0	4.6	5.4	6.5	11.0	1.3	2.2	4.7	27.0	65.8	7.3
Hungary	—	—	—	—	—	—	27.0	8.3	na	45.3	5.0
Denmark	0.8	4.3	8.7	9.3	2.7	4.7	4.6	5.3	4.6	45.0	5.0
Spain	1.4	1.2	2.4	2.3	2.5	3.3	2.8	8.6	8.0	32.4	3.6
Greece	0.4	0.8	1.4	4.2	6.9	8.4	3.0	6.2	na	31.4	3.5
Norway	0.2	0.3	0.8	2.7	8.6	6.6	4.4	4.0	3.0	30.7	3.4
Yugoslavia	1.8	2.8	2.0	2.9	3.1	4.3	7.1	2.5	na	26.5	2.9
Finland	—	—	—	—	0.1	0.1	0.2	2.5	2.1	4.9	0.5
Portugal	—	0.4	0.1	0.3	0.4	0.3	0.2	0.1	na	1.7	0.2
Eurpean Community	56.2	71.9	134.0	163.9	129.7	170.6	230.4	338.1	436.5	1,731.4	192.4
Nordic countries	4.0	16.6	24.0	26.6	29.5	30.9	39.6	40.8	36.2	248.2	27.6
All countries	75.0	101.6	167.7	201.3	181.9	233.7	345.8	453.2	537.0	2,297.2	255.2

Notes: The French figure for 1983 includes Indochinese who arrived under the French settlement quota. Nordic countries comprise Denmark, Norway, Sweden and Finland. Throughout the table, blanks indicate less than 50 applications; na = not available.

Source: UNHCR.

process. One of the most drastic measures was the reform, including a tripling of the budget, of the French Office for the Protection of Refugees and Stateless Persons (OFPRA) in 1990. Following the acceleration in the processing of claims and the reduction of backlogs, the French government abolished the right to work for asylum-seekers in October 1991. In July 1991, the government launched a programme to regularise the status of those asylum-seekers who had waited at least two years for a decision on their asylum application. To qualify, an asylum-seeker must have entered France before 1 January 1989 and must show proof of gainful employment. By the end of 1991, some 50,000 persons had applied for the programme (SOPEMI 1992).

During 1983–91, Sweden, the third largest country of destination for asylum applicants over the nine-year period, received almost 300,000 or 13 per cent of all claims submitted in Europe. But, as in France, applications in Sweden started to fall in 1990. In 1991 the country ranked only seventh on the list of receiving countries with almost 27,000 new applications. In December 1989 the Swedish government reacted to the sharp increase in asylum applications by suspending its normal refugee procedures. Under the new arrangement, asylum was granted only to refugees under the 1951 United Nations Refugee Convention, while the paragraphs in the Aliens Act referring to the entry of persons resisting military conscription and *de facto* refugees were cancelled.[5] The suspension of the normal asylum procedure was revoked in late 1991.

Since 1945, Austria has received an estimated 2 million refugees, most of whom arrived from the former USSR and the former communist countries in Central and Eastern Europe. While some 600,000 refugees have taken up local residence, most others were resettled in Australia, Canada and the United States. By the late 1980s, the number of spontaneously arriving asylum-seekers in Austria increased rapidly due to the relaxation in travel restrictions in the former Eastern bloc (see Table 11.1). At the same time, however, overseas resettlement countries became less willing to absorb these refugees due to their sheer numbers and the changed political conditions in their countries of origin. The new situation prompted the Austrian government to introduce a new asylum law in April 1990. Under the new law, 'manifestly unfounded' claims are dismissed without further investigation and asylum-seekers can be returned to third countries where they have not been persecuted. Other recent measures include the imposition of visa requirements on countries in Central and Eastern Europe and on Turkey and the deployment of the army to control undocumented migration at Austria's eastern borders (US Committee for Refugees 1992).

In recent years, Denmark has shown a remarkably stable number of new asylum applications: following a peak of around 9,000 applications in 1985 and 1986 and a decline to less than 3,000 in 1987, the country has received about 5,000 asylum claims annually since 1988 (Table 11.1). The strong fluctuation in the number of asylum-seekers in the mid-1980s was closely related to changes in the country's asylum policy. Thus in 1984, the country adopted a liberal refugee legislation, which made it difficult to repatriate asylum-seekers who were not granted refugee status (Froslev 1986). In October 1986, the Aliens Act was amended in an effort to reduce the inflow of asylum-seekers. The new Act made it possible to repatriate asylum applicants without valid visas to countries of transit or first asylum, provided that these countries would be safe. In addition, the new law provided that asylum applicants can be refused entry to Denmark until a decision on their refugee claim has been made and that airlines can be fined for bringing in foreigners without proper travel documentation (Boland 1987).

Norway, which had received quite a lot of refugees under UNHCR resettlement programmes, proved to be unprepared for the sudden increase in the number of individual asylum-seekers, which rose from 800 in 1985 to 8,600 in 1987. The Norwegian government responded to this trend, which resulted in part from tougher admission procedures in neighbouring countries, by creating a new Directorate for Immigration and by introducing a new refugee law. Among other things, the principle of first asylum was applied more strictly and visa restrictions were imposed on Chileans. In addition, a speedier asylum adjudication process was adopted (Crisp 1987; Crisp and Parker 1988). Since the introduction of the new measures in 1988, the number of new asylum applications has decreased steadily to an estimated 3,000 in 1991.

In both Belgium and The Netherlands, the number of asylum applications more than doubled between 1988 and 1990. On 1 January 1992, the Dutch government introduced a new model for the admission and reception of asylum-seekers aimed at reducing the processing time of asylum applications and at separating 'manifestly unfounded' from genuine claims. Under the new procedure, decisions in the first instance are expected to be made within one month.[6]

In Italy the number of asylum applications jumped from 5,000 in 1990 to 27,000 in 1991, mostly due to the influx of Albanian 'boat people'. Unlike those who had arrived in March 1991, the Albanians coming to Italy five months later in August were not allowed to apply for asylum but were repatriated. In the summer of 1991 the Italian government provided substantial aid to Albania while the Albanian government agreed to accept returnees and to discourage further massive departures (US Committee for Refugees 1992). The steep decline in asylum applications in 1988 (from 11,000 to 1,300) resulted from the government's decision to refuse new applications of Eastern Europeans who had transited through other countries. Despite the increase in 1991, Italy received considerably less asylum applications than France and the United Kingdom, countries with comparable levels of economic development and similar-sized populations.

Table 11.2   Asylum applications by region of destination and region of origin, 1983–89 (%)

Region of destination/origin	1983	1984	1985	1986	1987	1988	1989	1983–89 ('000)
European Community								
Africa	20	20	18	18	20	18	24	186.8
Americas	5	4	2	2	3	2	2	22.0
Asia	56	58	65	63	45	40	47	486.8
Europe	20	19	15	17	32	40	28	242.7
All regions ('000)	54.0	70.7	128.8	155.4	129.4	170.4	229.7	938.3
Nordic countries								
Africa	—	2	4	7	9	11	14	13.5
Americas	—	5	8	10	22	19	3	17.1
Asia	—	82	73	71	54	52	49	91.1
Europe	—	11	15	11	15	18	34	29.1
All regions ('000)	—	12.2	22.4	25.1	25.9	27.7	37.5	150.9
Europe								
Africa	18	16	16	16	16	15	18	208.0
Americas	5	4	3	3	5	4	2	42.2
Asia	50	55	63	60	45	41	43	627.4
Europe	27	25	19	21	33	40	37	390.7
All regions ('000)	69.5	96.2	160.9	191.4	178.0	230.0	342.5	1,268.4

Notes: Excludes stateless persons and those whose nationality could not be determined. Nordic countries are Denmark, Norway, Sweden and Finland.

Source: UNHCR.

Patterns of asylum migration

Region of origin and region of destination

Between 1983 and 1989, Asia was the main continental-scale region of origin of asylum applicants accounting for 50 per cent of all claims submitted in Europe, followed by Europe (31 per cent), Africa (16 per cent) and Central America, South America and the Caribbean (3 per cent). Table 11.2 gives the more detailed figures.

Compared to the first part of the 1980s, the second part witnessed an increase in the proportion of European asylum-seekers and a decline in Asians seeking asylum in Europe. In 1988 and 1989, the proportion of asylum applicants originating from the Americas not only declined in relative but also in absolute terms, indicating that reasons for flight from the region have generally diminished.

In the 1980s the Nordic countries, that is Denmark, Finland, Norway and Sweden, witnessed a strong diversification in the origin of asylum-seekers. Thus, while from 1984 to 1989 the proportion of Asians declined

Table 11.3 Asylum applications by country of destination and region of origin, 1983–90 (%)

Country of asylum	Africa	Region of origin Americas	Asia	Europe	Total ('000)
Austria	1.2	0.2	17.7	81.0	99.7
Belgium	37.5	2.0	43.9	16.6	51.6
Denmark	5.1	0.4	80.4	14.1	38.6
Finland	48.8	0.6	12.1	38.5	1.7
France	39.5	5.5	47.7	7.3	252.1
Germany	10.7	0.2	52.2	36.9	689.1
Greece	14.3	0.0	47.8	37.9	31.3
Hungary	0.1	0.0	0.1	99.7	45.3
Italy	15.1	0.5	14.6	69.8	38.8
Netherlands	32.4	6.9	49.0	11.7	57.2
Norway	16.8	16.6	46.7	19.9	25.7
Portugal	84.6	0.7	8.1	6.6	1.7
Spain	23.1	17.5	24.1	35.3	22.7
Sweden	11.2	11.7	54.4	22.7	114.7
Switzerland	9.9	2.6	73.2	14.3	120.5
United Kingdom	39.7	0.9	57.1	2.3	58.2
Yugoslavia	0.8	0.2	4.0	95.0	26.4
All	17.0	2.8	47.9	32.3	1,675.3

Note: Excludes asylum applications from stateless persons and those whose nationality could not be determined.

Source: UNHCR.

from 82 per cent to 49 per cent, the proportion of European asylum-seekers increased from 11 per cent to 34 per cent. During the same period, the share of Africans in the Nordic region increased from 2 per cent to 14 per cent. Nevertheless, in 1989 the proportion of Africans in countries of the EC was still considerably higher, 24 per cent. Another major difference between the Nordic region and the EC is their varying roles in asylum migration from the Americas. While during 1984–9 some 11 per cent of all asylum applicants in the Nordic region originated from the Americas, they formed only 2 per cent of all applicants in the EC. However, by 1989, both the EC and the Nordic countries received less than 5 per cent of all asylum applications from the Americas.

Region of origin and country of destination

Table 11.3 depicts for each European country of asylum the region of origin of the asylum applicants. Based on the dominant region of origin, four different groups of asylum countries can be distinguished.

Four countries, Austria, Hungary, Italy and Yugoslavia, received more than twice the average proportion of asylum applications from Europeans. Historically, Austria has attracted numerous refugees from Central and Eastern Europe, first as a country of transit, but increasingly as a country of destination. The high proportion of Europeans seeking asylum in Hungary is primarily caused by the inflow of ethnic Hungarians from Romania. Italy, like Austria, has traditionally served as a country of transit for European refugees seeking resettlement overseas, although these persons, as in Austria, have probably been excluded from the country's asylum statistics. Until February 1990, when Italy repealed the geographical limitation to the 1951 United Nations Convention, it granted asylum exclusively to Europeans.

Belgium, France, The Netherlands and the United Kingdom each received a significantly higher than average proportion (17 per cent) of their asylum applications from Africans. Except for The Netherlands, these countries had a strong colonial presence in Africa, which may in part explain their relative accessibility for African asylum-seekers. The United Kingdom differs from all other major asylum countries in Europe through the virtual absence of European asylum-seekers (2.3 per cent).

Asylum applicants from the Americas, accounting for less than 3 per cent of all claims during 1983–90, showed a particular preference for Spain, where they made up 17.5 per cent of asylum-seekers, Norway (16.6 per cent) and Sweden (11.7 per cent) and to a lesser degree for France and The Netherlands. While in the cases of France, The Netherlands and Spain colonial and related factors (language, culture) seem relevant, the preference for Nordic countries may lie in the political orientation of the refugees. As indicated in Table 11.4, it was in particular the Chileans, escaping a right-wing dictatorship, who found a safe haven in the progressive Swedish society of the 1980s.

Lastly, Denmark and Switzerland and, to a lesser degree, Germany, Sweden and the United Kingdom received a disproportionately large number of claims from Asia (Table 11.3). In 1983–90, the region accounted for almost half of asylum applications submitted in Europe, the major source countries being Iran, Sri Lanka and Turkey.

Information on trends in the regional origins of asylum-seekers by country is summarised in Figure 11.1. The proportion of European asylum-seekers in Germany increased from about 20 per cent in 1984–6 to 55 per cent in 1988 and then tapered off to about 40 per cent in 1988–90. In the late 1980s, France and in particular The Netherlands and the United Kingdom experienced a relatively strong increase in African asylum applications. In Sweden, the relative decline in applications from Asia and the Americas and the growing importance of Africa and Europe provided the country with a pattern of migration that closely resembled that of other 'mainstream' European asylum countries by the end of the decade. As in Sweden, asylum migration from the Americas to The Netherlands tapered off towards the end of the decade. In Spain, however, asylum-seekers from the Americas remained an important

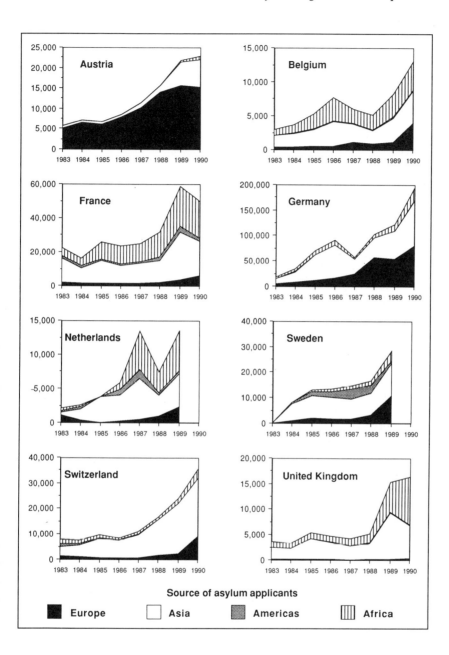

Figure 11.1 Asylum applicants by continent of origin for selected European countries, 1983–90

Source: UNHCR.

group, submitting 12 per cent of all asylum applications in 1989 and 1990. In contrast to Germany and Sweden, Austria experienced a marked decline in the proportion of Europeans seeking asylum. Thus, in 1990 two-thirds of all asylum applicants in Austria came from Europe, down from 90 per cent earlier in the decade. Asylum-seekers from Asia, in particular from Turkey, compensated this trend (see Table 11.4). In Switzerland, almost 75 per cent of all applications during 1983–90 were submitted by Asians, although the number of European asylum claims rose strongly in 1990 (Figure 11.1).

While comparisons between the receiving countries reveal some significant trends, it must be kept in mind that Germany was by far the leading receiving country of claimants from Asia and Europe. In 1983–90, Germany received 360,000 claims from Asians, while the second largest recipient of Asian asylum claims, France, received 120,000 claims. In addition, Germany received 250,000 asylum claims from Europeans, three times the number received by Austria, the second largest destination country of European asylum-seekers. In 1983–90, France was the leading country in receiving African asylum-seekers (100,000), followed closely by Germany (75,000).

The main source countries

Before discussing the leading countries of origin of asylum applicants, a few words must be devoted to the limitations of the data presented here. First, source countries that are important for individual countries but not for Europe in general, or source countries that have become important only recently, are not always distinguished in the European asylum statistics. This affected in particular the listings for France and the United Kingdom in Table 11.4. Thus, Guinea and Mali, important source countries for France in the late 1980s, were not included, while India and Uganda are absent from the list for the United Kingdom. Second, the available classification of source countries has not been stable over time. For example, from 1984 to 1990, the number of individually distinguished African countries doubled. In general, however, Tables 11.4 and 11.5 provide a useful picture of the most important source countries of asylum-seekers in Europe, the first by country of destination, the second by year.

From these two tables it can be observed that the majority of asylum applicants in Europe come only from relatively few source countries. In 1984–90, the top three source countries contributed between 36 per cent and 44 per cent of all asylum applicants annually, while 12 to 15 countries accounted for three-quarters of the annual number of asylum applicants. In addition, the pattern of asylum migration appears rather fixed: most leading countries of origin have been an important source country for a number of years. Thus, until 1989, Turkey, Poland and

Table 11.4 Country of citizenship of asylum applicants in the main European countries of asylum, 1983–90 (%)

Netherlands	France	Sweden	Germany	United Kingdom	Belgium	Switzerland	Austria
Sri Lanka 9.1	Turkey 19.4	Iran 23.9	Poland 14.7	Sri Lanka 16.7	Ghana 20.0	Turkey 36.8	Romania 27.9
Turkey 8.7	Zaïre 11.9	Chile 9.0	Turkey 12.8	Iran 12.3	Turkey 12.9	Sri Lanka 14.4	Czechoslovakia 15.9
Ghana 7.8	Sri Lanka 8.0	Lebanon 7.9	Yugoslavia 9.9	Turkey 10.6	Zaïre 8.6	Lebanon 7.6	Poland 15.0
Iran 7.2	Ghana 4.5	Ethiopia 6.0	Iran 8.8	Somalia 8.7	India 8.5	Yugoslavia 6.9	Hungary 13.7
Somalia 5.9	Angola 4.4	Iraq 5.8	Sri Lanka 7.1	Ethiopia 5.4	Pakistan 6.4	Pakistan 3.8	Turkey 6.4
Lebanon 4.7	Cambodia 4.1	Romania 4.2	Romania 6.6	Iraq 5.1	Iran 5.2	India 3.4	
Ethiopia 4.6	Laos 3.4	Bulgaria 4.1	Lebanon 6.5	Zaïre 4.8	Poland 5.1	Zaïre 3.2	
Zaïre 4.4	Haiti 3.3	Yugoslavia 4.0	India 3.6	Ghana 4.4	Yugoslavia 5.0		
India 4.1	Pakistan 3.0	Turkey 3.7	Ghana 3.3	India 4.0	Romania 4.5		
Poland 3.8	Romania 2.9	Poland 3.2	Afghanistan 3.1	Pakistan 3.9			
Surinam 3.7	Iran 2.4	Stateless 2.6					
Pakistan 2.2	Poland 2.4	Syria 2.3					
Bangladesh 2.0	Vietnam 2.0						
Nigeria 1.7	India 1.7						
Romania 1.7	China 1.4						
Yugoslavia 1.5	Senegal 1.1						
Iraq 1.4							
Afghanistan 1.4							
Total 75.8	75.9	76.8	76.4	75.8	76.2	76.1	79.0
No. of countries 18	16	12	10	10	9	7	5

Note: Asylum-seekers whose citizenship was unspecified have been excluded.

Source: UNHCR.

Table 11.5 Country of citizenship of asylum applicants, by year, 1983–90 (%)

1983	1984	1985	1986	1987	1988	1989	1990
Sri Lanka 8.8	Sri Lanka 13.4	Sri Lanka 17.7	Iran 19.0	Turkey 14.5	Poland 19.0	Turkey 16.9	Romania 19.0
Iran 8.0	Iran 11.6	Iran 12.7	Poland 10.3	Poland 11.6	Turkey 15.1	Romania 13.6	Turkey 11.5
Turkey 8.0	Poland 11.0	Turkey 9.9	Turkey 9.8	Iran 11.2	Yugoslavia 10.3	Poland 9.8	Yugoslavia 7.7
Poland 7.8	Turkey 10.7	Poland 8.5	Lebanon 6.1	USSR 5.6	Iran 8.4	Yugoslavia 7.5	Lebanon 6.9
Czechoslovakia 6.6	Czechoslovakia 5.3	Lebanon 5.2	Ghana 5.3	Sri Lanka 4.4	Romania 4.6	Sri Lanka 5.8	Sri Lanka 4.0
Vietnam 5.9	Ghana 5.2	Ghana 5.1	Sri Lanka 5.2	Yugoslavia 4.2	Sri Lanka 3.5	Iran 4.3	Iran 3.9
Cambodia 5.0	Romania 3.5	India 3.4	India 4.0	Hungary 3.8	Lebanon 2.9	Lebanon 4.3	Poland 3.7
Ghana 4.8	Lebanon 3.4	Czechoslovakia 2.9	Romania 3.5	Romania 3.7	Zaire 2.9	Zaire 3.1	Bulgaria 3.1
Zaire 4.7	Ethiopia 3.4	Pakistan 2.9	Pakistan 2.5	Chile 3.7	Chile 2.8	Somalia 2.8	Zaire 2.7
Romania 4.5	Pakistan 3.2	Romania 2.7	Czechoslovakia 2.4	Ghana 3.3	Hungary 2.6	Bulgaria 2.3	India 2.7
Hungary 3.0	Zaire 2.4	Ethiopia 2.6	Ethiopia 2.1	Zaire 3.2	Pakistan 2.3	Ghana 2.3	Vietnam 2.5
India 3.0	Iraq 2.3	Zaire 2.2	Zaire 2.1	Czechoslovakia 2.8	Ghana 2.2	Czechoslovakia 2.2	Somalia 2.4
Chile 2.7			Hungary 2.0	Pakistan 2.6		Pakistan 2.0	Pakistan 2.3
Pakistan 2.5			Chile 1.7	Ethiopia 2.6			Ghana 2.1
							Afghanistan 2.1
Total 75.4	75.2	75.6	76.0	77.4	76.4	76.7	76.5
No. of countries 14	12	12	14	14	12	13	15

Note: Asylum-seekers whose citizenship was unspecified have been excluded.

Source: UNHCR.

Iran have ranked invariably among the top four source countries, while Lebanon and Sri Lanka have equally been important countries of origin for years (see Table 11.5).

The political changes in Central and Eastern Europe in the late 1980s had a clear impact on the ranking of the major source countries. In 1990, Czechoslovakia, Hungary and Poland ranked much lower than they had during the 1980s, while Romania and Yugoslavia climbed up the list.

The relatively limited number of source countries of asylum applicants is even more striking when we look at some of the main countries of asylum (Table 11.4). In Austria, for instance, only five countries accounted for 79 per cent of all applications submitted in 1983–90. The origin of asylum applicants in Austria clearly reflects the country's traditional orientation towards East and Central European refugees. The Netherlands showed the widest distribution in the origin of asylum-seekers: here, 18 different countries accounted for three-quarters of all claims submitted in 1983–90.

Tables 11.4 and 11.5 also allow for a comparison between the main receiving countries and Europe as a whole. For example, in 1983–90, Switzerland received 37 per cent of all asylum applications from Turkey, while Turkey on average accounted for 10–15 per cent of all claims in Europe. Poles were strongly present in Germany and Austria (15 per cent in each country compared to about 10 per cent in Europe). In The Netherlands, Surinam ranked relatively high as a source country of asylum applicants and in France, Turkey, Angola, Haiti and Zaïre. Sweden received, comparatively, many Iranians (24 per cent), Chileans (9 per cent) and stateless persons. Sri Lankans, Iranians and Iraqis showed a strong preference for the United Kingdom. Belgium received a high proportion of asylum-seekers from Ghana (20 per cent), Zaïre and India (9 per cent each).

Major trends in East–West asylum migration

From 1983 to 1990, the annual number of asylum applications submitted by Europeans increased from 19,000 to more than 150,000. Almost 80 per cent of all European asylum applications were submitted by Poles, Romanians and citizens of the former Republic of Yugoslavia (Table 11.6).

The trends in East–West asylum migration reflect the political changes that took place in Central and Eastern Europe in the late 1980s and that have been referred to in other chapters in this book — see especially Chapter 8. Thus, the number of asylum applicants from Czechoslovakia, Hungary and Poland peaked in the late 1980s, reflecting the relaxation in travel restrictions in the former communist states. By the end of the 1980s, however, these countries had introduced new democratic

Table 11.6 Annual asylum applications from European countries, 1983–90 ('000)

Country of origin	1983	1984	1985	1986	1987	1988	1989	1990	Total
Poland	5.6	11.1	14.2	20.7	21.1	44.3	33.8	15.0	165.8
Romania	3.2	3.6	4.5	7.0	6.7	10.7	47.0	78.1	160.8
Yugoslavia	0.9	1.0	2.1	2.7	7.7	24.1	26.0	31.7	96.2
Czechoslovakia	4.7	5.3	4.8	4.8	5.1	4.6	7.4	1.7	38.5
Hungary	2.2	2.3	3.1	4.1	7.0	6.0	3.4	0.9	28.9
Bulgaria	0.3	0.4	0.4	0.5	0.4	0.6	8.0	12.5	23.1
USSR	0.1	0.1	0.1	0.1	10.2	0.5	1.3	5.1	17.5
Albania	0.5	0.4	0.5	0.3	0.2	0.2	0.2	5.9	8.2
Other	1.3	0.1	0.1	0.4	0.1	0.1	0.4	0.3	2.8
Total	18.8	24.4	29.8	40.6	58.5	91.1	127.6	151.2	541.9

Source: UNHCR.

structures making their citizens in general ineligible for refugee status in the West, although 15,000 Poles were able to apply for asylum in 1990. Measures imposed by Western countries to halt the influx of Central and Eastern European asylum-seekers included imposing visa restrictions, informing potential applicants about their reduced chances for asylum, introducing summary status determination procedures, and rejecting claims on the basis of 'safe country' considerations.

By 1990, Romania and the former Republic of Yugoslavia had become the most important source countries of European asylum-seekers, accounting for close to 75 per cent of all claims. In addition, the number of Bulgarian asylum applicants increased significantly towards the end of the 1980s. After 1990, Europe experienced major new outflows of asylum-seekers. In 1991, some 22,000 Albanians were allowed to apply for asylum in Italy, while many others were returned without having entered the asylum adjudication process. During the same year, tens of thousands of Albanians, many of them of Greek descent, entered Greece where some of them were allowed to apply for asylum while others were repatriated (US Committee for Refugees 1992).

According to UNHCR, the war in Yugoslavia has generated the largest refugee flow in Europe since the end of the Second World War. In late July 1992, the High Commissioner estimated that 1.8 million persons were displaced within the borders of the former Republic of Yugoslavia, while another 500,000 had sought refuge in other countries. Chapter 8 of this volume has more details of this tragic situation. The crisis in Yugoslavia confronted Europe with refugee-producing conditions that are more similar to those mentioned by the Cartagena Declaration and OAU Convention on refugees than those included in the 1951 United Nations Convention. Most European countries responded to the crisis by granting temporary asylum on a group basis rather than by individual status determination. By mid-1992, Germany had accepted at least 275,000 refugees, Hungary some 50,000, Sweden 40,000, Austria 30,000, and, Turkey and Switzerland each about 20,000.[7] However, other major European asylum countries, including France and the United Kingdom, accepted considerably smaller numbers, favouring instead refugee reception 'in the region'. The limits of this latter approach became visible when in late 1992 the Croatian government, despite its accession to the main international instruments of refugee protection, refused to accept Bosnian refugees on the grounds that it had already absorbed more than 600,000.

Finally, Table 11.7 illustrates the predominant role of Germany in East–West asylum migration during the 1980s. Citizens of Bulgaria, Poland, Romania and the former Republic of Yugoslavia chose Germany as their main destination. In all, Germany received almost half of all asylum-seekers from Europe and the former USSR who applied for asylum in 1983–90. The leading role of Austria in receiving Hungarians and Czechoslovakians, that of Hungary in receiving Romanians and that

Table 11.7   European asylum applications by European destination country, 1983–90 (%)

Country of destination	Alb.	Bul.	Cze.	Hun.	Pol.	Rom.	USSR	Yug.	Other	All
Germany (West)	17	41	31	30	62	29	17	73	3	47
Austria	7	13	42	48	9	17	5	4	1	15
Hungary	2	0	0	0	0	28	3	0	0	8
Italy	35	2	3	3	5	2	58	0	0	5
Sweden	1	23	3	10	3	3	7	6	12	5
Yugoslavia	14	7	13	0	1	10	2	0	11	5
France	7	4	1	2	4	5	3	2	10	3
Switzerland	3	4	3	3	1	2	1	9	3	3
Greece	12	1	0	0	5	1	1	0	0	2
Belgium	1	2	0	1	2	1	1	3	1	2
Spain	0	1	1	1	4	0	0	0	3	1
Netherlands	1	1	0	2	1	1	1	1	49	1
Denmark	0	1	0	1	2	1	1	0	1	1
Norway	0	0	0	0	1	0	0	3	1	1
United Kingdom	0	0	0	0	0	0	0	0	5	0
Finland	0	0	0	0	0	0	1	0	0	0
All ('000)	8.2	23.0	38.5	28.9	165.8	160.8	17.5	96.2	2.8	541.8

Note: 'Other' includes persons with unknown citizenship.

Source: UNHCR.

of Italy in receiving Albanians was discussed earlier. The high ranking of Germany (47 per cent), Austria (15 per cent) and Hungary (8 per cent) in receiving applications for asylum from Central and Eastern European citizens supports the view that refugees are predominantly absorbed within their region of origin. Major countries of asylum, situated further to the west, including France, The Netherlands, Switzerland and the United Kingdom, received only few of these claims.

Conclusion: determinants of asylum migration

Table 11.3 indicated that historical ties between countries seem to function as a major determinant of asylum migration. The former colonial powers tended to receive a disproportionately large number of asylum applicants from regions where they had their overseas possessions. Thus, as a region of origin of asylum applicants, Africa ranked relatively high in Belgium (38 per cent), France (40 per cent), Portugal (85 per cent) and the United Kingdom (40 per cent). France, The Netherlands and Spain received a larger than average proportion of asylum claims from the

Americas, because of their historical, cultural and linguistic linkages with refugee-producing countries in that region.

The validity of historical and related ties as important factors in asylum migration was also broadly confirmed by the information on individual source countries (Table 11.4). At the same time, however, anomalies to this pattern demonstrate that other forces are also at work. Ghanaians, for example, applied mostly for asylum in Belgium and The Netherlands, rather than in the United Kingdom, Thus, the existence of historical ties in itself is far from being a sufficient precondition for generating flows of asylum-seekers. Rather, it would seem that historical ties guide refugee flows in times of political instability or massive human rights violations. The high ranking of Sri Lanka in the United Kingdom, of Zaïre in Belgium, of Surinam in The Netherlands and of Haiti in France in Table 11.4 may illustrate this point.

Historical ties between the former motherland and its former colonies are often expressed in preferential visa legislation, However, the elimination of internal borders in the European Community, envisaged for 1993, has created the need to harmonise national administration policies. As a first step towards such harmonisation, the countries that signed the Convention on the application of the Schengen Agreement (Belgium, France, Germany, Italy, Luxembourg, The Netherlands, Portugal and Spain) agreed in principle on a list of 110 countries whose citizens need a visa to enter the 'Schengen-space'. In the past, the unilateral imposition of visa requirements by a country of destination often deflected the flow of asylum-seekers to a neighbouring country rather than halting it.

It was suggested earlier that the strong preference of asylum applicants from the Americas for the Nordic countries, consisting largely of Chileans seeking asylum in Sweden, was inspired by political factors. Sweden, with its social-democrat government during the 1980s, seems to have been an attractive environment for those fleeing a right-wing dictatorship.

A strong presence in a country of destination of foreigners of one nationality may enhance further migration of persons of the same nationality. This principle seems to apply to Turkish citizens, who form not only the largest group of foreigners in Europe, but also represented the largest group of asylum-seekers during 1983–90. These Turkish *Gastarbeiter* and asylum links are largely with Germany — as the appropriate column of Table 11.4 shows.

In brief, there seems much support for the view that ties, or networks, whether of a historical, cultural, political or other nature, are important determinants of patterns of asylum migration. National visa policies may account for sudden changes in these patterns. However, strict *ad hoc* reasons, including unconfirmed reports about a country's lenient admission policy, should not be dismissed as factors influencing the process of asylum migration.

Notes

1. The views expressed in this chapter are those of the author and do not imply any opinion on the part of the United Nations Secretariat. The author wishes to thank Hania Zlotnik, Acting Chief of the Mortality and Migration Section, for her invaluable support and critical comments. The author also wishes to acknowledge the financial support provided by the Directorate-General International Cooperation (DGIS) of the Dutch Ministry of Foreign Affairs.
2. The 1951 United Nations Convention relating to the Status of Refugees and its 1967 Protocol form the basis of international refugee protection. As of 31 March 1991, 104 states had ratified the 1951 Convention and 105 states had ratified the Protocol. The Protocol was added in 1967 because the 1951 Convention applied only to persons who had become refugees as a result of events that had occurred before 1951. The Protocol not only eliminated the temporal limitation but also made it impossible for new states that signed the Convention to restrict the application of the Convention to events that had occurred in Europe. The 1951 Convention had provided for a temporal and a geographical limitation because it was basically designed to cope with refugee flows that had resulted from the Second World War.
3. For example, the British government believes that a large number of migrants who do not qualify for an extension of their normal visa use the current asylum procedure to extend their stay. See 'Government introduces rules to curb asylum abuse', *Financial Times*, 3 July 1991.
4. See *SOPEMI Report 1988*, OECD, Paris, 1989, p. 33.
5. In Sweden, persons in refugee-like situations, or *de facto* refugees, are considered: (i) those who would qualify for official refugee status under the 1951 United Nations Convention but who, for various reasons, do not desire such status; (ii) persons who are in conditions comparable to, but less serious than, those cited by the Convention; and (iii) those who are forced out of their country, but who are not covered by the United Nations Convention (Nobel 1990). Apart from Convention refugees, war resisters and *de facto* refugees, the Swedish law allows for the granting of asylum on humanitarian grounds to those who are in need of protection. See the document *A comprehensive refugee and immigration policy*, Ministry of Labour, Stockholm, 1990.
6. See Ministerie van Justitie, *Jaarverslag 1991*, DVZ, The Hague, 1992.
7. See 'Spreading the burden', *The Economist*, 15 July 1992, p. 48.

References

Boland, R., 1987, *Annual review of population law*, United Nations Population Fund, New York.

Crisp, J., 1987, 'Asylum policy: the humanitarian dilemma', *Refugees*, 44: 13–15.

Crisp, J. and Parker, A., 1988, 'Coping with new arrivals', *Refugees*, 50: 35–6.

Frelick, B., 1992, 'Call them what they are, refugees', in *World refugee survey*, US Committee for Refugees, Washington, DC, 12–17.

Froslev, L., 1986, 'Interview with the Minister of Foreign Affairs of Denmark', *Refugees*, 33: 42–3.

Goodwin-Gill, G., 1987, 'The standard texts', *Refugees*, 46: 28.

Goodwin-Gill, G., 1989, 'The language of protection', *International Journal of Refugee Law*, 1(1): 6–19.

Inzunza, R., 1990, 'The Refugee Act of 1980 ten years after: still the way to go?' *International Journal of Refugee Law*, 2(3): 413–27.

King, R., 1993, 'European international migration 1945–90: a statistical and geographical overview', in King, R. (ed.), *Mass migrations in Europe: the legacy and the future*, Belhaven, London, 19–39.

McNamara, D., 1988, 'The responsibility of UNHCR', *Refugees*, 57: 21–2.

Nobel, P., 1990, 'What happened with Sweden's refugee policies?' *International Journal of Refugee Law*, 2(2): 265–73.

Salt, J., 1993, 'Skilled international migration in Europe: the shape of things to come?' in King, R. (ed.), *Mass migrations in Europe: the legacy and the future*, Belhaven, London, 293–309.

SOPEMI, 1992, *Trends in international migration*, OECD, Paris.

US Committee for Refugees, 1992, *World refugee survey 1992*, USCR, Washington, DC.

Chapter 12

Brain drain, brain gain, brain waste: reflections on the emigration of highly educated and scientific personnel from Eastern Europe[1]

Barbara Rhode

Introduction: brain drain and the Berlin Wall

Today it is often forgotten that the Berlin Wall was constructed by the German Democratic Republic in 1961 in order to stop the destabilising flood of brain drain migrants from East Germany to the West. Approximately 3.7 million of the 18 million Germans who were living in the territory of the GDR had already crossed the open border to West Germany. The amount of educated, academic and professional migrants amongst them was very high. They detested the 'dictatorship of the proletariat' which had ruled since the foundation of the GDR in 1949.

The ideological affiliation of the academic class to the value system of the bourgeoisie had made them declared enemies of the regime in all communist countries. Their previous material privileges had been drastically cut, their property — if it was not collectivised — lost its market value and the chances of their children to get access to good education were virtually suspended. Many engineers, doctors, lawyers, professors and teachers therefore left the GDR, taking their families with them. During 1961 their numbers were increasing from day to day.

Hence, it was the contrast in the social structure and the great discrepancies in the treatment of the educated classes which forced the GDR at a certain critical moment in the acceleration of this clandestine loss to close the border. Brain drain had to be curtailed in order to secure stability for the historical experiment of shaping a new system of collective interactions.

In November 1989 the counter-event, the opening of the Wall, was imposed again by a massive wave of migrants slipping through the Hungarian hole in the Iron Curtain — in the same East–West direction. In between the two events, migration from the East was minimal. It had been successfully stopped by the fortified border and defended against would-be migrants by the *Schiessbefehl* — the order to shoot at those who wanted to escape the GDR without permission to leave.

In 1989, too, it seemed that a very high proportion of the migrants were well educated with many of them holding a university degree. However, comparatively little is known about precise numbers amongst the newly initiated brain drain, except for some figures and estimates for single nationalities and ethnic groups. For instance, in 1991 the Hungarian Academy of Sciences estimated that 15 per cent of all Hungarian researchers were working abroad, and that the majority of these 4,200 absent scientists were intending to stay abroad for several years.[2] One year later, it would appear that the number of Hungarian *émigré* scientists had decreased, although no data are available to support such a statement.

The general indication is that the brain drain from Eastern Europe and the former USSR is substantial. Relevant figures, however, are being collected only now: a consortium of ten countries is cooperating on clarification of the ongoing process in all relevant countries of Central and Eastern Europe.

The next part of this chapter involves a discussion of the theoretical and normative aspects of brain drain, including exploration of the concept of 'brain waste'. The chapter then moves to an account of various historical and contemporary waves of brain drain migration, with particular attention paid to the Polish and Jewish cases, and closes with an analysis of brain drain from Eastern Europe today.

Brain drain: the theoretical concept

The theoretical notion of brain drain is not merely that of a simple statistical flow of qualified labour which crosses international borders. Rather, it expresses a normative concept evaluating the complex labour market relations between different countries. The 'actors' addressed by the mechanism of brain drain — the sending country, the receiving country and the migrants themselves — will be of a different background and in a different position in different historical periods.

In the literature on Western European migration, brain drain was first used in the 1960s to describe the outflow of British doctors, engineers and scientists to the United States (Adams 1968). Later it was applied more widely to net skill transfers between countries, and it has come to be a term which is more and more applied to the loss of highly educated people from Third World countries in favour of highly developed countries such as the United States, Great Britain and Australia where the lure of well-paid and fulfilling jobs is all too obvious (Glaser 1978). Two central ideas behind the brain drain concept are, firstly, that educational programmes are public costs, and, secondly, that the investment made in education to develop 'human capital' is a way of strengthening and supporting the economic potential of a country.

The concept of human capital has been developed by economists as part of their concern with the nature and explanation of economic growth. They pointed out that increases in the inputs to production could not adequately explain growth in economic output and it was suggested that a qualitative factor aided growth. Human capital was useful in that it reduced this 'unexplained' residual, helped the diffusion of ideas and technology, and fostered creativity and new inventions (Becker 1975). There are obvious connections between this human capital perspective on economic growth and ideas on 'skilling' and 'post-industrial society' in which investment is needed in education to improve the quality of the labour force to meet the employment demands of Western Europe's service-sector information economy.

It is true that there are some objections to the human capital approach. Firstly, there is a debate about the effectiveness of education raising skills and the appropriateness of educational curricula for labour market needs: more education does not necessarily mean better or suitable education. Secondly, it has been argued that education, far from creating human capital, is a cynical means by which entry to jobs is regulated and social control maintained. However, human capital can be used as a relevant framework to assess the costs and benefits of brain drain migration.

Costs and benefits of brain drain: nationalist and internationalist approaches

With a cost–benefit framework, two opposing views of brain drain can be identified. These approaches will be referred to as the nationalist and the internationalist view. The hidden meaning in the term 'brain drain' is most readily associated with the nationalist approach whereby a nation's human capital resources may be carefully husbanded. The internationalist approach, on the other hand, is often linked with a neo-classical analysis of the costs and benefits of migration to both migrant and nation; in this analysis the notion of brain drain may be replaced by 'brain exchange' or by the broader phenomenon of skilled international migration.[3]

The key to the nationalist approach is the perception of the harm of skilled migration to the source countries. Put simply, governments invest public money in the education and training of individuals. If these individuals then leave the country for personal gain, it is the economy of another country which is profiting from the investment in education donated by the country of origin. Moreover this loss of highly educated manpower deprives the source nations of human capital and represents a loss of productivity potential rather than the emigration of surplus population. Where the sending nations are underdeveloped Third World states and the receiving nations are rich countries of the West, as in the classic brain drain model, a clearly inequitable situation arises (Bhagwati

1979). From an economic point of view such migration is a loss of education expenditure and revenue from taxation. Money spent on the education of migrants is usually unrecoverable and the 'reverse transfer' of financial and human resources from poor to rich countries raises questions of equity and justice. Some writers on the subject of the migration of skilled and educated migrants from less developed countries have gone so far as to argue in Rostowian terms that a certain number of highly educated personnel is necessary to achieve a critical mass for economic take-off, and that brain drain may be a crucially disruptive loss from this critical mass (Beijer 1967; Patinkin 1968).

The internationalist conception of skilled migration can be approached using the idea of 'brain overflow': the emigration of a surplus educated élite (Baldwin 1970). In the country of origin the skilled person may be underemployed or unemployed and thus fail to realise his/her potential. There is plenty of evidence to show that some societies (a good example would be Sri Lanka) suffer from the chronic inability fully to employ educated personnel because of imperfections in the labour market and the over-expansion of educational facilities leading to 'skill inflation' (Bhagwati and Hamada 1974; Dore 1976). The use of labour in the country of origin is thus seen as being economically inefficient and skilled labour would be used with greater economic efficiency if it were freely mobile. By leaving its country of origin this underemployed but highly educated labour will be able to achieve three objectives (Johnson 1968). First, it will seek to maximise personal returns and thus individual welfare. Second, it will benefit the country of immigration by increasing labour input and by avoiding the costs of training. And, third, it will generate global externalities — for example by creating new industrial processes. In certain special cases the country of emigration may also experience definite benefits (relief from social tension, enhancement of international prestige, inflow of industrial investment, return of experienced migrants at some future date, etc.). Thus by the simple act of moving from a low-wage to a high-wage area skilled migration will create both individual and social benefits. The internationalist approach evaluates these benefits from a supranational or global perspective, arguing that skilled migration within a free market for trained manpower leads to an internationally efficient distribution of educated labour as a factor of production (Gish 1970).

Even within a nationalist perspective, however, it can be argued that brain drain is a rational strategy. Where education has a low opportunity cost, a nation can occupy a position in the international division of labour as an exporter of brains. This strategy has been explicitly followed by Egypt which has encouraged the export of skilled labour to the rest of the Arab world as part of a development plan whose objectives included the reduction of unemployment, the earning of foreign exchange, and the raising of GDP per capita.

Against the aggregate analyses of the nationalist and internationalist theses can be set the behavioural perspective of the individual migrant. When an educated person emigrates, he or she carries with them their acquired qualifications. One share of these qualifications derives from public investment in the educational and vocational system of the home country, the other share is linked to individual learning capacity and personal ambitions to achieve something in life. The second component makes the migrants look for a better future for their own or their children's lives, neglecting the other share contributed by their home country. The migrant makes a personal decision seeking a maximal return for the efforts of having achieved a certain standard of education (Rhode 1991, p. 28). The individual perspective may be to reward parents' investment in education rather than worrying about the possible wastage of public investment in education.

Impediments to change

In practice, of course, natural barriers and other restrictions hinder a totally free movement of actors in the international labour market. These impediments operate variously from the side of the country of origin, from the host country, and also from the individual potential migrant.

The process of personal decision-making is the most complex of these. The balance of the so-called push and pull factors differs very much according to deeply rooted cultural patterns, and this balance changes as part of any cultural and social change. No prediction can be made without knowing the migrant's cultural ties, visions and dreams of a different and better future. These images are communicated and formed through many different sorts of cultural agents: peer groups, media, cinema, literature, relatives and friends who have emigrated, political messages. Studying the personal motives of brain drain migrants is not possible without a thorough anthropological analysis of the special conditions of the specific groups in the different countries.

Second, there are the more objective impediments to movement, many of them erected by the nations themselves or enshrined within the very essence of their sovereignty. These objective conditions also impinge on the individual's decision-making process about whether to become a migrant, and if so where to go. Amongst these external barriers are linguistic and cultural factors and the limited acceptance of foreign degrees and diplomas as entry qualifications to certain professions and trades. Non-transferability of welfare and security entitlements may be another barrier to migration: older people and citizens in their productive middle ages will not dare to give up their allowances without having an alternative, whereas young people have less to lose and more to gain in this respect. Work permits and visa requirements may also discourage access to foreign labour markets. Host countries often screen for special skills, cultural and linguistic abilities or better education amongst the immigrants. Residential permits in most countries are linked with a work permit.

Just as no country would be willing to lose their most intelligent and highly educated workers to another country, so highly competitive host economies will not accept too many applicants for entry into their labour forces if they are not successful in attaining employment. Those migrants who do not get access to the labour market and who do not negotiate the often complicated bureaucratic procedures regarding permits to stay, work and establish a new residence (and perhaps citizenship) will not have much opportunity to remain in the labour market of their choice.

The normative element of brain drain

The 1960s view of brain drain as net skill transfer between countries seems too simple today. As a typical concept of the labour market disparities of the 1960s, it reflected an attitude towards a social phenomenon at a certain historical period when the advanced economies had not yet equipped themselves for the needs of a qualified labour force. During the 1960s, in nearly all industrialised Western societies, the labour force in general — and not just the highly qualified — was getting in short supply. The huge investment in education and professional qualifications was only just getting under way and had not yet paid off. Between the industrialised countries, competition for scientists, technicians and specialists of any kind was great. Thus, brain drain from economically disadvantaged countries was met by a 'brain gain' for the richer, receiving countries.

It was not until the early 1970s (later in some European countries) that the educational revolution provided enough qualified personnel to supply the labour markets. Figure 12.1 shows the growth in higher education provision in the main EC countries since the early 1970s. By the late 1980s, most member states had around 20 per cent of their 18–24 year olds in higher education; the most significant exceptions were Britain and Portugal where the proportion was only about 10 per cent. Already in the 1970s, however, unemployment for academics and other highly qualified persons occurred for the first time in the advanced countries of Western Europe. In the USA too, the brain drain argument lost its force when the national labour forces contributed sufficient qualified staff. In the 1970s and 1980s only the rich oil-exporting Arab countries still needed more experts and specialists than they could train themselves.

For the moment, nearly all the highly industrialised countries can cover their average needs for highly qualified sectors of labour themselves. The manner of how to reproduce and select people with top qualifications has become more professional and systematic. Career patterns often follow the structures of big national and multinational organisations, and transfers of highly skilled personnel between countries are initiated and

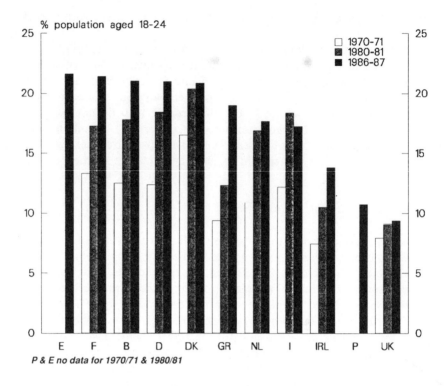

Figure 12.1   Share of 18–24 age group in higher education in EC member states

planned by the multinational companies themselves (Salt 1984; 1988).

These changes in the general condition of the international labour market for skilled personnel do not, of course, exclude the buying up of top specialists in certain fields, amongst them Nobel Prize winners and football stars. The continued frequent mobility of well-educated individuals has become part of the internationalisation of labour markets. Moreover some well-entrenched patterns of brain drain migration survive into the 1980s and 1990s. There is still a constant loss of top scientists and academics from the United Kingdom to the USA; if not really reflected by numbers it can be identified by seniority and the best-quality talent (Royal Society and Fellowship of Engineering 1987). At the same time, there is a constant influx into the UK of highly educated Commonwealth citizens.

In general, however, the situation has changed: the host countries can only take advantage of the incoming migrants by using them to put downward pressure on wages. This is possible only in certain sectors. If the labour market cannot absorb the migrants at the level of their qualifications, the phenomenon changes its nature: brain drain from the sending countries becomes 'brain waste' for the migrants.[4] This arises because the disparities in the wage system have grown to be so large that life chances are of much lower quality for the specialised and highly qualified labour forces of one country than they are for the ordinary worker in a more highly developed country. Under these circumstance, people may start to migrate even if they can no longer expect to get access to qualified jobs in other countries.

Brain drain thus becomes a different problem. There is no profiting actor on the other side to appreciate the no-cost external qualifications. The host countries do not encourage the influx of qualified personnel who cannot be placed because of lack of appropriate jobs, linguistic barriers and other cultural problems. From an individual perspective, the effect of being no use to the host societies, despite expensively acquired qualifications, can be disastrous. Educated personnel enter a cycle of 'dequalification' in exchange for the chance of achieving better material living standards. Academic migrants start off in their new host countries by selling newspapers or flowers, working as waiters in restaurants, or as cleaners and other unqualified jobs. In these circumstances, taxi driving may be regarded as a good job for an educated migrant from a poor country.

But an evaluation of the future development needs of the Western industrial, or post-industrial, states must also take into account other parameters. By the end of this decade a demographic gap will occur: the demands of the labour markets will no longer be adequately met by internally produced human capital. Whether this future additional demand will be quantitative or only of a qualitative nature has yet to be worked out. Certainly it seems that, with falling birth rates, the pervasion of West European societies by information technologies will require more highly trained young labour market entrants than the national demographic and educational system will be able to contribute. But some countries are afraid to tackle this problem with migration flows, the solution of the 1960s. Before, the dynamics of induced migration led to effects which could not be handled, neither by the countries of origin, nor by the host countries, nor by the individual migrants. The effects of the international migration process accelerated at a time when the restructuring of industry made great swathes of unskilled work redundant.

In the future, however, the anticipated shortfall of labour is expected to be of a skilled nature — a different pattern from the 1960s. Brain drain might therefore be managed as a selection from mass migration. Screening programmes could shape the target and flows which, however, will still negatively affect the countries of origin. Further analyses of these aspects and a careful monitoring of evolving patterns are needed, both for the countries of origin and for the host countries.

Waves of brain drain migration

Migration from Eastern Europe over the past 40–50 years only occurred as refugee waves following political turmoil and ethnic persecution. Migration across the Iron Curtain as a normal exchange with neighbours simply did not exist. The outflows that did take place during the period between 1946 and 1989 were always brain drains. The political ideal of proletarian autocracy hardly appealed to critical intellectuals, artists and scientists; neither did the system tolerate criticism in general or an active opposition. Each wave of refugees from Eastern Europe was a loss for the remaining intelligentsia. Moreover, continued intellectual haemor-rhage surely contributed to the torpidity and deterioration of the communist systems. The peaks of brain drain (of course, they were never labelled as such by the socialist regimes) coincided with waves of refugees after political upheavals.

The first of these waves concerned the Germans. It was, in terms of today's national borders, an internal German migration. In 1953 outflows from the Soviet-occupied territory of Eastern Germany (later the GDR) to West Germany developed into an avalanche; they ended only with the construction of the Berlin Wall. Between 1949 and 1961 about 3.7 million *Überseidler* transferred from East to West Germany (Kosiński 1970). Meanwhile German migration from Eastern Europe (excluding the GDR) to the Federal Republic involved approximately 8 million refugees and expellees between 1944 and 1950, and a further 2 million *Ausseidler* or ethnic Germans during 1950–89 (62 per cent from Poland, 12 per cent from USSR and 12 per cent from Romania).

The next politically triggered refugee wave followed in 1956 from Hungary: after the failed uprising about 200,000 Hungarians — mainly intellectuals, scientists and students — left the country. However, unlike the reaction in the GDR and elsewhere, the Hungarian regime did not totally suppress intellectual life and a slow reconstruction of science and a measure of academic freedom followed.

Brain drain next occurred in 1968 in Czechoslovakia after the 'Prague Spring' had been stopped by Soviet tanks. Again approximately 200,000 left. Here academics were widely expelled from their jobs and those who would not accept work as cleaners or warehouse personnel tried to leave the country. In this way Czechoslovakia lost the majority of its intellec-tual élite.

Poland, too, was unstable and witnessed organised opposition several times: first in 1956, then the anti-Semitic campaign of 1968 when many Jewish people left the country, the first workers' movement in Gdansk in 1970, and the more far-reaching *Solidarnosc* movements which started in Gdansk in 1980 and ended when Poland was put under Martial Law in December 1981. The refugee exodus peaked before the borders were closed, but shortly afterwards the rigorous regulations were relaxed. In fact, the Polish wave never really stopped, changing slowly into the present-day open-border movements. The Polish case will be considered in more detail shortly.

Setting aside the waves of emigration mentioned above — the sudden politically motivated effluxes of scientists, intellectuals and students — the estimate for emigration from all Warsaw Pact countries (i.e. excluding Yugoslavia) for the period 1970–85 was only around 100,000 per year: a small figure when related to a population of almost 400 million.

The Polish case

Poland was a special case. Compared to the other former Warsaw Treaty states, Poland always allowed its people a greater degree of geographical mobility. Since 1959 everyone who could show a written invitation by anybody could travel. Between 1959 and 1979 approximately 795,000 Poles emigrated, including 460,000 to West Germany and 300,000 to the United States. Mobility was somewhat restricted during martial law in 1981–2, but it quickly became liberal again. Even under the old regime, the problem of brain drain was discussed openly, since the Polish social sciences were never suppressed as much as in other countries. Since 1989 everybody can travel whenever they want, but as a reaction many Western countries introduced visas and fees for entry.

The push factors for Polish brain drain have been very strong. Living conditions were in nearly all respects unremittingly depressing. The economic situation was very poor and the ecological environment, especially in industrial areas, was one of the worst in Eastern Europe. Life expectancy is significantly lower than in Western countries, and in Upper Silesia 45 per cent of all pregnancies are reported to be abnormal. Under the communist regimes the wage system discouraged any academic career: the average monthly income of a professor was only $25. Thus, the proportion of highly qualified people who left the country during the 1980s was very high, although estimates are hard to verify because different figures cover different time-spans.

To quote an example: emigration from Poland during 1980–9 totalled some 600,000, of whom 20 per cent went to West Germany (plus another 2.5 per cent to West Berlin), 15 per cent went to the United States, 12.5 per cent to France, 8.3 per cent to Norway, 7.5 per cent to Sweden, and 6.7 per cent each to Canada and South Africa (Oschlies 1989). Emigration peaked at 230,000 in 1988 when the 'passport for everybody' policy was implemented. Focusing more specifically on brain drain, during 1980–7 approximately 76,300 academics left; during the years 1983–7 the brain drain comprised 36,000 technicians, 11,100 engineers, 10,000 students, 4,800 economists, 4,000 scientists (physicists, chemists, biologists, mathematicians) and 3,600 medical doctors (Oschlies 1989). Other reports from the early and mid-1980s indicate that young Poles embarked on higher education specifically to get a better start in the West. In other words, at an individual level, the brain drain was planned on purpose at an early age in order to give future migrants better bargaining power on the labour markets of foreign countries.

In addition to these more or less officially recorded emigrants, there has been substantial unrecorded emigration — people who leave as tourists but do not return. This, too, is a mechanism of brain drain. For example, of the 690,000 Poles who made a trip to the West in 1987, more than 130,000 held a university degree. There is no accurate information on the 'non-returners', but an estimate of 533,000 for unofficial emigration during 1981–8 is given by Okolski (1992, p. 95).

A study which brings the data up to the most recent years estimates that, during the 11 years 1980–91, 9.5 per cent of scientific personnel left the country (Hryniewicz et al. 1992). However, the rate of flight now seems to be decelerating: an annual loss of 0.86 per cent on average during 1981–91, but only 0.67 per cent during 1989–91. A slowing down of the brain drain since 1989 is also confirmed by Korcelli (1992) although this author points out the complications arising from different criteria for measuring migration over the past few years.

Hryniewicz et al. (1992) distinguish two types of brain drain: external brain drain (emigration), and internal brain drain into industry and the private sector. In addition to the 9.5 per cent of scientific brains who emigrated during 1981–91, 15.1 per cent left the scientific world to transfer to other work in the private sector. Thus the science sector lost a quarter of its staff during the decade. However, experts in Poland and in other Central and Eastern European countries tend to agree that the internal brain drain may be a positive element, reducing the overstaffing of the scientific system and mobilising the industrial system. Moreover some other benefits are resulting from earlier waves of brain drain. *Émigré* Polish scholars are able to activate links between the reformed Polish academic world and universities in Western Europe and the United States; and 'brain returnees' are beginning to help the country in the difficult transition that is currently being effected.

Jewish migration

The best-documented group of brain drain emigrants from the former Eastern bloc countries are Jews who headed for Israel. Although located geographically south of Eastern Europe rather than to the west, Israel definitely belongs, in a wider context, to the 'Western World'. In the past, Jewish migration from the Soviet Union was mainly via Vienna, Budapest and Bucharest. The total quantity of Jewish emigrants leaving Eastern Europe was of course higher than the flow to Israel only. The United States was always a major country of Jewish immigration, second only to Israel.

Data on immigration to Israel reflect the different phases of ethnic and religious persecution and changing policy patterns. The biggest immigration wave occurred in the aftermath of the Second World War, the Holocaust and in conjunction with the foundation of the State of Israel. Between 1948 and 1951, 332,000 Jews left Europe and went to Israel, 93 per cent of them coming from East European countries. During the 1960s the numbers of Jewish migrants were slowly decreasing amidst a rather insecure situation: on the one hand, migration policies in the socialist countries became more restrictive until escape was virtually impossible; on the other hand, anti-Semitism sprung up from time to time in different countries. Jews from the intellectual and well-educated classes were prominent in political opposition in Hungary and Czechoslovakia.

Over the entire period between 1948 and 1990 about 1 million Jews emigrated from Europe to Israel. However, with the opening up of Eastern Europe and the increasing pressure on the Jewish population in the USSR, the biggest-ever total arrived at the end of this period: in 1990, 184,600 Jews left the Soviet Union for Israel, equivalent to more than 18 per cent of the total post-war Europe to Israel flow. During the early and mid-1980s, up to 1988, Israel was the destination of about one-quarter of the emigrants leaving the USSR; after 1989 the proportion grew to one-half (Öberg and Boubnova 1993, p. 246).

The enormous increase in the yearly numbers of migrants from Russia to Israel is occurring at a difficult and politically unstable time in the Middle East. This very large wave of immigrants into Israel certainly does nothing to ease tension in the region. Despite the fact that this exodus contains a very significant brain drain, migration to Israel is a family-oriented ethnic migration, not a work-oriented economic migration. The reason why Russian Jews come to settle in Israel is because they want to find a place for themselves and their families where they can feel accepted and welcomed; for them the economic advantages do not play a pre-eminent role. Real brain drain migrants would opt for a country which would offer them more from an economic point of view. The fact that Jews could be described as pursuing 'ethnic migration' rather than economically induced brain drain makes the very high degree of brain drain even more surprising. Amongst the 1990 immigration of working population from Russia to Israel an astonishing 39 per cent were classified as 'scientific and academic workers', the vast majority of them (64.5 per cent) being engineers and architects.

The loss of the Jewish population may well constitute a factor in the economic decline of the CIS countries. During 1991 an estimated 90,000 scientists departed, probably including the most highly qualified members of the scientific élite. If the figures are reliable this is an annual loss rate of 3 per cent of the scientific personnel. The importance of the ethnic dimension is indicated by the destination countries of these migratory scientists: 44.9 per cent to Israel, 37.5 per cent to Germany, 12.4 per cent to the United States, and 1.2 per cent to Central and Eastern Europe.

Israel's reaction, on the other hand, is totally different. Unlike all other destination countries of 'new' European migrants, Israel has a clear picture of future immigration. It may be the only country in the Western World to show an explicitly stated appreciation of the flood of scientists and academics to come. The Minister of Science and Technology opened his annual address to the Knesset in April 1991 with the following words:

The current mass immigration from the Soviet Union presents a historic opportunity and unprecedented challenge for Israeli science . . . . Since there are
approximately 2,000 scientists and researchers per 100,000 immigrants, some
additional 20,000 additional scientists and researchers can be expected. This
would increase the Israeli scientist population by approximately 40% . . . . By
1995 Israel's scientific and technological manpower would rival that of
Switzerland, Sweden, Norway and Belgium. Israel would become a leader in
several key technological fields, with all the economic benefits that implies . . . .
An enormous amount of money has been invested — by others — in these
highly-trained people. This investment will be wasted if we cannot harness it for
Israel's benefit.

The Jewish migration described above is mainly due to ethnic reasons, much less to religion *per se*, and hardly at all to economic motives. Nevertheless the fact remains that it is not officially recognised as a brain drain by the 'loser' countries. The case of the Jewish migration shows the affinity of an ethnic group towards a certain state of education and professional involvement. It demonstrates the economic function of a particular ethnic group within a national society. If they leave in great numbers that particular function is missing. The Jews were often called the glue of Eastern European societies. If the glue drains away and the necessary tolerance of the other cultures diminishes, the first signs of socio-economic disintegration become visible. The special case of Israel on the other hand is unique in the sense that the host country welcomes the influx and is preparing a prospective policy. A similarity to other European countries exists only in the sense that, as in the case of Hungary or Germany, there is a state which feels responsible for a population which has not lived within the boundaries of the defined territories. And the state where the majority of the ethnicity (Hungarians, Germans, etc.) is living is by law obliged to accept and to integrate the newly arriving population which has been living outside the territory. But, more than just having the obligation to take in this ethnically related population, Israel is 'using' the incoming population in the real brain gain manner. No other country is addressing the problem in the same direct way. Israel transforms the ethnic gain into a real brain gain by adjusting its policies to the phenomenon.

Brain drain from Eastern Europe today

We saw earlier in this chapter that the artificial self-isolation of the socialist systems of Eastern Europe suppressed any equilibrating flows of exchange. The geographical proximity of better returns for qualified labour would have induced a flow of brain drain migrants earlier if the artificially reinforced borders had not hindered them. The Berlin Wall and the military fortification of the Iron Curtain were established to isolate the system and to hinder any cross-border entropy. Now, the problem has occurred all of a sudden with the opening of the borders. However, the labour markets of the West European countries are satisfied for the moment; in fact there is a steady unemployment of academics, technicians and all sorts of qualified people. The chances offered to brain drain migrants from the East are rather poor.

The discussion of the openness of host countries towards educated migrants is ambiguous. Demographers have started to warn of the decrease in the number of young workers in Western Europe in the next decades (see e.g. Lutz 1991). Assuming unchanging activity rates, the under-25 labour force of the EC twelve will fall from 27.8 million in 1990 to 22.1 million in the year 2000. As a reaction to the coming shortages in the labour force, there are clear signs of a willingness to make investments in new labour-saving technologies. How this will impact on the potential supply of skilled workers from the East has yet to be analysed. If Western Europe has yet to decide what opportunities to offer to talented and qualified people from Eastern Europe, the United States has already defined quotas for the next few years, especially for persons with family connections to people already settled there. Many Central and East European ethnic groups are oriented to the United States. And, as we have seen, Israel is also developing a policy of reception and integration of highly qualified immigrants.

In the West, public feelings towards the immigrants from the East are contradictory. There is sympathy, of course, for the revolutions against the old regimes, but as time passes these sympathetic feelings diminish. Yet there is a certain feeling of a shared European identity — which may mean that migrants from Eastern Europe will be more readily accepted than those from Africa, Asia or the Arab states. These feelings vary strongly between the different host countries according to their various historical backgrounds and cultural links. The feelings may also be differentiated by the nationality or ethnicity of the migrants, some of whom may be more favourably regarded than others. In general, however, most ethnic groups in Eastern Europe are not yet known to the Western European nations. One exception might be the media coverage of the civil war in Yugoslavia, where the visible violence and cruelty irritate or outrage the value-systems of most West Europeans.

A big problem concerning academics migrating from the countries of Central and Eastern Europe is that their style of academic life was quite different from that in the West. The strongly competitive access which is normal in Western Europe was not usual in the academic institutions of Eastern Europe. The Academies of Sciences, in particular, were symbols of prestige but required party membership. They were too big, too bureaucratic and highly inefficient. Under-funding was another key problem. The academic style was heavy and inflexible. Many departments were overstaffed, with a high rate of hidden unemployment.[5] This leads to an interesting question: did the overstaffing lead to a mentality supportive of continuity and afraid of changes? Are the 'brain migrants' therefore *really* the more flexible and adaptable members of the population?

During the past three years, however, staffing in the science and research sectors has been reduced in most Eastern European countries. In Bulgaria, for example, which has a total population of 8.8 million, the figures for employment of scientific staff dropped from 88,900 in 1988 to 70,400 in 1991, i.e. by 20.8 per cent (Tchalakov 1992). In Russia (population 148 million) the number of scientists in the public sector dropped by approximately 300,000 over the past five years, reaching a total of about 3 million employees in 1991. Between June 1991 and June 1992 scientific employment was reduced by a further 13.7 per cent. In Poland (population 38.2 million) the total number of employees in the science sector 'as scientists proper' was approximately 65,000 in 1991 — a very low quota compared to other Central and East European countries (Hryniewicz *et al.* 1992). The patterns and scale of Polish brain drain were described earlier.

From these figures, it is clear that the size and structure of the brain drain problem in CIS countries is enormous compared to the trends in the Central European countries. If the figures are correct, Russia has 46 times more scientists than Poland and a brain drain rate that is 4.5 times as high.

Another problem influencing 'brain migration' is the political nature of appointments, sackings and reappointments. Academics were hired and fired according to party affiliations. Especially in Czechoslovakia, scientists who had been expelled or degraded in 1968 have been reinstated in their old institutes, whilst former party members have lost their posts. Brain drain resulting from these changes may be considered less a loss to these reforming countries than a helping hand towards political cleansing. The real and harmful brain drain took place during the socialist period when intellectuals fled or were expelled.

After years of restricted mobility, the right of free movement is regarded as fundamental to the newly established democracies. Today many scientific and technical staff see a period abroad — possibly only for a relatively short time — as vital to achieving better qualifications and furthering the development of their institutes. Technically and managerially, education at many universities in Central and Eastern Europe is backward. Isolation during the socialist era, lack of intellectual exchange programmes and authoritarian management all hampered educational standards and achievements.

The neglect of the previous brain drain conceals also the opportunity of today — to encourage return migration by special incentives. Many refugees from communism have made successful careers in Western higher education institutions, companies and other organisations. Programmes to 'win them back' have been developed, notably by the United Nations Development Programme. Return migrants could help to import a more open style of teaching, research and management. Instead of encouraging academics and scientists to leave the country for a while for training or work experience abroad, aid programmes could help to found centres of excellence in research and education inside the countries, led by high-ranking scientists of native origin. Supplying returning academics with laboratory equipment and better libraries would also help to staunch the continuing brain outflow.[6]

Conclusion

All in all, the present conditions in Central and Eastern European universities are not very good. University teachers need better contacts with Western European universities; exchange programmes therefore are vital, and these are being established, both for students and staff. But fellowships for travel and study abroad are a double-edged sword, for many beneficiaries extend their stays abroad and seek to stay away for good. Hence brain drain may be initiated by educational support and exchange programmes. Motives for students not returning should be studied in much the same way as they have been already for Third World students who stay in the West and do not return (see for instance Abraham 1968; Glaser 1978; Kannappan 1968; Naficy 1967; Watanabe 1969). Programmes to help students to return should be established and their effects monitored. A closer degree of contact can also be achieved by promoting visits by qualified academics from outside; this may be more effective than sending East European scholars abroad, which may lead to brain drain.

The most dangerous development which brain drain might lead to is escalation to a critical mass beyond which it will be very difficult to keep the system operating effectively. If the best people are constantly leaving the country this will have two deleterious effects. First, the potential to restructure and overhaul the economy will be diminished. The speed at which necessary changes can take place will be reduced. This is the internal effect. The second effect is that 'colonies' are established outside the country which act as magnets for further brain drain, especially if the situation inside the country deteriorates. Brain drain thus develops as a form of chain migration, and mass emigration may follow, leading to large-scale regional destabilisation.

Notes

1. This chapter is a shortened and updated version of a larger study prepared as part of the COST (European Cooperation in the Field of Scientific and Technical research) programme of the Commission of the European Communities — see Rhode (1991).
2. See *Weekly Bulletin* of the MII, Hungarian News Agency, Budapest, 10 May 1991.
3. Skilled international migration (SIM) has been much studied by geographers in recent years (Findlay 1987; Findlay and Gould 1989; Salt 1984, 1988, 1992). Within Western Europe SIM has developed as an important facet of the 1980s migration scene, spurred on by the transformation of European economies to a post-industrial state and often lubricated by the internal labour markets of multinational companies; the role of the career structures of companies and of individual migrants is also very relevant. In such a conceptualisation SIM is multidirectional and most of the flows are reasonably well balanced between countries. For the time being at least, SIM flows concerning Eastern Europe are mostly one-way: hence the term 'brain drain', usually now reserved for Third World settings, is appropriate.
4. The term 'brain waste' was first suggested by R. Münz at the COST Pilot Seminar in 1991; see Rhode (1991, pp. 3–5).
5. For instance, Bulgaria had one of the highest ratios of scientists in the world — 5,641 per million inhabitants — but a very low level of investment in research equipment ($13,969 per year in 1987, dropping to only $1,068 in 1990). For comparison, the United States had 3,317 scientists per million people in 1988 (less than 60 per cent of the Bulgarian level), but an annual investment of $156,640 per scientist (Tchalakov 1992).
6. An approach of this kind is being developed at the Centre for Science and Technology in Moscow, set up jointly by Russia, the EC, Japan and the United States. The Centre should make two important contributions: research on conversion projects for the former military industries; and reduction of brain drain, especially of scientists formerly working on (sometimes top secret) military projects.

References

Abraham, P.M., 1968, 'Regaining high-level Indian manpower from abroad', *Manpower Journal*, 3(4): 83–117.

Adams, W. (ed.), 1968, *The brain drain*, Collier-Macmillan, London.

Baldwin, G., 1970, 'Brain drain or brain overflow?' *Foreign Affairs*, 48(2): 358–72.

Becker, G.S., 1975, *Human Capital*, Columbia University Press, New York.

Beijer, G., 1967, 'The brain drain from the developing countries and the need for immigration of intellectuals and professionals', *International Migration*, 5(3–4): 228–36.

Bhagwati, J., 1979, 'The international migration of the highly skilled', *Third World Quarterly*, 1(3): 17–30.

Bhagwati, J. and Hamada, K., 1974, 'The brain drain, international integration of markets for professionals and unemployment: a theoretical analysis', *Journal of Development Economics*, 1(1): 19–42.

Dore, R., 1976, *The diploma disease*, Allen and Unwin, London.

Findlay, A., 1987, *The development implications of skilled international migration for host and sender countries*, University of Glasgow, Department of Geography, Occasional Paper 20.

Findlay, A. and Gould, W.T., 1989, 'Skilled international migration: a research agenda', *Area*, 21(1): 3–11.

Gish, O., 1970, 'Brain drain: some critical comments', *International Migration*, 8(4): 203–4.

Glaser, W., 1978, *The brain drain: emigration and return*, Pergamon, Oxford.

Hryniewicz, J., Jalowiecki, B. and Mync, A., 1992, *The brain drain in Poland*, University of Warsaw, European Institute for Regional and Local Development.

Johnson, H., 1968, 'An internationalist model of brain drain', in Adams, W. (ed.), *The brain drain*, Collier-Macmillan, London, 69–91.

Kannappan, S., 1968, 'The brain drain and developing countries', *International Labour review*, 98(1): 1–26.

Korcelli, P., 1992, 'International migrations in Europe: Polish perspectives for the 1990s', *International Migration Review*, 26(2): 292–304.

Kosiński, L., 1970, *The population of Europe*, Longman, London.

Lutz, W. (ed.), 1991, *Future demographic trends in Europe and North America*, Academic Press, London.

Naficy, H., 1967, 'Brain drain: the case of the Iranian non-returnees', in Singer, H.W., de Kun, N. and Ordoobadi, A. (eds), *International development*, Oceana Publications, New York, 64–72.

Öberg, S. and Boubnova, H., 1993, 'Ethnicity, nationality and migration potentials in Eastern Europe', in King, R. (ed.), *Mass migrations in Europe: the legacy and the future*, Belhaven, London, 234–56.

Okolski, M., 1992, 'Migratory movements from countries of Central and Eastern Europe', in *People on the move: new migration flows in Europe*, Council of Europe Press, Strasbourg, 83–116.

Oschlies, W., 1989, 'Polnischer "Drang nach Westen": Dynamik und Motive der jünsten Emigrationswelle aus Polen', *Berichte des Bundesinstituts für ostwissenschaftliche und internationale Studien*, 30.

Patinkin, D., 1968, 'A nationalist model of brain drain', in Adams, W. (ed.), *The brain drain*, Collier-Macmillan, London, 92–108.

Rhode, B., 1991, *East–West migration/brain drain*, Commission of the European Communities, Brussels.

Royal Society and Fellowship of Engineering, 1987, *The migration of scientists and engineers to and from the UK*, SEPSU Policy Study 1, London.

Salt, J., 1984, 'High-level manpower movements in North–West Europe and the role of careers', *International Migration Review*, 17(4): 633–51.

Salt, J., 1988, 'Highly-skilled international migrants, careers and international labour markets', *Geoforum*, 19(4): 387–99.

Salt, J., 1992, 'Migration processes among the highly skilled in Europe', *International Migration Review*, 26(2): 484–505.

Tchalakov, I., 1992, *External migration amongst Bulgarian scientists in the beginning of 1990*, Institute of Sociology, Sofia.

Watanabe, S., 1969, 'The brain drain from developing to developed countries', *International Labour Review*, 99(4): 401–33.

Chapter 13

The geographical impact of migration in Europe: lessons for Europe from the New World[1]

John Salt

Introduction

This volume opened with an introductory overview of the 'migration issue' in the Western World which set recent and current European migration trends within a global context, paying particular attention to the US experience. The book closes on a similar comparative note, examining the evidence from the United States, Canada and Australia on the economic and geographical impact of immigration for lessons which can be drawn for Europe.

The growing political interest in Europe's international migrants during the last few years has been accompanied by concern about their role in national economies and labour markets. However, appropriate economic impact studies have been lacking, mainly due to data problems. In contrast, in the immigration countries of the New World, notably Australia, Canada and the United States, considerable effort has been expended by researchers into assessing the labour market effects of successive waves of immigrants. It is likely that the experiences of the New World may inform European migration scholars and policy-makers about the desirability of particular migration regimes. This is especially important in the face of continued difficulties in controlling immigration flows into and within Europe, the growing anti-migration feeling manifest in popular xenophobic reactions to immigrants, and in the policy concept of 'fortress Europe'.

This chapter reviews the literature on the economic impact of immigration in these countries, with the intention of developing lessons for contemporary Europe. It seeks to differentiate between the effects of successive cohorts of immigrants on their predecessors and on the indigenous population. It presents the results of aggregate analyses of the economics of immigration, focusing on labour market impacts. Its main argument is that, although the aggregate impact of immigration is broadly neutral, the distributional effects are anything but. These effects are geographical and sectoral, and they vary according to migrant origins and characteristics. Most attention is focused on the United States, where a large amount of research has addressed the impact of immigration, although the Australian and Canadian situation will also be alluded to.

Problems of analysis

At first sight such a comparison would seem of dubious value, since the New World countries continue to have large-scale immigration programmes, unlike their Old World counterparts. There are thus conceptual difficulties in attempting to compare permanent settlement immigration to the New World with temporary worker movement in Europe. Nevertheless, there are sufficient similarities to sustain a comparison between their experiences. The family preference system in Australia, Canada and the United States is paralleled by the family reunion which has occurred in much of Western Europe since the early 1970s. Both areas have programmes for accepting refugees and others on humanitarian grounds. In Europe both of these immigration categories, family and humanitarian, have led to more or less permanent settlement, with consequent entry to the labour force of the second generation and other family members, usually in low-status jobs. The New World and Europe, too, import labour from Third World sources. In both cases this is now usually a highly selective process. Both, too, are experiencing increasing immigration pressure and more illegal immigration (though Australia suffers less in this regard), with a growing informal sector. The problem of balancing entry between the three major categories — family, humanitarian, labour market — exercises both sets of governments.

There are, however, methodological problems in the analysis. Some doubt must be expressed about whether it is possible accurately to assess the economic impact of migration on a country even in general terms. The US Department of Labor (1989) concluded that a definitive assessment of the effects of immigration on the US labour market and economy 'remains essentially elusive'. It is not difficult to see why. The data are generally inadequate, especially relating to labour demand. Most studies rely on the census which occurs infrequently and can really only be used for cross-section analysis. The degree of detail on employer and occupational type means that demand factors may be assessed imperfectly at best.

A further problem is in the levels of data aggregation. A macro-regional scale inevitably obscures many local effects. It may also be important to look at sectoral subdivisions, for which data are not readily available and recourse is necessary to special surveys with limited sample size. It is difficult, too, to isolate the labour market behaviour of different groups, e.g. nationalities and arrival cohorts, particularly in view of the reliance on census information which is not designed to provide longitudinal data. The importance of cohort analysis is demonstrated by Borjas and Tienda (1987), among others.

The labour market for immigrants in Europe: a brief overview

Despite the massive literature on Europe's migrant workers, the sorts of economic analyses of their labour market impact carried out in the New World, and especially in the United States, are lacking. A major problem is lack of data, especially on qualifications, concentration by sector, access to training, promotion possibilities and entrepreneurship. Few attempts have been made recently, as Böhning and Maillat (1974) did for the first guestworker phase, to bring together extant research material and data in order to assess the overall labour market impact of both new- and earlier-generation immigrants. Macro-economic modelling exercises are generally lacking.

Where information is available it suggests that migrants are generally in a weak labour market position. In contrast to the United States, Canada, and Australia, it would appear that in Europe the majority of migrants still occupy the kinds of jobs for which they were originally recruited. Many of them have moved from manufacturing to service employment, in line with economic restructuring, but they are still concentrated in jobs at the bottom end of the labour market. Furthermore, at the individual enterprise level they frequently 'end up working with the oldest machinery and materials' (de Beijl 1990, p.45), meaning low productivity, more injuries and more sick leave. To keep their jobs migrants need to perform better than average under worse working conditions. They earn lower wages than native-born workers, even where they are doing the same job and their unemployment levels are higher. There is abundant evidence that second-generation immigrants are similarly afflicted.

Not all of Europe's immigrants are low-skilled. There is growing evidence that substantial numbers of highly skilled professional, managerial and technical staff move more or less freely within, into and from Europe (Salt 1992). Many of these are transferred within the internal labour markets of large employing organisations. The high level of expertise they possess ensures that the role they play in the European (and global) economy is much more powerful than their modest numbers would suggest. In the United Kingdom, for example, so highly valued are corporate transferees to their employers that an estimated £4–5 billion is spent per annum on their relocations.

The number of migrants in self-employment has been growing, an indication of growing economic integration. Most businesses, however, require comparatively little capital investment or skills, although available information is limited. Types of business vary, but there seems to be one thing in common between European countries. Many immigrant-owned businesses serve only the immigrant community, and can be seen as part of the enclave economy. They use family labour or rely upon ethnic recruitment networks to provide the cheap, flexible labour force that gives them competitive strength.

The economic impact of immigration: a general view from the United States

There is no clear consensus on the economic impact of immigration in New World countries. Some of the earliest and most durable econometric findings relating to the United States were those of Chiswick (1978; 1982). Using single census cross-section data he argued that the situation of immigrants relative to the native-born gradually improves and eventually a crossover occurs so that they appear to have a stronger labour market position than non-immigrants. Simon (1989) concluded optimistically that new immigrants do not displace native-born workers, at least at the aggregate level, and that their presence in fact *creates* employment. He found that they do not consume more than their share of welfare benefits when compared with natives, at least in the long run. The US Department of Labor (1989) reached a similar upbeat conclusion: immigrants are successfully absorbed into the US labour market, and the overall benefits of their presence exceed the liabilities.

A more cautionary view was put forward by Martin in Chapter 1 of this volume. His conclusion was that continuation of the immigration *status quo* of the mid-1980s would lead to an increasingly polarised labour market and therefore a more unequal society in the United States. Heavy immigration was seen to distort the economy, creating large numbers of low-paid, marginal jobs that would disappear with only a small wage increase; such jobs had the effect of preventing industrial restructuring.

More innovatively, Borjas (1990) has developed the thesis that an immigration market exists in which countries compete for the physical and human capital of immigrants. Because of changes in US immigration policy and of changing economic and political conditions in the United States and abroad, the United States is currently attracting relatively unskilled immigrants. In doing so it is losing out to Canada and Australia, which are able to attract 'desirable' immigrants through their emphasis on points systems rather than family preference. Borjas claims that the skill composition of immigrants to the United States has fallen over the last 20–30 years. Although these less skilled immigrants do not greatly affect earnings or opportunities for the native-born, they may have an important long-run impact. Borjas argues that they have little chance of attaining economic parity with native-born during their lifetimes, a conclusion at odds with those of Chiswick (1982) and Simon (1989), and hence they are likely to experience higher than average poverty rates. This will in turn give them a high propensity to use the welfare system, while national income and tax revenues will be substantially lower than they would have been had the United States attracted a more skilled immigrant flow.

Occupational characteristics of new immigrants to the United States

Migration flows have their own geographies, linking origins and destinations in networks of varying complexity. It is important not to regard migrant flows as homogeneous, but to disaggregate them according to migrant characteristics. The recorded occupations of migrants may reflect their qualifications upon arrival, the jobs employers are prepared to give them, or both. In fact, most discussions about the occupational characteristics of immigrants are based on the jobs in which they are engaged after arrival, but there is good reason to believe that in many cases these are not a fair reflection of the skills possessed. Many immigrants take jobs for which they are over-qualified — the process described in Australia as 'occupational skidding'. In fact, one of the weaknesses of the literature on new migrants is the lack of information on the qualifications they possess upon entry to the United States (and to other countries). Of course, qualifications and experience obtained elsewhere may not be appropriate for the new economy, particularly where skills are in redundant technologies.[2]

The generally low skill of Europe's immigrants, and their seeming lack of advancement over two or three decades, was alluded to above. Immigrants who arrived in the United States during the 1970s were on average less skilled than those who arrived earlier and their earnings did not rise as rapidly as was anticipated from earlier evidence. Partly this reflects the sluggish national economy in the 1970s, but it is also a reflection of national origin. Mexicans and other Hispanics predominated among the least skilled and attracted lower wages than others, particularly Asians. Nearly three-quarters of recent Mexican immigrants to Los Angeles had completed no more than eight years' schooling; in contrast nearly half of recent Asian immigrants had attended high school or college and over a third had four or more years of college (Muller and Espanshade 1985).

In Los Angeles also, differences in education levels of recent Mexican and Asian immigrants are reflected in occupational status. Whereas most Asians hold white-collar jobs, Mexicans have gravitated to low-skill, low-wage, blue-collar and service jobs. Many Mexicans have gone into manufacturing (especially food, clothing, textiles and furniture), which employed half of recent immigrants during the 1970s.

In contrast, the experience of Puerto Ricans suggests that change in the quality of immigrants from particular sources over time may not necessarily imply a change in the selection process. Data from the 1960, 1970 and 1980 censuses suggests that more recent Puerto Rican immigrants are better educated and more skilled than their predecessors. However, this is not because emigrants have become a more select part of the island's population, but because of a general improvement in education and training on the island. Later cohorts show some differences in both destination location and occupational status from those who came earlier (Ortiz 1986).

Nevertheless, the relationship between occupation and migrant origin is not clear. Papademetriou and Muller (1987) found that Asians were generally well educated, entering with a level and range of skills that enabled them to retain jobs in a broad spectrum of occupations and industries. Among recent immigrants, their earnings were high, nearly as much as those of native-born whites. In contrast, Dominicans were poorly educated and the lowest earners, and, along with recently entered Puerto Ricans, had higher than average unemployment rates.

Explanation for these relationships may be found in part in category of entry. South-East Asian refugees share with other immigrants a concentration in lower-skilled jobs. However, three-quarters of South-East Asian refugees were white-collar workers in their own country, but only 17 per cent had found similar jobs in the United States. Moreover, they were disproportionately found in manufacturing, especially manual jobs, like other groups of immigrants. Gender is also significant, since occupational differences between nationalities are not necessarily replicated by both sexes. Colombian men have better jobs, greater experience and more occupational mobility than Dominicans, but there are no such differences between the women.

It is suggested that the fact that new immigrants are less skilled has led to a reduction in the US national income. Borjas (1990) reckons that if people who came during 1975–9 had been as skilled as those of the early 1960s, US national income would have been $6 billion higher per annum. Because recent immigrants are less skilled they are more likely to have recourse to welfare, and the longer they stay in the United States the greater the probability of using the welfare system.

Differences occur between immigrant waves. Recent waves are more polarised, containing more college graduates but also more who never entered high school. There are differences, too, in the labour market experiences of the different waves. Borjas uses the 1940–80 censuses to show that the gap between immigrants and natives in various labour market characteristics has been growing over time. Trends provide 'irrefutable evidence of a significant deterioration in skill level and labour market performance of successive immigration waves' (Borjas 1990, p. 51). There are also significant demographic and labour market differences by national origin. The analysis shows that those from the Philippines, for example, are much better educated than Mexicans despite similar levels of attainment of the populations of those countries. This suggests that those Filipinos who migrate to the United States are better educated than those who do not. The reason for the relative decline in educational attainment among successive waves would seem to lie in the changing national origin mix of the immigration flow. Differences between the origin groups reflect the comparative rewards for schooling in the origin countries and the United States. Where the latter are greater, immigration is more likely. Hence a major area for analysis is which types of people select themselves to come to a particular country.

A comparison of the experiences of the United States with those of Canada shows that the Canadians have also experienced a decline in the relative skills of immigrants over successive cohorts. But the reverse is the case in Australia. Borjas argues that a global sorting of skills occurs. It means that there is no such thing as 'the' impact of immigration because the skill levels of immigrant groups differ markedly among host countries. Australia and Canada get better-educated migrants. They screen them via a points system, but this has not stopped decline in Canadian quality, perhaps because family union means that not all are screened. However, a points system, awarding entry to the highly skilled, cannot ensure that only the most productive, highly educated workers are attracted. Whether or not they come will ultimately depend upon the deal they are offered in the immigration market — that is, the extent to which the host country rewards skills in comparison with their origins and with competitors.

Ultimately, then, no one conceptual model explains the differences between the labour market experiences of overseas and native-born. Papademetriou and Muller (1987) suggest that a dual model is helpful, with an upper tier of stable and well-paid jobs and a lower one where conditions are less secure, wages lower and prospects dimmer. However, most immigrants go into poor (lower-tier) jobs, but some are in high-paying ones: e.g. 30 per cent of female doctors in New York State are Asians, who comprise only a small fraction of all females. It would seem that the labour market is very segmented and a dual model is a gross over-simplification.

The geographical impact of immigration in the United States

Much of the analysis of the economic effects of immigration has been at the aggregate national level. Yet most views of immigrant entry are fabricated in the light of local and regional circumstances. One consequence is that the labour market impact of immigrants can easily be magnified by their uneven regional distribution. In 1980 nearly 80 per cent of foreign-born lived in only ten states; California, New York and Florida between them had over half. It is not surprising, therefore, that most studies of the impact of immigration have been in these states, and most local studies have focused on New York and Los Angeles. Studies are therefore biased towards those places with high concentrations of immigrants. The indirect effects of immigration in areas of low foreign settlement have received little attention. These effects include redirection of stemming of internal migration flows which may hitherto have gone to areas of immigrant concentration, or increased out-migration from these last areas. Furthermore, the particular circumstances of local and regional labour markets themselves influence the impact of immigrants, whose 'effects are not merely superimposed on a region; they evolve out of the unique history of economic development within each geographical setting' (US Department of Labor 1987, p. 47).

For example, evidence from Chicago and the north-east region indicates a relatively low socio-economic achievement among Mexicans and other Hispanics compared with elsewhere in the United States. This would seem to be related to industrial restructuring in the regional economy, where the decline of heavy industry has encouraged some employers to de-skill the production process to reduce the wage bill. Immigrants have been relied upon to accomplish this. This region also demonstrates the significance of the regional economy in influencing the range of occupations available. Opportunities for new immigrants are increasingly in services rather than manufacturing. These factors may help explain geographical variations in the treatment of illegal immigrants. Chiswick's (1978) study of a small sample of illegal Mexicans in Chicago suggests they were less exploited in low-paying, dead-end jobs than their counterparts in California.

Most migrants have settled in the large metropolitan areas. However, there are major differences between the different origin streams. Europeans and Asians have distributed themselves in similar fashion to the population as a whole, while Hispanics are more concentrated in particular locales. Secondary migrations of immigrants within the United States, unlike native internal migrants, do not seem to respond to wage differences, but to other criteria, in particular proximity to those from similar national origins.

Despite the local importance of immigrants on the labour market, there is little research on the determinants of immigrant location decisions (US Department of Labor 1989, p. 49). Of particular interest is the extent to which immigrants choose where to live and work on the basis of prevailing labour market conditions. This choice will not only reflect the realities of supply and demand in particular sectors and occupations, but immigrants' perceptions of these, as well as a host of social factors like family and friends in the area. In this context, ethnic recruitment networks undoubtedly play a major role.

A major area of uncertainty is the relationship between internal and international migration. Waldinger (1987), using shift-share analysis, showed how the out-movement of the indigenous workforce was creating opportunities for immigrants. He found that numbers of whites in employment in New York were falling quickly during 1970–80 because of trends towards suburbanisation of both labour and jobs. This process then led to new opportunities in the city for other — immigrant — groups. The implication is that the white population moved voluntarily rather than being displaced. There was also some movement of immigrants from declining blue-collar manufacturing jobs into vacancies in white-collar public service jobs. Jobs in the blue-collar sector were then often taken by newly entering migrants. In sum, the flight of the white population set in motion a process of ethnic succession, with blacks moving into white-collar and public sector jobs and immigrants into blue-collar and manufacturing jobs. Each ethnic category thus became concentrated into distinctive employment niches close to their skills and/or relative ability to organise their labour supply. At the same time, immigrants created their own demand for labour in low-wage immigration industries, like garments, which have survived by employing labour-intensive production processes.

The immigrant population has also been moving out, chasing after job opportunities away from city centres. For example, recent Puerto Rican immigrants are less concentrated in New York than their predecessors. This is because earlier Puerto Ricans have moved out of New York, partly in response to the decline in unskilled manufacturing jobs that tempted them in the first place. This movement has, ironically, created vacancies in New York into which new immigrants from the island have come. However, their capacity to progress into white-collar and skilled jobs depends on their being able to obtain employment in these sectors in the first place, something that is becoming increasingly difficult (Ortiz 1986).

Most of the literature on the impact of immigration focuses upon areas of migrant concentration. It is important also to consider the impact of immigration beyond the areas most immediately affected, lest a false picture of the overall effect is presented. There is come evidence that immigration into California has had a geographical displacement effect on indigenous workers and jobs (Marshall 1988). Between 1955 and 1960 California had a net migration gain of 1.1 million from other states; during 1970–83 the net gain fell to only 11,000. It is blue-collar workers who have been most affected. During the latter period there was a net inflow of 205,000 white-collar workers, but a net loss of 134,000 blue-collar. Amongst blacks, in-migration from the rest of the United States exceeded out-migration by 102 per cent during 1970–5, declining to 62 per cent during 1975–80 and 11 per cent during 1980–3.

This rising out-migration of blue-collar Americans may help explain why job displacement in California is not reflected in the area's relatively favourable employment and labour market participation rates, and why complementarity has seemingly developed between Mexican and black workers. California now seems to be exporting to, rather than importing from, the rest of the United States those less-skilled workers who most directly compete with Mexicans. Hence it is possible that those who become unemployed or discouraged workers in California appear in the statistics of other states.

The corollary, of course, is that other states may gain either because they become recipients of internal migrants who might otherwise have gone to California, or because they retain their own potential emigrants. The consequential labour market effects of this process may be similar to those created by immigrants in California and elsewhere, but until more research is carried out we cannot be sure.

The wages impact of immigration

The evidence does not support the thesis that immigrants unduly depress overall wages. Immigrants (including illegals) have had a small impact on the earnings of the native-born (a 10 per cent increase in immigrant numbers decreases the wages of native-born by only 0.2 per cent). The effect on earlier immigrants is more significant, a 10 per cent increase in immigrants reducing wages of foreign-born workers by 2 per cent (Borjas 1990).

A large volume of econometric research has attempted to estimate the aggregate effect of immigration on the wages of both native workers and those of other immigrants. The consensus of results is that substitution is more apparent among ethnic and gender groups than among groups defined by skill levels (US Department of Labor 1989, p. 61). However, the 'own wage' effect (i.e. within a group) may be greater for unskilled workers of the same ethnicity (Grossman 1982). The overall conclusion, though, is that an increase in the supply of immigrant workers on the earnings of native workers is small.

The studies of Chiswick (1982) and others, using census data, have suggested that new immigrants start at lower incomes and at some stage cross over to higher incomes than native-born workers. However, it cannot be assumed that this will happen for all cohorts, as is evident from a comparison of Chiswick's results using the 1970 census with those of Borjas (1985) using both 1970 and 1980 data. Incorporating 1980 census data showed recent migrants doing less well than similar people had ten years earlier; this may have been because the labour market was worse than it had been ten years earlier.

Of some concern in the United States is the effects new migrants might have on the least advantaged, especially black workers. Borjas (1985), again using census data, found that in general male immigrants do not affect the earnings of black males (though Cardenas (1976) found that in San Antonio in the mid-1970s Mexican-Americans fared better than blacks) but have small negative effects on the earnings of white males. This relationship does not hold for all immigrant groups. Substitution between white native males and immigrants has been found to exist for Asians, Hispanics and legal Mexican-origin immigrants. Puerto Rican and Cuban men, however, have been found to complement white men, and thus to have positive effects on their earnings. The slight substitution effect between immigrants and the native-born population was confirmed in 1987 by Borjas and Tienda.

It seems, in fact, that the greatest wage effect may be on earlier immigrants (Borjas and Tienda 1987; Grossman 1982). In California Mexican immigration has tended to depress the wages of Hispanics already there (McCarthy and Valdez 1985). The wage growth of the latter was 40 per cent less than the national average during the 1970s; illegal migrants were an important reason for this (Muller and Espanshade

1985). The wages of low-skilled Mexican-Americans are generally lower in local labour markets with high concentrations of Mexicans, implying that new entrants depress the wages of those who came ahead of them. Cardenas (1976), however, found that there was no significant difference between the earnings of Mexican illegals and 'Anglos' (white Americans), concluding that the former were not being exploited. His results for Texas concur with those from elsewhere, that illegal workers have only a small effect on wages and employment within a locality.

The state of the local economy is not neutral in setting wage rates. There was a small immigration effect on New York's wage growth in the 1970s, influenced by the poor state of the local economy at that time, but this disappeared during the 1980s as the regional economy improved (Papademetriou and Muller 1987).

Labour market impacts in Canada and Australia: general summary

A study on the medium- and long-term macro-economic implications of increased immigration concluded that although uncertainties about the composition of immigration and the behaviour of the Canadian economy made precision impossible, 'immigrants lead to a larger economy, and have little effect on long-term disposable income per capita' (Informetrica 1989, p. 31). There may be transitional negative income effects, but these are likely to be insignificant. The study regarded immigrants in aggregate only, making no attempt at a breakdown of origin, though it was suggested that where highly qualified immigrants from less developed countries were involved, their emigration might reduce real income in potential Canadian export markets. A recent report by the Economic Council of Canada (1991) concluded that there are net economic benefits to immigration, but they are very small.

In many ways Australian experience of immigration in the last two decades or so parallels that of the United States. In the Australian case the immigration has been large relative to the native-born population, and this has increased the national consciousness about its effects. In contrast to the United States, however, illegal immigration is much less of a problem. In Australia macro-economic models of the impact of immigration are generally agreed that immigration had brought a net positive employment benefit, and no wage loss, since the mid-1970s, although there have been some industries where disadvantage has ensued. These are especially in those local labour markets already in surplus, and where migrants are concentrated (Withers 1987). During the 1980s a growing emphasis has been placed on encouraging the immigration of skills and youth. There is less evidence in Australia than in Canada, and especially the United States, that immigrants have been used to bolster declining sectors. Indeed, immigrants have tended to settle and work in growing regions and industries.

Conclusion

The experience of the New World countries allows no definite conclusion on whether immigration during the period since the 1960s has resulted in clear net costs or benefits, or for whom — migrants or citizens of the host nation. There is no evidence that at the aggregate national level immigration has held back economic growth. This may also be true at the macroregional level within the United States. Conversely it cannot be argued conclusively, on the evidence available, that immigration has strengthened economic growth. Indeed, its impact on earnings and unemployment may well be neutral. There is, though, some evidence that greater selectivity in immigration, with the aim of improving labour quality by focusing on the young and skilled, is likely to have a more favourable labour market impact. The implication is that where immigration is less selective the economy will perform worse than one taking in higher-quality immigrants. Hence the concept of an immigration market, with host countries in competition with each other to improve the quality of their immigrant flows, is highly pertinent. The operation of such a market is well illustrated in the attempts of some countries to attract business immigrants from Hong Kong.

Increasingly, then, the quality of new immigrants has become more important, especially in Australia and to a lesser extent in Canada, with labour market considerations paramount. In the United States the debate about quality has recently become more vociferous, spilling over into a concern about the wisdom of immigration in general. The Immigration Act of 1990, while reaffirming the importance of family entry, also represents an attempt by the United States to compete with the other New World immigration countries for skills. Although all three accept immigrant settlers for family reunion and for humanitarian reasons, there has been a growing feeling that these entry categories may 'dilute' the quality of the intake. Indeed, there is some evidence that the process of chaining through the family category has done just that. In Europe there is little evidence that most new migrants (those who have entered from Eastern Europe may be an exception) have entered more skilled occupations than those who came in the earlier phase of migration. This applies to the second generation as well as to most humanitarian entrants from outside Europe.

The immigration market concept has become more important as the world's economies have fused into a global whole, even now trying to incorporate the former socialist economies of Eastern Europe, and with the prospect of the CIS economies joining the club. The economic restructuring that has occurred in both the New World and Europe has changed the nature of labour demand, putting a premium on skills, at least in the formal sector. This applies also to the new destinations in southern Europe. They may have come late on to the scene as labour immigration countries, but there is no reason to expect that their labour demands will echo those of the European destinations a quarter of a century ago. The economies of Italy, Spain and Greece are high technology and post-industrial, and they require more or less the same skills as their northern neighbours, as we saw in Chapter 10.

Above all else, the experience of the New World countries demonstrates the need for disaggregation in assessing the costs and benefits of immigration. Studies of the impact of individual birthplace streams are required, as well as those of the total economic effect derived from macro modelling exercises. Much US research demonstrates the usefulness of such a breakdown. It is clear also that the effects of new migrants are sector- and geographically specific, so more studies are required of individual industries and local labour markets. The inter-regional impact of immigration is largely unknown. The evidence from California shows it to be considerable, but as long as most of our assessments come only from studies carried out in areas of immigrant concentration, the wider effects will escape attention. This is particularly important in the present European context. Studies based on immigration pressure points, in regions of Germany, Italy and Spain for example, may give a false impression of the impact of new migrants, unless they are accompanied by analyses which include labour market areas more marginally affected.

Notes

1. The present paper is derived from a larger comparative study, carried out by the author as consultant to the OECD, on the economic impact of new migrants in the New World and Europe.
2. This would seem to apply *a fortiori* to present-day East Europeans.

References

Böhning, W.R. and Maillat, D., 1974, *The effects of the employment of foreign workers*, Paris, OECD.

Borjas, G.J., 1985, 'Assimilation, changes in cohort quality and the earnings of immigrants', *Journal of Labor Economics*, 3(4): 463–89.

Borjas, G.J., 1990, *Friends or strangers? The impact of immigrants on the US economy*, Basic Books, New York.

Borjas, G.J. and Tienda, M., 1987, 'The economic consequences of immigration', *Science*, 235(4789): 645–51.

Cardenas, G., 1976, *Manpower impact and problems of Mexican illegal aliens in an urban labor market*, Center for Advanced Computation, University of Illinois, Urbana, IL.

Chiswick, B.R., 1978, 'Illegal immigration and immigration control', *Journal of Economic Perspectives*, 2(3): 101–15.

Chiswick, B.R. (ed.), 1982, *The gateway: US immigration issues and policies*, American Enterprise Institute for Public Policy Research, Washington, DC.

de Beijl, R.Z., 1990, *Discrimination of migrant workers in Western Europe*,

International Migration for Employment, Working Paper 49, ILO, Geneva.

Economic Council of Canada, 1991, *New faces in the crowd: economic and social impacts of immigration*, Ottawa.

Grossman, J.B., 1982, 'The substitutability of natives and immigrants in production', *Review of Economics and Statistics*, 64(4): 596–603.

Informetrica, 1989, *Medium and long-term implications of increased immigration: final report*, Consultant Report to the Canadian Government, Ottawa.

McCarthy, K.F. and Valdez, R.B., 1985, *Current and future effects of Mexican immigration in California: executive summary*, Rand, Santa Monica, CA.

Marshall, R., 1988, 'Jobs: the shifting structure of global employment', in Sewell, J.W. and Tucker, S.K. (eds), *Growth, exports and jobs in a changing world economy: agenda 1988*, Overseas Development Council, New Brunswick, 167–94.

Muller, T. and Espanshade, T.J., 1985, *The fourth wave: California's newest immigrants*, Urban Institute Press, Washington, DC.

Ortiz, V., 1986, 'Changes in the characteristics of Puerto Rican migrants from 1955 to 1980', *International Migration Review*, 20(3): 612–28.

Papademetriou, D.G. and Muller, T., 1987, *Recent immigration to New York: labour market and social policy issues*, Report for the National Commission on Employment Policy, Washington, DC.

Salt, J., 1992, 'Migration processes among the highly skilled in Europe', *International Migration Review*, 26(2): 484–505.

Simon, J.L., 1989, *The economic consequences of immigration*, Blackwell, Oxford.

US Department of Labor, 1987, *Geographic profile of employment and unemployment*, Bureau of Labour Statistics Bulletin 2279, Government Printing Office, Washington, DC.

US Department of Labor, 1989, *The effects of immigration on the US economy and labor market*, Bureau of International Labor Affairs Research Report 1, Government Printing Office, Washington, DC.

Waldinger, R., 1987, 'Changing ladders and musical chairs: ethnicity and opportunity in post-industrial New York', *Politics and Society*, 15(4): 369–401.

Withers, G., 1987, 'Migrants and the labour market: the Australian evidence', in *The future of migration*, OECD, Paris, 210–33.

Index